Understand Roman Ci

In loving memory of my brother-in-law Mike Barratt (1943–2011)

Understand Roman Civilization

Paula James

Hodder Education

338 Euston Road, London NW1 3BH.

Hodder Education is an Hachette UK company

First published in UK 1999 by Hodder Education

First published in US 1999 by The McGraw-Hill Companies, Inc.

This edition published 2012

British Library Cataloguing in Publication Data: a catalogue record
for this title is available from the British Library.

Library of Congress Catalog Card Number: on file.

10 9 8 7 6 5 4 3 2 1

The publisher has used its best endeavours to ensure that any
website addresses referred to in this book are correct and active at
the time of going to press. However, the publisher and the author
have no responsibility for the websites and can make no guarantee
that a site will remain live or that the content will remain relevant,
decent or appropriate.

The publisher has made every effort to mark as such all words
which it believes to be trademarks. The publisher should also
like to make it clear that the presence of a word in the book,
whether marked or unmarked, in no way affects its legal status as
a trademark.

Every reasonable effort has been made by the publisher to trace the
copyright holders of material in this book. Any errors or omissions
should be notified in writing to the publisher, who will endeavour
to rectify the situation for any reprints and future editions.

Hachette UK's policy is to use papers that are natural, renewable
and recyclable products and made from wood grown in sustainable
forests. The logging and manufacturing processes are expected to
conform to the environmental regulations of the country of origin.

www.hoddereducation.co.uk

Cover image ©Keith Wheatley – Fotolia

Typeset by Cenveo Publisher Services.

Printed in Great Britain by CPI Group (UK) Ltd, Croydon, CR0 4YY.

Contents

Meet the author

Welcome to *Understand Roman Civilization*!

Back in 1998 I found myself on a journey of discovery for I quickly realized that the writing of an introduction to Roman civilization could never be just a factual account. A scholar of this pivotal period in human history can find that familiar territory rapidly becomes a changing landscape as popular perceptions and portrayals of Rome reimagine its realities (with varying degrees of historical authenticity and some surprising and fruitful outcomes). In the meantime, painstaking and insightful academic researches reveal new truths about how life was lived and how the world was variously viewed by a society in which a huge underclass of slaves and labourers toiled throughout the Mediterranean to create the material wealth of the empire. In short, a lot has happened in Roman scholarship since the end of the twentieth century.

Studying the Classical world is a never-ending activity which constantly disturbs my cultural complacency. The past can become a place where we confront our own prejudices and preconceptions as well as subjecting Roman ideologies and practices to scrutiny. I have always believed in foregrounding the Roman voice and presence (in epitaphs, graffiti and all branches of visual art and literary genres), but this does not mean that everything we hear or see 'straight' from the past is reliable evidence for universal trends (although everything taken together will contribute to the general picture and most sources provide 'unwitting testimony').

After all, history (and this book is a contribution to cultural history) should be a study more than his or her story; it is an academic discipline that demands attention to context, a commitment to a comprehensive approach and an awareness of our own political partisanship as we conduct our research and disseminate our findings. I hope you will both enjoy and at times take issue with this introduction. There is so much more to read and to see about Roman civilization.

Paula James

In one minute

Educated Romans would have been surprised at some of the commonplace artefacts and the archaeological traces of the 'lowly' we find so fascinating for a study of their civilization. Archaeologists continue to discover and preserve the tombstones of slaves, labourers and craftsmen and women. And we have to remember that glorious mosaics, monumental sculptures, paintings, portraits and elegant and functional pottery are the products of such people. Some workshop and factory owners became wealthy benefactors of their cities but many who grafted for them are neither named nor known to us, although their trade associations (precursors of medieval guilds) may be identifiable through emblems and commemorative inscriptions.

In this short book I have taken a tour of Rome and its empire through a selection of the literature, art and architecture this complex society left as its legacy to subsequent generations. The educated and privileged Romans who did not have to toil or beg for the means to live found time to be both contemplative and creative in their descriptions and in their interpretations of the world they knew, its social structures, its politics and ideologies, its philosophy, religions and cultures. So I have let them speak through their letters, histories, poetry and discursive essays on ethical matters from how to live (and how to die) to natural history, scientific enquiry, the gods, the universe and, well, pretty much everything.

I have chosen the father of Latin epic, Virgil, to explore the myth and history of early Rome, and Ovid and Horace, also acclaimed poets, to give a less lofty and more ironic picture of the capital and the countryside it had colonized in the Italian peninsula.

A monument – the Altar of Peace – is analysed for its visual 'sermon' on the Golden Age ushered in (allegedly) by the emperor Augustus with another poet of this time, Tibullus, thrown in for good measure. Literary vignettes (especially those penned by the satirist Juvenal) picturing and problematizing the contrasts between an urban and a rural existence lead into discussions on material conditions and also aspects of leisure and labour, social stratification and cultural legacies. The chapter on Roman relationships, with a focus on the orator and statesman Cicero, conjures with the beliefs and emotions of those in public and political life, and the grief and the elation of losing and holding on to property, power and personal security.

A variety of sources are brought into play for an exploration of Roman colonization and the concept and realities of empire. This sketch of the Romans abroad spans a broad chronological swathe and includes a few snapshots of late antiquity, when the character of Rome and its empire – much beleaguered by 'barbarian' incursions – is significantly changed but also still operating in a cultural continuum.

In this new edition I have used the Insight boxes to conjure with the knottier problems that surround the Roman experience. They illustrate where individual pictures are indicative of universal conditions, where self-images are partial and misleading and, last but by no means least, where I have changed my views in the light of new interpretations and a salutary dose of reflection.

1

Introduction: clearing the ground

Learning about any civilization is a challenge, a discipline and a joy. Teaching yourself about other ways of life should shift the emphasis away from being a passive consumer of information about the Romans to becoming an active agent in the process of discovery. This introduction to Roman civilization invites you to take part in an exploration of that civilization. I shall be providing background information and establishing a frame of reference, a context, for the society you have started to study. The idea is that you develop rewarding ways of looking at a foreign culture and that, by the end of the book, you feel confident about working on your own with the type of material and the evidence that has survived from the culture itself.

Evidence – a sneak preview

My dear Marcus, I am truly grateful at what you have done about Tiro, judging his former condition to be beneath him and preferring us to have him as a friend rather than a slave. Believe me, I jumped for joy when I read your letter and his. Thank you and congratulations.

Letter received by Cicero from his brother, Quintus, Gaul, May 53 BCE, *Letters to Friends* 16.6

My dear Lepidina, greetings. I am inviting you to my birthday party on the third day before the Ides of September. Do come. It will be so much nicer if you are there. Give greetings from me to your Cerialis. My Aelius and my little son also send greetings. I'll be expecting you, sister, my sweetheart, hail and fare you well as I hope to fare well myself.

Birthday invitation from Claudia Severa to Sulpicia Lepidina, Roman military fort at Vindolanda, *c.* 100 CE

Bronze bust of Emperor Augustus

Modern drain cover in Rome (SPQR = Senatus populus que Romanus)

What is up with you? You promise to come to dinner and then you don't turn up! I shall have the law on to you: you can jolly well repay me for this and it won't be cheap. We had a lettuce each all laid out, three snails apiece, and two eggs, barley cake and wine with honey (chilled too – and you can count this as part of the debt since it's an expense which melts away in the dish), and there were olives, beetroots, gherkins and onions and a thousand other similar treats. You could have heard comic recitals or some serious reading or a musician, or the lot; that's how generous I am.

> Pliny to Septicius Clarus, Italy, c. 100 CE, *Letters* 1.15

Marcus loves Spendusa
Serena detests Isidore.
I have had many girls here!
I scored here, then I went home.
Successus was here.
Lovers like bees lead a life of honey.
I can't believe this wall hasn't collapsed under the weight of all these boring clichés from sad scrawlers.

> Pompeian graffiti (preserved under Vesuvius' volcanic ash from the first century CE)

That was a random sample of the sights of the Roman world. Throughout this book, you will be meeting more of the same in a number of different contexts, evidence ranging from epitaphs, mosaics and monuments to famous literary works. The sources are rich, varied and plentiful but they can be frustratingly fragmentary. To a certain extent the material above speaks for itself. At other times, gaps in the text (the Latin term is *lacunae*) or problems of provenance (i.e. who wrote something and when, what was the original location and function of this or that artefact) have set scholars of the Roman world puzzling over the meaning and significance of many texts.

All roads lead to Rome

There are disturbing as well as uplifting discoveries to be made when we start to investigate the past. Visiting ancient Rome as a foreign country: we might bring too much of our own cultural baggage with us (an inevitable tourist trap) and sometimes the journey proves uncomfortable. If it is possible, it is certainly preferable to travel light in terms of our own preconceptions. We need to exercise some caution about judging Roman life and customs from a twenty-first-century perspective – modern views can be varied and have their own cultural tensions.

Think for just a moment about different attitudes to public execution and legalized retribution in the modern world. The Roman games will raise these issues and you may already be acquainted, through films and historical novels, with disturbing aspects of a society where death and suffering were mass entertainment. The existence and acceptance of slavery (witness the letter above about Cicero's slave secretary, Tiro) is likely to reinforce a feeling of 'them and us', although it is only within the last 200 years that Europe and America abolished their slave trades. At other times we seem to be no distance away from the feelings and anxieties of a people who lived 2,000 years ago.

> When the report reached me of the death of your daughter, Tullia, I was indeed deeply and grievously sorry, and I felt that the blow had struck us both. Had I been in Rome, I should have been with you and shown you my grief in person. And yet that is a melancholy and bitter sort of comfort. Those who should offer it, relations and friends, are themselves no less afflicted. They cannot make the attempt without many tears, and rather seem themselves in need of comfort from others than to be doing their friendly office for others. None the less, I have resolved to set briefly before you the reflections that come to my mind in this hour, not that I suppose you are unaware of them, but perhaps your grief makes them harder to perceive.
>
> Letter from Servius Sulpicius to Cicero, *Letters to Friends* 4.5

Being 'taught' about Rome

THE LANGUAGE ROUTE

The Monty Python team, in the film *Life of Brian*, summed up the popular assumption about the formal learning of Latin as a way of getting to know about Roman society. One scene has Brian, a new recruit to the rebel forces of Judaea, writing 'Romans go home' in Latin on the wall only to be discovered by a military patrol. John Cleese is cast as a Roman centurion who chastises Brian for all the grammatical mistakes in his protest graffito. Having corrected the Latin like a tyrannical schoolmaster, the Roman commander moves on, leaving Brian to write out his subversive message 100 times. Anyone of my generation who did Latin at school will appreciate the joke.

Learning an ancient language has, in the past, limited access to studying ancient societies. Latin has gained, and to a certain extent retains, a fearsome reputation as both difficult and boring while also being an élitist and exclusive subject. The old rhyme about Latin being 'a language as dead as dead can be/it killed the ancient Romans and now it's killing me' takes some living down but, as an eminent scholar once pointed out, Latin is a dead language only if we kill it. Today, it is taught in a much livelier way and Roman culture quickly captures the imagination of the school class.

Getting to grips with Latin is well worth the effort because, if taught in its cultural context, the language of any society provides a fast track into access to that culture. I shall be seasoning this study with some memorable phrases and sayings in the original Latin (all translated) in the hope that this will whet your appetite for the future. Occasionally you will be given the original Latin text below the English translation, partly for your interest but also to illustrate how and why some words translate as they do and the distinctively *Roman* thinking behind the terms and concepts.

The primary aim of this book, however, is to show you several ways into Roman society. Roman civilization is much more widely accessible to us than it was in previous centuries, not just because of ongoing discoveries by archaeologists and the general advances in evidence gathering on past cultures, but through the introduction of classical courses in translation which are proving popular in schools and colleges. Classical Civilization holds its own as an A level subject and schools, colleges and universities can bring a buzz to cultural history and language courses by the use of online resources. At one end of the educational spectrum the Minimus lunchtime clubs (created by Barbara Bell) have brought light-touch Latin to primary age children, while in higher education large numbers of adult part-time learners have since 2000 relished the chance to study Latin from scratch with the Open University. Lorna Robinson has championed Latin in State schools and has pioneered Open Air workshops in Classical Language and Civilization.

As a subject, Classical civilization is well and truly on the map in education; study of the ancient world is no longer a restricted area. In the 1990s there was an explosion in the communication of information allowing far greater access to a vast range of subjects. The ancient world is no exception. Nowadays, in one form or another, many of us can afford to 'visit' ancient Rome.

BOLDLY GOING

Having cautioned you earlier about preconceptions, I would like, at this point, to draw upon what you know about the Romans.

You might be aware of archaeological activity on Classical sites or know something about how historians handle historical sources and how these techniques are applied to ancient writers, or to epitaphs and inscriptions. Maybe you are interested in relating principles of art criticism or literary theory to Classical texts. You will be surprised how easily some of these approaches will come to you if you are prepared to meet them halfway. The richness of learning about Classical civilization is its multidisciplinary nature, and that in itself expands your options for study.

A moment's pause – more first impressions. What exposure have you had to the Roman world? Think about what you might have learned through holidays, television or school; recent or dimly recalled, these are the strengths you, personally, bring to a study of the Romans.

PLACES

You probably came up with a variety of things. Rome is a popular tourist capital. You might have seen the Colosseum in Rome close up or from a distance. Although it has often looked incongruous, for many years sitting in the centre of a busy junction for instance, it has never ceased to be an impressive ruin. You may have been in the South of Italy and visited the ruins of Pompeii and Herculaneum, burned, buried and partly preserved after the eruption of Vesuvius in 79 CE. Some remains are more haunting than others.

There is no need to stop at Italy. The Roman empire has left its mark through Europe, Asia and Africa. Perhaps you have admired an aqueduct or been surprised at the central-heating systems installed in many of the villas. Not everyone expects such levels of sophistication in an ancient society but the underfloor columns of the Roman

The Colosseum

hypocaust structure, laid bare in many remains throughout the world, are proof of the ingenuity of Roman design and construction.

Tantalizing remnants of wall paintings and mosaics are featured in museums or preserved on their archaeological sites. Artefacts tend to communicate to the imagination much better if they are, where possible, preserved in their 'find spots' (the archaeological term for the location of the discovery as opposed to a place of display such as in the museum). You will be taken on a tour of a decorative Roman villa in Chapter 3 and will have the opportunity to work out how the inhabitants might have organized their domestic space and arranged their creature comforts.

PEOPLE

Excavations help us to uncover the Roman empire in all its variety. The 'low life' tend to 'speak' to us more through archaeological remains than through the literature of the period, which is often monopolized by the educated, affluent and, invariably, male part of the population. When the past meets the present it is the upper classes and the wealthy who are most visible, whether the medium is fiction or history. In fact, the ancient historians and

A Pompeii street

biographers had an eye for the salacious anecdote and for the dramatic possibilities in the affairs of the ruling classes. Their approach to recording events and social trends was coloured by a belief that history produced positive and negative exemplars and the historian's job was to illuminate these. This might require reordering and telescoping events, selecting and embellishing the most interesting eyewitness reports and, generally, filling in the gaps to keep the pattern of history coherent.

These historians and the biographers, the emperors and great generals of the empire led lives deserving of careful scrutiny. They were seen as making history, far more than objective processes and movements from below. Economics and sociology are relatively modern disciplines, and the Romans looked first and foremost to the role of the individual in history for explanations. Success stories came from the strong-willed and forceful personalities of the past; Rome had always faltered in the hands of the weak and the wicked.

I find it fascinating that the ancient historians might regularly reconstruct past events and add colour to their accounts of pivotal moments with speeches and other dramatic devices. This could capture the mood or highlight an historical process even if it

Roman aqueduct – the Via Appia

Hypocaust and mosaic, Bignor Roman Museum, UK. Bignor Roman Villa by kind permission of the Tupper family (and thanks to photographer, Roger Morris).

compromised authenticity, rather as movie makers and even television docudramas punctuated with reconstructions give us strong if fanciful visualizations of what it was like to 'be there' (of which more later). You may have enjoyed reading the thrillers of Lindsay Davis (her detective Marcus Didius Falco pursues his investigations in a meticulously researched Roman world) or the Stephen Saylor books. Historical novels such as Helen Dunmore's *Counting the Stars* (2008) about the poet Catullus illustrates that the Roman world constantly captures the imaginations of writers and their readers.

What was never in question was that the Romans were, by nature and character, conquerors and controllers. A key underlying assumption, shared by Greek and Roman historians in the empire, was that the destiny of Rome to rule had been decided from its humble and rural beginnings. The gods, especially Jupiter, had approved it and as long as the rulers and people kept respectful and cordial relations with the Olympian deities, the eternity of Rome and its worldwide territory were assured. Looking for patterns in the past that pointed to the reality of the present is a tendency you will encounter in Chapter 2. In this case the evidence does not come from the prose work of an historian; instead, you will be looking at a poet's view of the foundation of Rome and the empire.

PICTURING PEOPLE

The focus on the lives of emperors, especially those behaving badly, and the exotic or erotic aspects of Roman imperial society has been common in popular treatments of Roman history. Robert Graves' books *I, Claudius* (1934) and *Claudius the God* (1935) stimulated and sustained interest in the lives of the emperors, focusing on power politics and how the rulers of Rome distorted and destroyed lives and relationships. These two novels were based on the writings of ancient authors such as Suetonius and Tacitus.

The serialization of both books as *I, Claudius* by BBC television in the 1970s struck a contemporary chord. Audiences were following the fortunes, on a weekly basis, of the emotionally dysfunctional family of the first Roman emperor, Caesar Augustus. It was not so unlike television soaps of the time, such as *Dynasty* and *Dallas*, which were also about ruthless and rich family groupings, stabbing each other in the back and competing for control over the corporate structures that were the source of their wealth. *Mad Men*, with its focus on a corporate 'family', might fit the bill better at the time of writing. *I, Claudius* remains a television classic and is a popular purchase on DVD.

BIG- AND SMALL-SCREEN ROME

Of course, things move on in the media when it comes to dramatizing the Classical past. In 2006 the combined efforts of HBO and the BBC resulted in a gritty and explicit miniseries, *Rome*. Shot on location at Cinecitta Studios, this had high production values and portrayed the seamier and sexier side of the capital across the whole social spectrum. An emphasis on the gangsterism of Roman politics possibly owed something to its own contemporary televisual world. The hard-hitting *Sopranos* springs to mind. *Rome* burst forth on twenty-first-century consumers of things Classical who had been primed by Ridley Scott's 2000 movie, *Gladiator*, itself a millennial resurrection of the Hollywood epic genre. Like previous large-scale screen productions dealing in the horrors of the arena, Scott's cinematic vision was partly inspired by famous paintings on this subject, particularly the arena as portrayed by the French academic painter Jean-Léon Gérôme.

These fanciful and graphic slices of Roman life can evoke social realities and highlight historical trends as well as doing violence to factual history. Edited essays on the ancient world on screen make very interesting reading, from contributions by scholarly consultants on set (often describing the frustrations of this role) to critiques of the cultural contexts of these recreated Romes (for *Gladiator*, Martin Winkler, 2004, and for *Rome*, Season One, Monica Cyrino, 2008). In 1998 (just ahead of *Gladiator*) Maria Wyke wrote a ground-breaking book (*Projecting the Past: Ancient Rome, Cinema and History*), which showed how movie makers interwove modern preoccupations (political, religious, social and cultural) within their representations of hotspots and larger-than-life figures from the Roman empire. Robert Rosenstone (1995 and 2006) has also forced many of us in the business of Classics to think outside the box with his stimulating arguments about the place and potential of film in the making of history.

CONFRONTING A FEW ASSUMPTIONS: GROOVY GREEKS AND ROTTEN ROMANS

The ancient Greeks are frequently represented as having a monopoly on finer feelings, of being the founding fathers of philosophy, as having penned the greatest plays and sculpted the best statues. Many facets of Greek civilization came to light in the nineteenth century, through archaeological finds and detailed scholarly work on the language. This process gave shape to the cultural landscape of ancient Greece and presented a seductive picture of freethinking, creative and aesthetically attuned people. They were seen as more attractive than the Romans, who followed them and who suffer from a first, but lasting, impression of being cold, calculating and colonizing, controlled and controlling, pragmatic and drily technical.

These impressions are not necessarily inaccurate; but they simply tend to tell only one part of the story. The stance adopted invariably relates to the direction our own society is taking and what past models of civilization are in and out of fashion. The Romans inspire popular admiration for their vigour in military matters, for their engineering ingenuity and for their legal and administrative systems, whereas in the field of art and literature they seem to be forever following in the footsteps of the Greeks. It has to be said that there were ancient voices that characterized the Romans in this way, for instance the commander and author Vegetius, whose view of his compatriots as disciplined warriors and good administrators but less cultivated than the Greeks is discussed in Giardina, 1995, p. 2.

Roman identities

The Romans adopted Greek gods and heroes, and instituted cults and rituals in their honour, quite early on in their history. The wider cultural debt to Greece became pronounced once mainland Greece had moved into the orbit of the Roman empire. The Latin poet Horace, writing in the last century BCE (one of his poems will be featured in Chapter 2), uttered a famous line about captive Greece taking her captor Rome captive in turn and introducing 'the arts' to rustic Latium: 'Graecia capta ferum victorem cepit et artis/intulit agresti Latio' (*Epistles* 2.1: 156–7).

A good example of the Greek influence in the field of literature is a poem which you shall look at shortly, the *Aeneid* of Virgil. Virgil, who lived at the same time as Horace, wrote his epic poem on the subject of the Trojans who were the legendary founders of Latium in central Italy and whose descendant Romulus established and expanded the settlement of Rome. The epic form was a recognized medium for the narrating of momentous events. Its verse was in a style suited to its subject matter, not necessarily pompous nor overblown, but a special poetic language which reinforced the heroic nature of the characters and the significance of their experiences.

In writing this kind of poetry, Virgil looked to the obvious and famous models from the Greek world. The *Iliad* and the *Odyssey* were the two great epics attributed to Homer and produced in written form in the eighth century BCE. The *Iliad* dealt with the siege of Troy, the battles and internal tensions of a few weeks during the ten years of hostilities. The *Odyssey* followed the adventures of the Greek hero Odysseus, who took another ten years to get home to Ithaca.

The *Aeneid* features a homecoming, in the sense that the Trojan prince Aeneas leads the Trojan refugees to a new home, a settlement of their own, in Italy. Virgil also drew upon Homer's *Iliad* for the battles between the Trojans and the indigenous race in Italy. There are other more subtle homages to Homer in motifs and themes, for instance the heroic imperative, the participation and power of the gods, the tragedy, as well as the glory, of war.

This was quite deliberate on Virgil's part; there was no shame in imitation, in following traditions and adapting the work of one's predecessors in Greek and Latin literature. Virgil drew upon a wide range of episodes and poetic techniques in Greek authors other than Homer, including the playwrights who had flourished in fifth-century Athens and the literary circle, known as the Hellenistic poets, whose cultural centre was third-century BCE Alexandria.

However, the very Roman texture of Virgil's epic poem, the *Aeneid*, places it firmly in the poet's own time and culture; the work broke new ground in its tone and treatment of the destiny of Rome and its empire. Virgil is proof that Roman patterns of creativity are distinct and fascinating in their own right. So, an important part of this book is to set you on some less familiar paths alongside some well-trodden ones, to demonstrate that our inheritance of things Greek has been mediated and enriched by things Roman.

POINTS TO REMEMBER...

1 Archaeologists continue to uncover the material culture of Rome, and the past is constantly on display.

2 Throughout the centuries Classical scholars have, with their translations, preserved the Roman voice for all of us to hear.

3 Although the messages might be mixed, we can make a start even from snippets of ancient sources in asking fruitful questions about Roman life and thought.

4 The Romans and their empire continue to capture the imagination of novelists, poets, dramatists, artists, film-makers, TV producers, inventors of Internet game scenarios and creators of graphic novel heroes.

5 Most people know something about ancient Rome, and the Latin language has permeated the English language, culture and institutions.

6 Documentaries about Rome can be lively and informative, but recreating the Roman experience is still a speculative process in many respects. Ancient authors, our primary source, liked to dramatize historical events.

7 The relationship between Romans and Greeks was a complex cultural interaction, not simply about one civilization 'borrowing' from another.

City tour

In this chapter you will be introduced to three poets, Virgil, Ovid and Horace, who wrote under the regime of the first Roman emperor, Augustus. All three poets tell us something about Roman identities and how these are tied up with the city and its empire. With Virgil and Ovid you will be touring famous areas of the city and learning something about their significance and history. Horace takes you on a trip through Italy which is revealing about the extent, the shape and the place of the peninsula within the empire as well as raising the issue of its relationship to Rome.

Excavations below the baths of the emperor Trajan (the Oppian Hill) in the 1990s revealed a 10-sq-m (108-sq-ft) fresco of a walled port from an aerial perspective. This was an exciting discovery – could it be a plan of an actual seaside development or an unrealized dream for a new Ostia or Naples? Fragments of a fresco, even if the picture does turn out to be a map of ancient Rome, do not by themselves reveal the significance or the atmosphere of the capital city. As the cover of Catharine Edwards' 1996 book, *Writing Rome*, points out: 'For the ancient inhabitant or visitor, the buildings of Rome, the public spaces of the city, were crowded with meanings and associations.'

Archaeologists invariably have to listen to stories that survive about a site, dig deep into the legends and sift for the significant facts as well as artefacts. Your first encounter with 'written' Rome will be a short extract from Virgil's epic poem, a scene from the early site of the Forum, followed by an alternative view of the city taken from the work of a slightly later poet, Ovid. The idea is to explore some of the meanings and associations mentioned in the quote above.

You can see from the chronological span of the Roman empire that we face a real challenge. This was a civilization as long temporally as it was broad geographically – and that's assuming some tidy ends and definite beginnings. As this *Teach Yourself* book is not a history of the Roman empire, we can do some darting about on its cultural map. You will soon realize that a great deal happened both before and after Virgil and you will need to get your bearings. All the sources from the Roman empire which you are going to encounter, whether visual or literary, come with a context – historical, social and political. A first step in any tour around a famous site, and the same goes for a famous text, is to locate the 'you are here' pointer.

This is the reason why you are asked to read a preamble before you read the poetry of Virgil, to find out where Virgil fits into the Roman scheme of things. This bit of background will set you down centre stage in exciting times, as Virgil lived through a turbulent era when the Republican government was cracking under various stresses and strains.

A few good men?

The Roman empire was not always ruled by an emperor. The senate, a body of élite and wealthy men, was the key assembly which ruled Rome for about 400 years (since the expulsion of kings from Rome; you might like to check out the timeline again). The senatorial class, basically the Roman aristocracy, had for many years monopolized the government at home and abroad. They only grudgingly and belatedly opened their ranks to the rich, but not nobly born, 'new' class, known as the *equites*. (*Eques* means a knight, someone who can furnish himself with horse and military equipment at his own expense; the title denoted a high-income status.) The substantial empire which Rome had acquired soon became not only an administrative challenge but a melting pot and maelstrom for the personal ambitions of assorted aristocrats and self-made men.

This is a complex political situation condensed into a paragraph, but the important thing to remember is that the last century BCE was one of strife and striving for power. Individual generals, such as

Julius Caesar, had been taking away control of the administration and army from the Senate. Pompey was Caesar's chief rival, ironically the man from whom Julius had learned a great deal in his bid for power. They had been uneasy allies for a time. Pompey married Caesar's daughter, Julia, and their brief marriage was evidently a very happy one. Julia's death in childbirth severed an important tie between the two generals.

Pompey had demonstrated better than any of his predecessors how one man with an army, money and contacts could extend his influence abroad and persuade individual kings and cities within Rome's orbit to become personal friends and political allies. In a later chapter we shall take a closer look at patrons and clients in Roman society, because this system was a fundamental way of making friends (and enemies) in a very hierarchical social structure.

Caesar won the final round in a damaging civil war against Pompey. He became, effectively, sole ruler of Rome and was assassinated in 44 BCE (the Ides of March on the timeline) by some of those senators whose role in the administration of the empire he had sought radically to redefine and marginalize. The conspirators, led by Brutus and Cassius (Shakespeare's man with the 'lean and hungry look' in his play *Julius Caesar*) aimed to restore the Republican order of things. They reckoned without Caesar's heir, Octavian, who, at the age of 18, found himself in possession of men, money and a whole network of power bases throughout the Roman world, his inheritance from his famous great-uncle.

Insight

HBO's *Rome* emphasized the ruthlessness of the young Octavian. Whether the historical Julius Caesar recognized his great-nephew's promise in this respect or had other motives for adopting him, the 'boy' (whom Cicero thought could be flattered, used and discarded) made astute use of his legacy (especially the legions). I suppose, to put it baldly, Octavian's choice at age 19 was to play the high-stakes game for the empire or face assassination.

Octavian was to become *princeps*, first citizen or, in other words, emperor. A hundred years of struggle had been resolved but this was a process with considerable cost. The famous final confrontation with Antony and Cleopatra took place at the Greek seaport of Actium and, within a year, Octavian had made Cleopatra's Egypt his personal property. Once he was established in the supreme position, he took a new name, Augustus, denoting authority and divine sanction.

The title Augustus was also a statement about rulership and about being at the head of a vast empire. The name suggested one who deserved reverence and obedience. It transformed the young Octavian from opportunist politician to being the father of the whole country (*pater patriae*, another of his titles and a 'badge' of the highest office).

For Virgil and his contemporaries civil war must have seemed a nightmarish norm for Rome and Italy. (He was about 42 when Octavian came to power.) The poet was a native of Mantua and he grieved over the tragic amount of damage to his beloved Italian countryside during the conflicts between the supporters of Caesar's assassins and the avenging Caesarians and then, later, between the rivals for Caesar's legacy of power.

Virgil was also no stranger to the ruthlessness of men determined to reach the top in Rome and the provinces. His family's land was confiscated by Octavian when the 'demobbed' veteran soldiers were settled throughout Italy (although eventually standing armies were to become a feature of military organization).

In spite of this, Virgil not only learned to look hopefully towards the new emperor as a 'fixer' in the positive sense, but he was eventually prepared to sell Augustus' image to the educated reading public of Rome and Italy. It could be argued that Virgil is more responsible than any other Roman writer for promoting the 'new deal' the emperor had in mind for the city and its empire and for giving an imaginative shape to the Golden Age Augustus claimed to be ushering in.

Back to the future

The *Aeneid*, Virgil's epic poem, is full of references to Roman perceptions of their past and hopes for the future now that the emperor Augustus has stabilized government and administration. Augustus encouraged Virgil to write a poem in celebration of the new era of peace and prosperity for Rome, but the poet chose not to deal with his own time. Instead of constructing an epic around the recent battle of Actium (a subject he considered for a short time), he went back to basics and, as you have heard, produced 12 long books (averaging about 800 to 900 lines each) about the journey and arrival of Aeneas and the Trojans in Italy.

In the following extract Virgil imagines how the site of Rome, before Rome, might have looked but, within this simple scenario, he also explores the legends, history and cultural milieu of the city in his own time. He brings an historical continuity to Rome's expansion, an intentionality if you like, and plots its progress from the very early days. In Italy, Aeneas finds an ally in the Arcadian king, Evander, who has created a modest settlement on what is destined to be the site of Rome. In this scene, the hospitable king takes Aeneas on a circuitous route to his humble palace. They keep to the valley possibly, as one commentator suggests, because Evander is old and a little frail, although a less prosaic explanation is that this enables Virgil, the poet, to point to key sites of the future.

> Evander spoke: Some god – we know not who – dwells here, in this wood, on this hill with its leafy crown... Jupiter himself, that's whom the Arcadians believe they have seen, with all the tell-tale signs, brandishing his black shield, summoning the storm clouds. You can see the walls in ruins, and the debris of two towns. Testament to a race long gone.
>
> *Aeneid* 8.351–6

If you follow this walk on the plan, you will see that the king and his guest follow a path close to the Capitoline, Palatine and Aventine hills. This area was to become the social and political pulse of the city, although the surrounding 'spur' hills also became densely populated. The Arcadians are living centre stage in more ways than one. This is a strange kind of city tour which looks both back and forward in time to the sacred and significant places of the imperial capital.

Although you are provided with a plan and can trace this walk on it as we travel through the text, it's never easy to visualize three-dimensional reality from the flat page. Rome is known as the City of Seven Hills, but these hills are not necessarily marked on every map of ancient Rome which you will find in other books. It is difficult, too, to recreate the sense of wonder the fictional hero, Aeneas, is encouraged to feel as he looks up and around at the slopes of the city. For instance, Evander takes Aeneas past the tangle of thicket which covered the Capitoline Hill. The king alludes to its awesome atmosphere and the belief that a divine presence pervades the place.

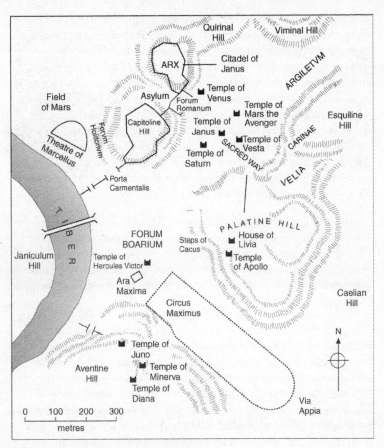

The rough guide to Rome (Evander, Aeneas and future landmarks)

Evander is circumspect about this lurking god's identity but
Virgil's readers would have tuned into the significant associations
immediately. The Capitoline Hill was destined to be the site of
the great golden temple of Jupiter Optimus Maximus (Best and
Greatest). Built by the Etruscans (from modern Tuscany), the
original wooden structure was restored in 83 BCE and repaired
and gilded by Augustus in 26 BCE. It's as if Jupiter has already
taken up residence and is ready to be revered by the race he
has chosen to enjoy empire without end ('imperium sine fine':
Aeneid 1.279).

Ruins of ancient Rome

Augustus dedicated another temple on the Capitoline in 22 BCE near the great triadic monument to Jupiter, Juno and Minerva. It was specifically dedicated to Jupiter Tonans (the god in his role as Thunderer) and built in gratitude for Augustus' escape from a lightning shaft in Spain. Suetonius (biographer of the Caesars – he has already had a brief mention) tells us that the god appeared to the emperor in a dream to complain about the rerouting of his worshippers. Augustus was visiting the new temple frequently and this set a trend which Jupiter viewed as a snub and a breach of religious etiquette (*The Twelve Caesars*, 'Augustus', 91). Augustus replied to Jupiter that this new temple was a mere vestibule to the main edifice, not a rival place of worship. The emperor was a keen traditionalist, not least in his belief in meaningful dreams.

Moving on

In the following extract, look at the Latin first and pick out the proper names. What signposting for the future does Virgil do in this passage?

> This citadel father Janus founded; and Saturn built his there. Thus the names attached, Janiculum and Saturnia. And so the conversation went, as they approached the dwelling of the unpretentious king, and saw on every side his herds mooing their way through the forum of Rome and the wealthy Carinae, our 'Ship Place.'
>
> ['hanc Janus pater, hanc Saturnus condidit arcem; Ianiculum huic, illi fuerat Saturnia nomen.' talibus inter se dictis ad tecta subibant pauperis Evandri, passimque armenta videbant Romanoque foro et lautis mugire Carinis.]

Aeneid 8.356–61

Finding the names of the gods, the king and the locations was straightforward; we print Latin names with capitals. The endings of these names in Latin will not necessarily correspond to the endings in English, as Latin is an inflected language. One feature of an inflected language is that the form of a noun changes depending on its role in the sentence. For instance, Evander is *Evandri* because the line translates as the house *of* Evander. Where we use 'of' to denote possession (or an apostrophe 's'), Latin always changes the ending.

The mention of past monuments by Evander gives an even greater sense of antiquity to the spot. The citadels of Saturn and Janus were already, in this time of early Italy, ruins from a bygone age. The legends about the Janiculum and Capitoline hills once being city sites themselves remind the reader that Evander was a relatively recent arrival and an exile too. The god Saturn was associated with the Greek Kronos. Saturn was supposed to have taken refuge in Italy when he was overthrown by the new generation of Olympian gods and forced to come down to earth. In this way, the site is established as a good place for new starts.

The Janiculum Hill rises opposite the city of Rome on the west bank of the river Tiber. Or it's possible that the Janiculum refers to the citadel on the Capitol itself, one of its summits in fact, in which case Aeneas did not have to look beyond the Saturnian settlement to make the proper gesture of politeness. Whatever the true explanation, the god Janus, a home-grown Roman deity, packed a punch for the Roman reader. As the god of doorways (our word 'janitor' is derived from his name), he symbolized the turn of the year and was often depicted as facing both ways. Janus is an appropriate god to single out at this point in the story. With the arrival of Aeneas, Roman history is at the crossroads and about to realize the first step towards its famous future. There is no turning back for Aeneas in his mission to found a new city.

Evander and Aeneas saunter on along the valley on the north-east side of the Palatine. Originally a swamp, the Roman Forum was to become the life and soul of Rome, a bustling business quarter and the heart of political and social life with a whole complex of public buildings. Virgil pictures the lowing cattle grazing through the Roman forum. This is not just a quaint vision for his contemporary reader. It's quite likely that the early settlers on the surrounding hills made this a meeting place and watering hole for their cattle. Ancient wells have been discovered there. It never lost its marshy nature, in spite of the draining which had been done at an early date. The river Tiber flooded five times in Augustus' reign alone and the poet Horace stresses the seriousness of the situation in the Forum area: 'We saw the yellow Tiber, its waves violently driven back from the Tuscan shore, threatening to overwhelm the regal building and the temple of Vesta' (*Odes* 1.2.13–16).

Past rusticity is in sharper relief on the Ship Place, or Carinae. By Virgil's and his audience's time this steep slope on the Esquiline Hill was a well-to-do and fashionable residential area, much more a place for consumers than producers and oozing sophisticated urbanity. This one brief reference could summon up one or two keen contrasts for Virgil's Roman readers, rural huts and town housing, the fragility of civilization in the face of the elements, even complacency versus humility when heroes walk with kings.

> On arrival at his home, 'This is the threshold', said the king, 'where our champion, Hercules, entered; this the palace that received him. Show your spirit, my guest, and your contempt for wealth. Behave like a god, as he did, come right in and do not be insulted by our modest means.'
>
> *Aeneid* 8.362–5

There is a Greek flavour to the scene. Evander is an Arcadian and Aeneas a foreign refugee who worships the same gods and is close culturally to his host. Arcadia was an area of Greece which loomed large in Roman imagination as an idyllic and pastoral place, the home of poetic inspiration, but also of innocence and vulnerability. (I recommend the interesting final chapters on the 'Arcadian dream'

in Beard and Henderson's *Classics: A very short introduction*.)
Hercules, a Greek hero (Greek name Herakles), had a cult centre at
Rome and Augustus encouraged a parallel to be made between the
Greek hero and himself as saviours of civilization.

> Try to note any names of gods and goddesses you believe to be either
> Greek or Roman. You have encountered the hero Hercules' original Greek
> name above. Readers will probably come up mostly with the Roman
> names for the Greek gods as these are in relatively common use in English.

Your list may well have included names like Neptune (Greek
Poseidon), Mars (Greek Ares), Apollo and Diana (Artemis), perhaps
Ceres (Demeter) and Athena. This warlike goddess of wisdom
and weaving tends to be better known by her Greek name. To the
Romans she was Minerva. Mercury (Greek Hermes) was associated
with merchants and thieves, also eloquence and travel. He was lower
down in the pecking order on Olympus, a kind of divine facilitator.
Mercury's name is given to the only metal that becomes liquid at
room temperature, also known as quicksilver, so he is a byword for
versatility and mutability. He is a familiar figure as well as name for
any form of communication. I imagine that you had heard of Jupiter
before you learned about his significance for the Romans from the
Virgil extracts. Holst's theme tune for Jupiter from *The Planets* suite
has become a popular piece. The full title of this section is 'Jupiter,
Bringer of Jollity'. For the Romans, it was the older god of an earlier
generation of divinities, Saturn, who was associated with licence,
leisure and generally having fun. The Romans endowed Jupiter
(Greek Zeus) with ultimate power and final arbitration in matters
of cosmic importance. Zeus played the same leading role in the
Greek pantheon. In either guise, stories about his philandering with
goddesses and mortal women, rather like a sex addiction which made
him forget himself, should demonstrate that it was power that made
the Greek and Roman gods worshipful and not moral superiority.

Insight

I have reflected on this statement suggesting wayward gods behaving badly
and wondered if we sometimes simplify and fudge the representation of the
Olympians in Latin literature and philosophy. The educated Romans adjusted
the image of the Greek pantheon to reflect, reinforce and sometimes subvert
their own social structures, norms and ethical systems. In the *Aeneid* Jupiter
is the keeper of destiny and all the gods ultimately abide by the rules when it
came to big issues, preserving the march of history for instance… Discuss.

Juno, Jupiter's wife and sister, corresponding to the Greek Hera, was a similar case in point, as she was vindictive and vengeful. She is the merciless persecutor of the Trojans in Virgil's poem. Venus, the goddess of love, Aeneas' mother, may also be known to you as the Greek Aphrodite. At some stage in the eternal scheme of things she was married to Vulcan (Greek Hephaistos), the blacksmith god who manufactured Jupiter's lightning shafts and thunderbolts. Her affair with the god of war, Roman Mars, Greek Ares, was a humorous scandal told by Homer in his epic story of Odysseus.

The major deities inhabited Olympus, a high and sacred mountain in Greece, although the Roman Dis (Greek Pluto or Hades), being king of the dead, was expected to remain in the underworld. Dis in Latin means 'rich' while Plouton in Greek is translated as 'Giver of Wealth'. The God of the Underworld was never short of subjects and, although the poets might depict him as bitter and resentful at his relegation to the nether regions, he ruled a realm buried in an abundance of minerals.

The members of the pantheon, both Greek and Roman versions, should alert you to something you may have already known. The Romans, like many civilizations at the time, worshipped a number of deities. In contrast to the Jews, and later the Christians, pagan Rome did not acknowledge one god as the creator and controller of all the affairs in the cosmos. Jupiter was in a central and leading role but the other gods had their particular spheres and were worshipped by their followers with the hope, sometimes even a clear expectation, that they would grant requests if rites and rituals were carried out appropriately.

If you look again at the city plan of Rome, you will soon gather which gods had special significance for the survival and success of Rome and her empire. Augustus encouraged commemoration of his final battle against Antony and Cleopatra with a heavy emphasis on the victory of Roman gods over those of Egypt. Apollo was presented as an active fighter for the emperor-to-be and when Egypt was finally in Augustus' control the temple of Apollo was officially consecrated in celebratory style. (The gods are listed in Appendix 4: The Roman Pantheon.)

Alluding to Augustus

In Virgil the contrast between early Rome and the great city which it became is clear. Ironically, the impressive buildings of Augustus' time (he boasted that he found Rome a city of brick and left it a city of marble) have not survived intact into the present day and there have been many occasions over the centuries when the visitor encountered a terrain much more like Evander's Rome than the great city of Augustus which Virgil and his readers knew.

Virgil's contemporary readers would have enjoyed this picture of early Rome. It played upon a fascination that educated Romans of the Augustan age often articulated about their new and improved city: 'quid tum Roma fuit?' the poet Propertius asked. 'What was Rome like then?' (*Poems* 4.4.9). This preoccupation was tied up with a belief that Romans were rougher and tougher in the early days and this stern character was what had made Rome great. The luxuries of empire had diluted the robust native nature and the frugal lifestyle of the early Republican ancestors. So, when Virgil portrays Evander as self-conscious about his dwelling, he is relying upon his readership to make the necessary connections and to appreciate the allusions. The king is described in the Latin as *pauper* but our word *pauper* would be to give a misleading picture of destitution. We shall discuss Latin 'poverty' further in Chapter 4.

Evander's home, then, was on 'the almost exact spot where stood the abode of Augustus' (Warde Fowler, 1918, p. 75). Augustus, according to the second-century CE historian Suetonius, kept his house relatively unostentatious but it was 'the first building to meet the traveller when he left the *summa sacra via* [the most sacred way] and the temple of Jupiter to enter the Palatine' (Warde Fowler, p. 76). Evander's claim that his humble palace received a conquering hero, Hercules, who was deified upon his death, lends it a prestige in the past which further raises its status in the present. Hercules' struggle with the local monster, Cacus, was dramatically narrated by the king earlier in Book 8 of the *Aeneid*. The hero earned the gratitude of the local settlers for his victory over Cacus, which heralded a new beginning. As Augustus liked to be linked with Hercules as a second saviour and restorer of Rome, Virgil manages to identify both guests of Evander, Hercules and Aeneas, with Augustus by a skilful use of the legends and a bit of neat geography. Better still, he can reinforce the idea that the leadership of the new emperor was a logical legacy from the first foundations of the empire.

There is a fair amount of choice if we want to move forward from Virgil's rustic dream and tour around the centre of the splendid new city of the poet's own day. Publius Ovidius Naso, or Ovid, as he is better known, was not the first nor the last Roman writer to take his reader around the colonnades and temples of the Augustan era, but he is one of the most entertaining guides. Naso means 'Nose', and you will find that the Roman citizen often had a quirky, even jokey, last name, which functioned as our first names do, to personalize and distinguish. Ovid was born in Sulmo in the Italian peninsula (modern Sulmona). Although technically he was a provincial, Rome was his cultural home and the centre of his universe.

Ovid's place on the cultural map

Ovid tells us in tones of awe that he saw the great Virgil only once, for he was a much younger contemporary of the *Aeneid* author. Ovid was a post-war baby. He grew up in the days of Augustus' early rule and suffered none of the trauma of civil strife which the emperor had skilfully, sometimes savagely, resolved. Consequently, Ovid felt free to take a rather mischievous and relaxed line about Augustus' political programme of works, his restoration of traditions, morals and buildings.

Look at his account of some of the sites of Rome. He is guiding the reader around good places to pick up a girl. The poem is *The Art of Love* (*Ars Amatoria*), a seduction manual full of comic scenes and tongue-in-cheek advice to the hesitant lover. I have translated Ovid's poetry into continuous prose but if you look at the samples from the original Latin, you can see its verse shape on the page. The *Ars* is written in elegiac couplets with a shorter line alternating with a longer one. It was a form the Romans adopted both for love poetry and for laments.

All you have to do is take a stroll under the shelter of Pompey when the sun is approaching the lion pelt of Hercules. Or go where the mother [Octavia, Augustus' sister] has added to the endowments of her son, a work wealthy in a marble finish. Nor should you neglect the colonnade which takes its name from its founder, Livia [the empress, Augustus' wife] and which has a random display of ancient paintings.

> [tu modo Pompeia lentus spatiare sub umbra
>   cum sol Herculei terga leonis adit:
> aut ubi muneribus nati sua munera mater
>   addidit, externo marmore dives opus.
> nec tibi vitetur quae, priscis sparsa tabellis,
>   porticus auctoris Livia nomen habet:]
>
> Ovid, *The Art of Love* 1.67–72

This is a rich passage for our purposes, although it's important
to find the fun in it as we tease out its many-sided references to
Roman myth, history and everyday life. If we unravel the names and
allusions, we find a real mix of new and restored colonnades and
temples (remember the boast of Augustus). Ovid first suggests the
portico of Pompey as a pick-up place. Shady and cool under the plane
trees and fountains, it was an inviting spot near the theatre of the
same name. Pompey, the great general of 50 years earlier and rival
supremo to Julius Caesar, reminds the reader not just of an eventful
past but also of a legendary loser in the high stakes of ruling Rome
and its empire.

The historical slides effortlessly into the mythical with the mention
of Hercules in the next line. Here Ovid is reminding the reader in
a roundabout way that it is the hottest point of summer. The sun
enters the zodiacal sign of Leo (the Nemean lion defeated by Hercules
in Greece) on 23 July. This is partly poetic padding (the term for
decorating a simple statement of time or place is periphrasis) and
also an astrological aside, as the constellations were represented by
the poets as *formae deorum*, the shapes of the gods. The Greek and
Roman myths have supplied us with virtually all the names of the star
clusters and galaxies. I would say that it gives us a sense of looking
down, an aerial perspective of the city, as well as a feeling of the lazy
days of high summer.

Next stop is the portico of Octavia, which she dedicated to her son
Marcellus. He had been groomed for imperial stardom, to succeed
his uncle Augustus, but had died young (his short life was celebrated
in Book 6 of the *Aeneid*; his mother was allegedly overcome with
emotion at a reading by Virgil). The marble finish conjures up
something exotic and colourful, 'setting off the brilliant white of the
Italian Carrara stone' according to Hollis in his 1977 commentary on

the *Ars Amatoria*. Rome had become very much an importing society on the acquisition of an empire.

The emperor's wife, Livia, to whom the Porticus Liviae was dedicated, had a random display of pictures throughout her portico. Ovid does not tell us what the old paintings were which he describes as 'scattered over the colonnade'. Written descriptions from the ancient world frequently outlast physical remains. The temple of Apollo, god of the fine arts and of healing, is well attested by other poets as it marked Augustus' victories over the pirates (led incidentally by the son of Pompey). This temple was finally consecrated to the god after the battle of Actium and the conquest of Egypt. Apollo was presented in architectural reliefs and by Augustus' poetic circle as a real and decisive presence at Actium, facing out and defeating the outlandish Eastern deities fighting on the side of Antony and Cleopatra.

> Then there's the portico with the statues of the Danaids, the granddaughters of Belos, boldly preparing death for their doomed cousins with their savage father standing by, sword drawn. And don't pass by the site of Adonis whom Venus wept for and the Sabbath venerated by the Syrian Jews. Do not shun the temple of Memphis sacred to the linen clothed heifer [the Egyptian goddess Isis]. Isis makes many girls in her image as a conquest of Jupiter's.
>
> Ovid, *The Art of Love* 1.74–8

In the portico connected to Apollo's temple, and in between its columns, stood the statues of the daughters of Danaos. In the Greek legend they were commanded by their father to slaughter their husbands on the wedding night. The tragic theme continues with the reference to Adonis, the beautiful young lover of Venus. Adonis was killed by a boar. His festival seems to have been observed particularly by the prostitutes of Rome. These Greek myths are ready to hand and the poet expects his audience to be attuned to them. The areas he suggests are not exactly romantic settings – the myths they evoke are more about the violence of passions than the game of seduction.

The allusion to the Sabbath is an indication that Jews and their synagogues were a familiar sight in Rome. Many Jewish prisoners of war, casualties of Pompey's capture of Jerusalem in 63 BCE, had, on gaining their freedom, settled in the city. They were evidence of

Rome's increasingly cosmopolitan character and also of a certain amount of calculated toleration of their beliefs and practices. Concessions to their religion were, however, an act of patronage. The Jewish high priest, Hyrcanus II, had ensured the services of his people to Julius Caesar and Augustus honoured the client relationship he inherited from his great-uncle.

The worship of the Egyptian goddess Isis caused more concern to the authorities in the city. There were moves to discourage worshippers of her cult but the goddess remained popular and was a source of both irritation and amusement to those poets whose mistresses were devotees, as the rites could involve periods of celibacy. In Apuleius' novel *The Golden Ass*, written in about 150 CE, this Romanized author (he came from North Africa) describes the rites of Isis in detail, from the perspective of a newly 'ordained' priest. The pull of such religions is understandable; they were exotic, mystical and akin to Christianity in their promise of personal and eternal salvation.

After all that background, read our last extract from Ovid below and remind yourself how this passage started out. What claims does Ovid make for the power of love when he latches on to the legal system?

Even the law courts (who would credit it?) lend themselves to love. Often passion's flames are found in the sharp-tongued court. Where the Appian nymph nestles under the marble shrine of Venus and beats the air with an upward jet of water, there, frequently, a lawyer is captivated by Love. The man who looks out for others has not looked out for himself.

And frequently in that spot the skilled speaker is at a loss for words. It's a brand-new case and it's his own cause that has to be pleaded. Across the way in her neighbouring temple, Venus laughs. He who handed out the favours is now in need of some himself.

[illo saepe loco desunt sua verba diserto,
    resque novae veniunt, causaque agenda sua est.
hunc Venus e templis, quae sunt confinia, ridet:
    qui modo patronus, nunc cupit esse cliens.]

Ovid, *The Art of Love* 1.85–8

Ovid's allusions come so thick and fast that we are in danger of being slowed down or even sidetracked on the guided walk. You have already been diverted into discussions about myths, religion and Roman politics. Ovid's shorthand results in a list of condensed images; he enjoys taking us on a narrative trip – every temple tells a story. For the educated audience of the poet's own time, these were familiar stories and probably gave the piece an anecdotal air, whereas we have to tease them out rather laboriously.

Ovid's message, amid all that mythological paraphernalia, seems to be that there are plenty of places with exotic associations as well as impressive surroundings where love could be courted or unexpectedly make its mark. The power of the Love gods, Venus and Cupid, knows no boundaries, or so Ovid would have us believe. The poet has created a lovers' lane around Augustus' proud avenue of restored buildings.

Not only that, Ovid livens up the picture of the law courts and makes a joke about slippery advocates getting their come-uppance at the hands of the Love god. In the Latin, the poet subverts the language of the law and makes it the language of love. A good example is the term *res novae*, literally 'new things' which was legal speak for an unprecedented case. It's no use the barrister consulting any treatises to cure him of love; they haven't been written. The words *patronus* and *cliens* refer to a relationship of giving and receiving a service. The barrister is now in need of advice himself and will be in the vulnerable position of having to return an obligation. Ovid is irreverent about this very Roman profession.

If you are enjoying the *Ars* and plan to read on, you will find that Ovid goes on in the same vein. His recommendation of the theatre for those on the lookout for love gives him an excuse to relate the story of Romulus, Rome's first king, who engineered the violent abduction of the neighbouring Sabine women; these reluctant brides realized too late that they had been trapped by attending a show. The Sabine women were seized at a primitive performance taking place in a natural and rough-turfed amphitheatre and the rape of the Sabine women became a home-grown legend masquerading as historical fact. The love poets enjoyed citing it as evidence for their lusty and lustful ancestors. In Ovid's account it serves the purpose of recommending the theatre as a place where women are vulnerable and on show themselves.

This is only a taste of Ovid and his inimitable style. A popular poet among the literate and educated circle at Rome, he nonetheless sadly ended his days in exile at Constanza in Romania. He wrote prolifically and pleadingly to Augustus and his successor, Tiberius, but there was no hint of a recall. Ovid tells us in the poetry and letters of lament that this poem, the *Ars Amatoria* was partly to blame for his banishment, since he says that he was punished because of a poem and a mistake ('carmen et error'). The mistake was perhaps witnessing something compromising to the emperor or his family.

The *Art of Love* had been in circulation for about ten years, so it was probably more of a prompt than a reason for Ovid's severe punishment. The poet describes his sense of isolation in the far-off outpost of empire with its frozen wastes and barbarian inhabitants. This is particularly poignant if we remember what he was missing about Rome, the new and improved city with its shady colonnades and, above all, the praise for his poetry at the cultural centre of the empire. Here are the elegiac couplets of lament that Ovid writes from exile:

> I turn from thoughts of the home I miss and my mind makes for the places of our lovely city. The imagination has its own eyes and I can see everything, at one moment the markets, then the temples, then the theatres with their marble façades while the level paved porticoes are right there before me. Now I see the Campus Martius. Its grassy plain overlooks lovely gardens, pools, canals and the water feature, Virgo.
>
> [atque domo rursus pulchrae loca vertor ad urbis,
>   cunctaque mens oculis pervidet usa suis.
> nunc fora, nunc aedes, nunc marmore tecta theatra,
>   nunc subit aequata porticus omnis humo.
> gramina nunc Campi pulchros spectantis in hortos,
>   stagna et euripi Virgineusque liquor.]
>
> Ovid, *Letters from Pontus* 1.8.33–8

Insight

Ovid was not the first of the poets who composed during the Augustan regime to lend a bohemian air to vignettes on life, leisure and love at Rome. However, he seems to have hit a nerve with the *Ars Amatoria* even though he was exiled ten years after its publication. His highly imaginative and sophisticated landscape of mythical transformations (the epic poem *Metamorphoses*) manages to weave together themes of fragile personal and social identities, of artistic freedom and the use and abuse of power.

Like his laments, Ovid's offending poem, *The Art of Love*, has survived the centuries and outlasted the Roman empire itself. Both poems are evidence not only for a Roman sense of fun, debunking austere and self-important images, but also a witness to the power of the first emperor who could censor and condemn at will. This was the downside of the 'beneficent' regime under Augustus.

Out of town

There is one final poet to meet from the era of Augustus. Quintus Horatius Flaccus, born in Venusia (modern Venosa in southern Italy) in 65 BCE, was also part of the emperor's literary circle. The extracts you will be reading describe his journey to Brundisium (Brindisi), and forms a bridge to the broader canvas of Chapter 3 on the Romans and the countryside.

Horace, the name by which the poet is more familiarly known to the modern reader (Flaccus, the 'nickname' element means 'flap-eared'), needs a brief introduction – remember the 'you are here' rule in relation to our ancient witnesses? Horace acquaints us in this poem below with the man who gathered up the talented group of writers in the service of Augustus. Maecenas was a rich member of the *eques* class and an influential adviser and administrator for the emperor from the early days. He functioned informally as a minister for culture, a role which suited him well because he seems to have had a particular talent for diplomacy in a variety of situations.

Horace was, like Virgil, economically embarrassed by the civil wars. In any case, he was lower down on the social ladder than other writers encouraged by Maecenas, being the son of a freed slave (his father was apparently a *libertus*, or freedman). By his own admission, he had been a brief fighter on the side of Caesar's assassins (one battle seems to have convinced him that he was not, primarily, a political animal). He enjoyed a definite upturn in his fortunes when he gained the friendship of Maecenas and he was able to devote a great deal of his time to writing poetry. In gratitude, he celebrated Maecenas' family and status in a number of his *Odes*. It was only natural, too, that he became an advocate for the Augustan regime.

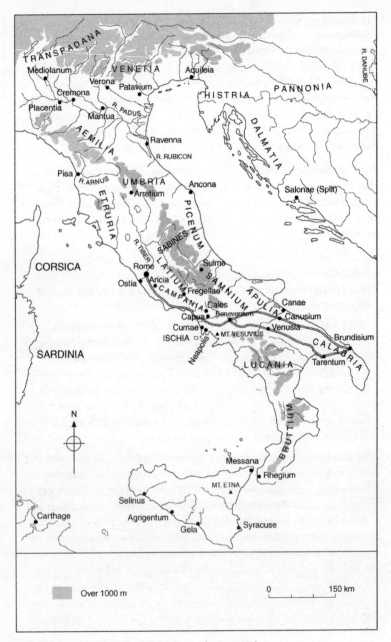

Map of Italy showing Horace's route from Rome to Brundisium (modern Brindisi)

He did not produce an epic, but he did commemorate in verse the emperor's achievements and the imperial family's military triumphs (*Odes* 4). Horace's *carmen saeculare* (centenary poem) was performed at the Secular Games in 17 BCE, an ambitious public occasion with fighting spectacles, sacrifices and sacred banquets. This was the kind of festival we might associate with the millennial celebrations of the year 2000 CE or the 2012 Olympics in London. You will not be surprised to learn that the Roman jamboree also came with a variety of political and propagandist agendas.

Now to the poem, *Satires* 1.5. In spite of the original Latin being in the stately hexameter (six metrical feet per line) verse of epic, these extracts read like a travel diary. Initially, that is how I would like you to approach the poem. Imagine you were using this piece of Horace as evidence for journeys in the Roman world.

What impressions do you gain and what questions are you prompted to ask about transport and terrain, comfort and accommodation? The map of Italy shows Horace's route and some of the towns and villages he passed through.

I left great Rome behind me, came to Aricia and found lodgings in a modest inn. Heliodorus the rhetorician, by far the most learned among the Greeks, was my companion. From there we went to the Appian market which was packed with boatmen and grasping innkeepers. We divided the journey over two days, although travellers in a hurry can do it in one. The Appian Way is not so punishing if you take your time. It was here that the water, filthy stuff, put me at war with my stomach and I waited impatiently while my companions dined.

By now night was making ready to cast her shadows over the earth and to scatter the stars across the sky. Then the slaves and the boatmen began to exchange insults: 'Hove to!' 'Whoa, that's plenty. You've got 300 on board.' A whole hour went by while fares were handed over and the mule got harnessed. The evil gnats and frogs from the fens murder sleep. In the meantime the boatman, sunk in sour wine, sang about his girlfriend and a passenger provided the counterpoint.

Finally the passenger was worn out and dropped off to sleep; the lazy boatman put his mule out to graze, anchored him to a rock and himself snored, flat out. Come dawn, we realized that the boat was not moving, nor did it until one hothead leapt out from the boat and set about the mule and the boatman with a willow cudgel and dealt him a series of body and head blows.

Eventually, at ten o'clock, we were just about landed and were washing our faces and hands in your stream, Feronia. [Five kilometres (3 miles) on at Anxur, Horace meets Maecenas and Cocceius whose mission on the journey is to settle feuds between certain friends. Together they go to Fundi and then on to the city of Mamurra.]

Murena was our host but Capito provided the meals. The next day was a most welcome one; for Plotius, Varius and Virgil met us at Sinuessa. The earth does not boast of any better souls than these and no one is more wedded to them than I am. What embraces and what rejoicing there was. There is nothing to match a delightful friend, when you are of sound enough mind to appreciate it.

We found shelter in a little stopover establishment [*villula*] close by the Campanian bridge where the state purveyors are obliged to furnish fuel and salt. Then on to Capua; here the mules were relieved of their saddle bags, not before time. Maecenas went off for a game, Virgil and I for a sleep. Games are no fun for the dyspeptic and sore-eyed. Next stop was Cocceius' well-stocked villa which lies above the inns of Caudium.

[Over supper the company enjoy an extempore comic duo between a freedman of Maecenas and a native Oscan.] At Beneventum the bustling host almost burned the place down. He was turning some lean thrushes on a spit when the fire escaped through the old kitchen and rapidly licked upwards to the roof. Then you should have seen us, starving guests and frightened slaves snatching up the supper and trying to put out the flames.

This is the area where Apulia [Horace's birthplace] starts to display her familiar hills to me. Those hills are scorched by the Sirocco [or Altino, a hot wind] and we would never have crawled through them without the hospitality of a villa near Trivicum; but it was eye-wateringly smoky because the stove burned green wood, leaves and all. I stayed up till midnight waiting for a girl who let me down. What a fool I was! That meant that I had a frustrating night and stained my nightshirt and supine stomach because of my graphically coarse dreams.

After Trivicum we were whirled off in carriages for a 39-kilometre (24-mile) stretch so spent the night in a little town. I cannot name it in verse but it can be made recognizable by its characteristics:

they sell water, cheapest of all things, but the bread is by far the best around. The seasoned traveller is in the habit of backpacking a supply for ahead, as at Canusium (the brave Diomedes founded the place long ago) the bread is gritty and you can't even fill a jug of water here. And this is where Varius departed. He was sad to go and his friends were in tears.

We arrived at Rubi worn out; we had done long stretch and the rain made it more miserable. The weather was better the next day but the road was worse right up to the walls of Barium, a fishing town. [But Horace manages to joke about a local legend concerning the springs of Gnatia.] Brundisium was journey's end and so ends my writing trip.

Horace, *Satires* 1.5

This is quite a substantial trip on a road running from the outskirts of Rome right down to the coast at Brundisium. Horace and his companion started off on the 64-kilometre (40-mile) stretch from the capital to the Appian market. They were taking their time, a leisurely two days. Main roads were generally of good quality and there were plenty of these, not only in Italy but also throughout the empire. In fact, the Italian network had been established by the end of the second century BCE and the traveller expected paved and well-drained roads on the established routes.

Between Rome and the Alban Hills the friends would have passed through an impressive avenue of tombs and other buildings. It was customary to line the roads approaching a city with burial monuments. The spirits of the dead were then at a safe distance from the dwellings of the living but the deceased were duly, and publicly, commemorated to all the passers-by.

The canal journey was a less happy experience. There were delays harnessing the mules, a great deal of noise from the boatmen and the slaves, to say nothing of the gnats and frogs of the fens: chaotic boat boarding, general delays and dicey transport; travel has not changed that much. Back on the road in Feronia and on to Capua, things seemed to be becoming marginally more civilized for the company.

Before the Romans had taken control of the peninsula, the Campanian region had originally been inhabited by the Oscan race. The area was overrun by the Etruscans in their early history and, later, by the Samnites who established themselves in the Capua area in the fifth century BCE. The Oscan language survived all these influences and there is a distinct hint of this local colour in the entertainment the company enjoys at Caudium. Caudium had been the site of a disastrous Roman defeat in 321 BCE during their wars with the Samnites for control of Campania.

The west coast of Campania had also been settled by the Greeks, but Horace's road now veered east from Capua towards the more mountainous region of Apulia. The Via Appia from Capua to Brundisium was the first Roman road to be built; it was completed in 312 BCE. The company stopped over in Beneventum (modern Benevento), a town close to Horace's home territory.

The relief shown on the map of Horace's route gives a clear idea of just how extensive the mountain range is and why the carriage had to start climbing. Beneventum's original name had been Maleventum but when the Romans established a colony there in the third century BCE they changed the ill-omened prefix *male*, meaning 'bad', to *bene* ('good').

Beneventum is a good example of Roman urbanization. A substantial Roman city had replaced the old Samnite colony (according to the historian Livy, *Histories* 9.27.14) and Roman resettlement techniques brought about a dilution of Oscan culture which had not occurred under previous invaders (a point made by Kathryn Lomas, in *Cultural Identity in the Roman Empire*, 1998, pp. 65–6).

Horace's birthplace Venusia (modern Venosa) was situated on the Appian Way. Many cities in Apulia had sided with the Carthaginian invader, Hannibal, on his march through Italy in the last quarter of the third century BCE. The region of Apulia had also been the headquarters of a significant Italian alliance which took Rome on in open war in 91 BCE. This did not endear them to Rome.

Journeying on

The pace of travel was quickening. Evidently it was feasible to cover over 48 kilometres (30 miles) a day in a carriage, though not necessarily pleasant to do so. Wagons and carts were less comfortable than litters carried by slaves. Horace mentions a *raeda*; translated as carriage, a misleadingly grandiose title, this was a large, open cart with wooden wheels, iron tyres and no springs.

The last lap of the journey was plagued with the rain and a bad road along the east coast.

Canusium (Canosa) on the right bank of the river Aufidus obviously and ironically suffered from a water shortage. Part of a splendid aqueduct remains there to this day but, unfortunately for Horace's party, it was not built until the second century CE by the wealthy Herodes Atticus. Evidently the stony nature of the bread was more difficult to cure. In the late nineteenth century visitors were still complaining about it and putting its bad quality down to defective millstones.

A successful trip?

Horace did enjoy himself in spite of the discomforts. There were, after all, no major disasters. There was evidently a real and present danger of banditry. In his commentary on the satire Michael Brown speculates on the security aspects of a journey like this: 'Since Italy in the early 30s was infested with brigands, whose removal Octavian undertook in 36, an armed bodyguard would probably have been required, of which Horace makes no mention.' (*Horace Satires*, 1993, p. 139)

The most Horace's company had to contend with was a fire in the kitchen at Beneventum, an episode which reads like a knockabout comedy ['nam vaga per veterem dilapso flamma culinam/Volcano summum properabat lambere tectum']. I have put the Latin in here so you can pick out *Volcanus* (Volcano), the Latin for Vulcan. The god of fire is used to describe the fire itself as it makes a purposeful escape (*dilapso*) out of the kitchen. It adds to the comic flavour: it is as if the god himself is bursting out of the confines of the cooking area.

Incidentally, barbecuing the thrushes gives you your second taste of a Roman menu. The stove in the villa at Trivicum conjured up smoky visions. Not all places were as well run or pleasant as Cocceius' country residence. The 'diary' goes on in wryly comical vein as Horace describes being let down and actually stood up by a deceitful girl. He spent the night with sex on the brain – some translations are coy here – Horace is clearly having wet dreams. Look at the Latin printed below and then look at the translation which is pretty much word for word:

> hic ego mendacem stultissimum usque puellam ad mediam noctem
> exspecto: somnus tamen aufert intentum veneri; tum immundo
> somnia visu nocturnam vestem maculant ventremque supinum.
>
> [I stayed up till midnight waiting for a girl who let me down. What
> a fool I was! That meant that I had a frustrating night and stained
> my nightshirt and supine stomach because of my graphically
> coarse dreams.]
>
> Horace, *Satires*, lines 82–5

Veneri in line 84 is a form of the noun *venus*. Venus is not just the goddess of sexual passion, she is also the word for it, just as the god of fire, Vulcan, could lend his name to the minor conflagration with the charcoaled thrushes. The disappointment at the inn is a relatively minor mishap on a successful trip. At least the travellers could plan their itinerary knowing that there were places to stay, a mixture of lodging houses, the hospitality of friends and the convenience of the *villula*, a distribution point where those travelling on public business could obtain provisions for their journey.

Hidden agendas

Michael Brown reminds us that writing an entertaining travelogue was a tradition of Roman satire (I shall be looking more closely at satire in Chapter 4). In that case Horace may be fitting his journey's episodes into a ready-made framework or tweaking them a little to correspond to a previous poetic model. The journey and the incidents were genuine enough but Horace is making poetic capital out of his adventure.

The description of the trip to Brundisium suggests that for Horace it was an entertaining and pleasurable holiday. Fellow poets and close friends are met along the way and pleasant evenings shared with plenty of good conversation. But this is clearly not the whole story. There is a brief allusion to Maecenas' and Cocceius' purpose in travelling to Brundisium. The reference to their being 'old hands at settling feuds' connects this journey with the embassy of 38 BCE, which was an attempt to patch up the alliance between Octavian and Mark Antony.

These two men, you might remember, had divided up the empire between them after defeating Brutus and Cassius and their armies.

The pact they had made at Brundisium two years before was not surviving too well. This particular mission was accomplished and the negotiations produced the treaty of Tarentum, but this too proved to be only a holding operation.

It is typical of Horace to exercise discretion. He was one of the 'resident' poets along for the ride. Allegedly, Horace did not get involved with the wheeling and dealing of the men in power and in those early days, before Octavian became the unchallenged ruler of the empire, it was no doubt wise to distance oneself from the political game. Of course, Horace's contemporaries did not believe in his neutral pose and frequently pestered him for insider information. Several of the poems involve Horace disingenuously stating that he had nothing but innocuous conversations with Maecenas on the various diplomatic excursions.

I would like to leave you with a revealing little exchange of precisely this nature. It is from Book 2 of Horace's *Satires* and you should have no trouble in relating to Maecenas' strategy for 'keeping off' politics. In that case, there are really only two safe subjects to discuss and 'flappy-eared' Horace had no intention of living up to the name he had inherited.

It's seven, no, nearly eight years – how time flies – since Maecenas first regarded me as one of his friends, in so far, anyway, as a travelling companion, someone he would like to take along as on a carriage journey and someone he could share some inconsequential conversation with. I quote 'What's the time?' or 'How do you rate the Thracian "Chicken" against Syrus?' [both gladiators in a forthcoming fighting match]. 'These morning frosts really are nippy. You can't be too careful.' This is the sort of stuff you can safely deposit into 'open' ears!

Horace, *Satires* 2.6.40–48

Insight

This poem is a celebration of Horace's rural retreat, his Sabine farm, where modest wining and dining with friends are contrasted with the pressures of public life in Rome. One of Horace's guests tells the story of the town mouse and his country cousin. This is a reworking of an Aesop fable but Horace adds various Roman layers, literary and social, to the narrative, which becomes a commentary upon the simplicity and wholesomeness of life away from politics in the capital.

POINTS TO REMEMBER...

1 The Roman empire is still very much in view across the world. We can travel physically and virtually to both restored and ruined places which resonate with Roman culture, uncovering the daily life of this diverse and stratified society through monuments, gravestones, workshops, palaces and public works.

2 We can also read the surviving texts (principally in Latin and a fair amount in Greek) from this vibrant and historically significant civilization. The wide range of writing (from history to poetic genres) reveals the complex relationships educated Romans developed with their literary predecessors and peers, their families, friends and the social structures that shaped their lives.

3 Studying Latin (and even just getting acquainted with its structure and vocabulary) prompts all kinds of questions about the way in which the language reflected and reinforced a distinctive Roman psychology and philosophy of life. We can go beyond simply tracing the survival of Latin words and expressions in modern times, interesting though basic etymology might be. There is also a strong argument that all great literature deserves to be read in its original language.

4 Rome had an empire before it had emperors. Octavian (Augustus means 'revered', 'esteemed') portrayed himself as the first citizen and the father of the country but he held his autocratic position by gathering all the reins of power into his hands from the treasury to control of the provinces and the imperial legions.

5 Talented poets like Horace and Virgil were encouraged to allude to a new age of peace and prosperity under Augustus. In his epic about the early and painful struggles to establish the Roman race, Virgil included visionary moments of future successes and setbacks. He presented Jupiter as the divine patron of Augustus whose destiny it was to restore the greatness of the empire and the grandeur of its capital.

6 The Greco-Roman gods had distinct personalities, spheres of influence, attributes and skills. They were simultaneously

possessors and embodiments of their crafts (e.g. weaving, fighting, forging) and known for their defining characteristics (e.g. passion, artistic creativity, inebriation). You might like to try matching the god to the attribute as you read through the chapters.

7   The Greeks settled in the south of the Italian peninsula and towns such as Pompeii preserved something of Greek urban lifestyles. A Greek king, Evander, appears (in the legendary tradition) as a local but rustic ruler in the area around Rome in Virgil's epic. The Romans remained in awe of and very influenced by the achievements of Greek culture, especially the art and literature of fifth-century BCE Athens and the works of writers in the Hellenistic period (the age of Alexander the Great; see Appendix 1: Timeline of Roman history).

8   Ovid was a versatile and prolific poet who fell foul of Augustus because he either witnessed or was somehow implicated in an indiscretion that had a political edge to it. His punishment illustrates the limitations Augustus placed upon the literary artists at Rome, even though he developed a system of patronage rather than blunt coercion.

9   Ovid's poetic epistles expressing his anguish at being exiled from the city of Rome have left us with impressions of the urban geography and of the ambience of the capital. It is not a factual account for posterity but we learn a great deal from all the poets whose works can function as a political and social barometer.

10 Horace's Italian journey sketches out many aspects of travel, politics and leisure in the late Republic. Maecenas also fell out of favour with Augustus after being a highly astute adviser and cultural ambassador when the emperor-to-be needed to construct a new image for himself as father and protector of the people.

3

Roman holiday

In this chapter your starting point will be a piece of architecture in contrast to the literary texts you became acquainted with in the tour of Rome and the journey through Italy. Of course, there will be a number of Roman voices, too, which can modify or verify our understanding of the images and symbols we see on works of art. The idea is that after reading this chapter you will feel that a link has been forged between the two forms of expression, visual arts and written literature, and that you can transfer skills of interpretation from one to the other. Pictures on a sculpture can be 'read' as well as viewed.

The Altar of Peace

The *Ara Pacis*, or Altar of Peace, survives as a continuous frieze of statements about Roman rituals, Roman ideals and Roman realities. It is almost a set of lectures on what Romans should value, in short how the Roman ideology was promoted by the men in power. This monument, constructed in honour of the peace that the emperor Augustus had established across the empire, tells us a great deal about the political as well as the cultural tone the new regime was planning to develop. So the next stage of understanding is to get to grips with techniques of Roman propaganda. A study of one of the important panels on this monument will lead you into an evaluation of Roman attitudes towards the countryside. The countryside is a key place to begin an exploration of Roman identity as it is important to recognize the significance of Rome's rural heart.

A VERY ROMAN MONUMENT

When I had successfully concluded affairs in Spain and Gaul and returned to Rome, in the year of the consulship of Tiberius Nero and Publius Quintilius, the Senate decreed that, in honour of my return, an altar of Augustan Peace should be consecrated on the Campus Martius, in which they ordered that the magistrates, priests and Vestal Virgins should make an annual sacrifice.

The Achievements of the Divine Augustus 12.2
(*Res Gestae divi Augusti*, usually *R.G.* for short)

The occasion for the proposal to build the *Ara Pacis* was the successful completion of Augustus' campaign to calm things down in the western provinces; ostensibly, the altar was not marking the end of civil war nor was it an explicit rejoicing that a damaging and divisive period for Roman society was over. The site of the altar honoured the emperor's return from abroad in that it faced the Via Flaminia, the road by which Augustus had re-entered the city.

The extract above is Augustus' version of how the altar came about. The source I have used is Augustus' *Res Gestae*, inscribed on bronze tablets and designed, in his own lifetime, as part of the emperor's mausoleum. A copy in Greek, set up on a monument in Ankara, Turkey, is about the best version scholars have had to work from, along with fragments of a Latin inscription. The document is a priceless source for the period as it is the emperor's own account of his policies and actions throughout his reign.

Augustus is sometimes eloquent for what he does not say, and every now and then ancient historians of the period obligingly record things this astute emperor omitted from his version of events. We should certainly treat with caution Augustus' claim that the idea of constructing the Altar of Augustan Peace was a spontaneous suggestion from the Senate floor. No doubt there was someone there primed to plant the idea that such a monument would be a fitting part of the celebrations when Augustus returned from successfully securing troublesome provinces.

One or two questions come to mind about this monument. What function would an altar have had in Roman times? Would there have been a temple and was there any particular god that would have been honoured and thanked for the peace?

This is one of those nodal points, or sticking places, for the student of Roman civilization. The military historian Vegetius ascribed the following, often quoted, policy to Roman imperial strategy: 'si vis pacem, para bellum' or 'igitur qui desiderat pacem, praeparet bellum' [If you want peace, prepare for war] (*De Re Militari* 3). What was this Altar of Peace designed to do? Was it built in the interests of promoting peace but, simultaneously, quite comfortable about glorifying war?

Insight

It is worth reflecting upon twentieth- and twenty-first-century rhetoric when predatory wars masquerade as peace or as the defence of democracy at home and abroad. The Romans can and should be judged harshly for their colonization with the wholesale destruction of cities (witness Carthage) and peoples. They, of course, would have argued that they were securing their borders and installing good government after these countless casualties.

Let's turn to a poetic source, and a poet introduced in Chapter 2, to find out how he viewed the monument. Ovid might have been present at the dedication ceremony of the Altar of Peace. He writes about the Altar of Peace in his work on the Religious Calendar, the *Fasti*. As Ovid was revising this poem while he was in exile, the fulsome tone of praise was probably calculated to conciliate the emperor he had offended. Whatever the personal agenda and psychological state which prompted this verse, Ovid is still a Roman, presenting a Roman perspective. It's probably true that a compliment can only be effective if it corresponds to commonly held perceptions:

My song has led me to the altar of Peace; the dedication day is the second from the month's end. Peace, be present, with your hair bound and the victory laurels of Actium decorating your head. Be indulgent and stay put throughout the whole world. Although a lack of enemies means a lack of reasons for triumphal processions, you will bring greater glory to our commanders than war! Let the soldier carry weapons only to restrain the armed attacker and let the fierce trumpet be the clarion call for the procession alone.

Let the world near and far regard with awe the descendants of Aeneas and if there is any land which fears Rome too little, let it be because it is a land that loves Rome. Priests, add incense to the flames burning on the Altar of Peace, let the white sacrificial animal be anointed and fall. Ask the gods who listen favourably to dutiful prayers, that Peace and the imperial house which guarantees Peace last a long time.

Ovid, *Fasti* 1.709–22.

An altar was a site where the individual could make a personal sacrifice, but also where everyone met to take part in rituals which ensured the safety, security and prosperity of the whole community. Ovid gets quite emotional about what the altar represents. The altar did not name an Olympian god but it was consecrated to the divine person of Peace. Peace is addressed as a goddess by Ovid. You might be wondering why the goddess Peace did not figure in the list of gods covered in Chapter 2, but Peace, in the guise of a goddess, would be perfectly acceptable to the Roman mentality.

The Romans were familiar with the idea of acknowledging and worshipping abstract concepts and these were frequently depicted in art and literature as recognizably human forms. They were personifications but the *persona* was a divine one. For instance, Honour, Virtue and Concord all had temples dedicated to them in Rome. Perhaps they were less important deities than the Olympians but they were significant enough to deserve attention and sacrifice. Augustus' altar promoted Peace, until then little heard of in the ancient sources, to a prominent position.

Once built, dedicated and ritually inaugurated, the altar remained as a civic and sacrificial area, but there was no temple attached to it. The altar had strong associations with Augustus and his achievements but the emperor would have felt uncomfortable about a full-scale sacred precinct (the literal meaning of temple, *templum*, is a circumscribed space for worship) as that might suggest that he was worthy of divine honours. Although Julius Caesar had been deified after his death, and emperor worship was practised in some of the provinces, for many centuries living rulers did not seek such godlike status in Rome.

Augustus, his rise to power and consolidation of his position at the helm of the empire did not have the support of all Romans. On the other hand the protracted civil wars had taken their toll. The consecration of an Altar of Peace must have encouraged co-operation in the task of repairing the physical and emotional traumas resulting from the strife both in the city and throughout Italy. This altar implied a celebration of the Augustan settlement, and an end to hostilities, but we need to return to the issue of war, and particularly foreign wars, before we can thoroughly digest Roman ideas about peace and monuments to Peace.

> The temple of Janus Quirinus, which our ancestors resolved should
> be shut whenever peace had been secured throughout the empire of
> the Roman people on land and sea by means of victories, and which,
> before I was born, according to tradition, had been shut only twice
> since the founding of the city, was ordered to be closed three times by
> the Senate while I was the leading citizen.
>
> Augustus, *R.G.* 13

The significant point here is that peace was associated with
military victory and implicit in the term 'peace' is the notion of
Roman conquest and success (The Ovid poem said as much).
Peace from civil war was the reality of the situation when the
Altar of Peace was commissioned but that would not be something
to celebrate openly, nor could it be publicly admitted that the
Roman system of administration and the security of its empire had
ever been put at risk. Even the battle of Actium was presented by
Augustus and the poets he patronized as a victory over the foreign
queen of Egypt, Cleopatra, and the role of Antony, the Roman
commander and Octavian Augustus' rival, was marginalized in art
and literature.

Insight

Apollo has special significance for the victory over Antony and Cleopatra
which marked the ascendancy of Octavian in Rome. Virgil's vivid
portrayal of Apollo facing down the outlandish Egyptian gods at the battle
of Actium (depicted on the shield made for Aeneas by Vulcan in Book 8 of
the *Aeneid*) was a powerful and influential image in the Augustan version
of events. Horace's joyous poem on the death of Cleopatra celebrated her
final defeat and visualized her flight from Actium. By committing suicide
some time after, Cleopatra cheated the Roman people of seeing her in
chains at a triumphal display in the capital. Horace's ode begins 'nunc
est bibendum' [Now is the right time for drinking!] as if festivities could
finally take place.

For the Romans peace was a condition which was actively achieved,
and generally achieved by force. The term 'Pax Romana' came to
be synonymous with the Roman empire, the area under Roman
dominion in which peace was maintained by military strength and
efficient government. Virgil, in his epic the *Aeneid* (the first poem
encountered in Chapter 2), summed up the situation and the reality
of the Roman empire by stating that Augustus, the representative of
Roman power and authority, would spare the submissive and wage

total war on the proud ('parcere subiectis et debellare superbos', *Aeneid* 6.853).

I suppose a clear case of a victory statement would be Trajan's column, an impressive spiral of scenes from the wars against Dacia in the Balkans. This triumphal monument from the second century CE is one long battle dispatch and a feast of facts for the historian of Roman soldiery. It is also a rich 'text' for understanding the nature of Roman rule and expansionism, the essence and implications of Pax Romana and the fate of those who opposed it.

'READING' THE ALTAR

The point of this preamble is to remind us of how important it is to know something of the background and context when looking at any evidence for Roman civilization. The *Ara Pacis* is a vital source for our understanding of how Augustus worked upon and exploited traditional attitudes towards the city, the country and the empire. It was an ambitious and large monument, a rectangular and roofless precinct wall measuring 7 metres (23 feet) high by 10.5 metres (34.5 feet) long, west to east, and 11.6 metres (38 feet) wide, north to south. Inside was the raised altar, all around which were sculpted reliefs on both the inside and outside faces of the walls.

Visualize yourself standing at this altar and taking a slow turn around to view the panels. The inner walls have been carved to look like the slats of a fence with all the equipment of a sacrifice hanging from them – bulls' skulls, ritual bowls and garlands. The garlands are made up of a wide variety of plants and fruits, representing the four seasons and the span of the sacrificial year, a comforting sight for the Roman onlooker suggesting that, after all the upheaval of the civil wars, things were back to normal. For the people and gods of Rome it was business as usual.

Walking around the outside of the structure, one would see decorated walls with a common border. The lower zone is made up of more foliage and small animals peep from under the sculpted leaves. Let's focus on the 'procession' panels in this visual narrative.

Try to work out at least some of this for yourself. Describe the dress and deportment of the figures and have a guess at the event in which they are participating.

Reliefs on the Ara Pacis

Discussion

The figures are taking part in a procession and they are all dressed formally, men, women and children in full-length clothes. The toga was worn by significant property-owning male citizens on state occasions and Augustus actually legislated that, cumbersome though it could be in a Mediterranean climate, this heavy and elaborate garment should be *de rigeur* in the conduct of public, legal and political business. Workaday clothes and also the dress for leisure were the thinner, shorter and more practical tunics. Augustus was determined to tighten up on the lax habits and appearance of those with status and to restore the dignity of the senatorial order. If that meant wearing the toga in summer in a hot and crowded amphitheatre, such was the *noblesse oblige* to which the upper-class citizen submitted.

Insight

The toga is worthy of study in the sociology of clothing. Putting on the manly toga (*toga virilis*) at around age 12 was a rite of passage, signifying that boyhood was over and the duties of citizenship were beginning in earnest, but at 6 metres (20 feet) in length it was not a practical everyday garment. Jerry Toner (1995, p. 104) suggests that the wearing of the toga in public by female prostitutes indicated that they had 'abandoned traditional female codes of dress and decorum' and so became quasi-masculine. Much later in the Roman empire (the fifth century CE) togas became garishly multi-coloured and were worn by senators at Rome as a display of wealth rather than a sign of dignified service to the state.

Dress codes can be revealing whatever society we study. On the frieze, Augustus and his chief minister and indispensable military commander, Agrippa, can be singled out as they are males with their heads covered. This marks them out as presiding magistrates and, as such, key figures in carrying out sacrifices on behalf of the state. Public and communal religious rites were the responsibility of governing officials and not the preserve of a priestly caste, but Augustus involved priestly colleges in the state rituals as a matter of course.

It is apparent that this event is some sort of religious festival, perhaps marking the safe return of Augustus or a general celebration of the peace, which would be appropriate to have as a decoration and statement on the Altar of Peace. Scholars and experts can make only an educated guess at the nature of the event represented. The altar took three and half years to complete and was dedicated at the end of January in 9 BCE so, possibly, the sculpture is showing

Sculpture of Augustus as High Priest (Pontifex Maximus)

us scenes from the dedication ceremony. (The figure of Augustus is damaged on the frieze but in the photo above you can see him striking a religious pose.)

> Whatever the occasion, what sort of message would the sculpture have conveyed at the time?

Discussion

This is a happy occasion as well as a formal one with many of the figures on the frieze appearing to be turning around and chatting to one another. Having the imperial group stand out and simultaneously blend in with the procession bonds Augustus and his family to the Roman people in the context of a civic ritual and thanksgiving. This is true social harmony. The artwork throughout the monument represents Augustus, the emperor, in more than one role – as presider over religious rites, bringer of prosperity, protector of the empire and, last but not least, as a good family man. Augustus is shown as an ideal citizen, worthy of admiration and respect both as an individual and a type, both father of the people (*pater patriae*) and a more abstract model of Roman virtues and authority.

MAKING CONNECTIONS – ONE LAST PANEL

The figure in the following illustration may represent Peace herself. She could also be a personification of Mother Earth or even Italy, as she has plenty of the produce at her feet which the Italian countryside could provide. She is flanked by figures who look like winds and waters in human shape. This particular panel will lead us into the discussion about Roman rural origins and how important agricultural life was to the Romans. It is finely carved and seems well preserved, but it must be remembered that it was restored in 1784 and eighteenth-century artists had fewer scruples about retaining the integrity of the original work than the restorers of today.

> Look at the panel and the general composition. How is prosperity conveyed?

Figure representing Peace or Italia or Earth?

Discussion

The lush landscape symbolizes the goddess's powers. At her feet are an ox and a sheep, an indication of plentiful herds and flocks. On her lap are two children, whose survival and success seem to depend on this happy state of affairs, the thriving rural community. The picture demonstrates that the image and imagery of the countryside have a vital part to play in a sophisticated urban milieu. Remember how Italy had been devastated in the civil wars, how Virgil lost his farm and many lost their livelihood.

You could conclude that this panel is all about Italy at peace and the rhythms of the farmer's year restored, and certainly that is an important part of the symbolism and the story Augustus wished the artists to tell. Digging deeper, we could ask ourselves what the Italian countryside meant to the Romans and whether their relationship to it changed over time. We tend to have a picture of packed cities – Rome possibly had up to about a million inhabitants in the early centuries CE and across the empire large towns and provincial capitals, such as Alexandria, Carthage and Antioch, teemed with people. The countryside with its organization and activity and interaction – economic or otherwise – with the town can be more of a mystery to the modern reader. The shape of the empire, town, country and borders, will be a topic for this book's concluding chapter so, for the present, confine yourself to considering whether Augustus could tap into continuous and underlying sentiments about the province of Italy which, after all, constituted the local landscape of Rome.

Back to the land

RURAL IDENTITIES

Reading through Roman literature does not leave an impression of romantically wild or scenic areas of mountains, forests and rivers untouched by human hand. Instead, the term countryside summoned up for the Roman writer images of agriculture with the well-run farms or estates which were a profitable haven of peace and orderliness. Virgil's Evander was graced with the title 'king' but he is a really a chieftain in a small and working agricultural community. Archaeological evidence generally corresponds to this picture, although there's no exact match with Roman myths and legends about their past.

Rome's foundation myth, the story of Romulus and Remus, tells how a site was chosen by the twin brothers, sons of the god Mars, and how the farming people quickly established themselves in the area.

The historian Livy (*Histories* 1.6) records one version of events which has Remus being killed by his brother for mocking the low walls of the early settlement. Rome may have started off in internecine strife but for the Romans this story emphasized the existence of a ruler and a nation who were not to be trifled with.

Preserved on the Palatine Hill stood an historical landmark for the Romans, the Hut of Romulus, a reconstruction of a primitive dwelling with walls of wattle and daub and a thatched roof. The hut was maintained by priests and rebuilt if necessary. It was destroyed more than once. There was at least one occasion when it burned down as a result of a ritual being carried out within it. From the time of Augustus onwards our literary sources refer to a similar hut on the Capitoline Hill. What was important to the Romans was the enduring symbolism, not the original site of the hut. It represented Rome's humble beginnings, the seedbed from which she had risen as a conquering nation and the place where Roman values and virtues had first been formed and tempered.

Both the hut of Romulus and the plentiful countryside portrayed on the *Ara Pacis* make significant statements about the rural identity of Rome and the Romans, but it would be naive to think that feelings about the country and country life were uncomplicated, when so many Roman citizens had made their home in the city with its superior amenities and sophisticated ambience. The town dweller considered himself to be urbane and cultured. *Urbanitas* conjured up a range of characteristics, all of them counterposed to the qualities of the countryman who constantly displayed *rusticitas*, a peasant mentality coupled with boorish behaviour. The ambivalent attitude to the simple life and those who lived that life will be touched upon in Chapter 4.

THE RESPECT FOR HUSBANDRY

Many wealthy Romans owned country estates and visited them regularly, particularly in summer when the heat and noise of Rome became unbearable. They had bailiffs to run the farms and slaves to work them (the bailiffs might be trusted slaves with skills of accountancy and management). The smallholder would have to toil away on his modest plot of land but even he could afford one or two slaves if he was able to make a go of things. In the following medley of literary sources several images of agriculture, real, ideal, practical and poetic, are shown. Let's start with Cicero, the Republican orator, lawyer and politician and a man whose career, public life and *raison d'être* were based in the capital city. Cicero wrote a treatise, *De Officiis, On Duty*, for the benefit of his son and it is Cicero's pronouncements on the dignity of landowning which are of interest here:

> Trade if the business is small should be considered vulgar; but if it is a large-scale business, importing many things from all over the world and distributing to many without sharp practice, it should not be greatly censured. Indeed, it would seem to be worthy of praise if those who engage in it, when sated with profit, or perhaps I should say satisfied with it, transfer their possessions from the port to the country estate, as they have often done so from the sea to the port. But of all occupations, from which gain is made, nothing is better than the cultivation of the land, nothing more profitable, nothing more delightful, nothing more worthy of a free man.
>
> Cicero, *On Duty* 1.151

What sort of country life might Cicero, an ex-consul and wealthy man, be recommending to his son?

Discussion

It is doubtful if he envisaged his son, young Marcus, grubbing about in the soil or getting his own hands dirty in any way. There was a story from the early days of the Republic about the consul Cincinnatus being called from the plough to go and sort out a crisis in Rome (he had to pause and pick his heavy toga up on the way there) but this was not how most gentlemen farmers expected to conduct themselves on the land. Marcus Cato, who was a role model for the stern, patriotic moralist brigade in Roman politics, saw farming as a business venture rather than an ostentatious display of one's wealth, but he was no more a working farmer than Cicero would have been:

> Once he applied himself more strenuously to the business of making money he saw agriculture more as a diversion than as a profitable venture, and he invested capital in sure and safe things: he bought ponds, hot springs, land rich in Fuller's earth, areas which produced pitch, land with natural pastures and woods – all of which brought a great deal of money in for him and could not, something he himself used to say, 'be ruined by Jupiter'.
>
> Plutarch, *Life of Marcus Cato*, 21.3

Can any conclusion be drawn from Plutarch's description? The cryptic phrase about Jupiter refers to bad weather, Jupiter being the god of the elements, storms, rain, etc. Fullers' earth was widely used for cleaning woollen garments. Cato may have decided that farming was best pursued as a hobby and not a place to make serious money. Evidently, he took up moneylending as his main profit-making activity. Senators were not supposed to engage in trade and commerce, but they could use slaves and freed slaves (freedmen) to invest for them while they remained silent partners.

Insight

The senatorial stratum clearly did own commercial enterprises and increasingly so as Roman manufacturing grew in size, diversification and complexity. See David Jones' detailed and elegant 2006 case study on *The Bankers of Puteoli: Finance, Trade and Industry in the Roman World.*

Obviously for Cato, even the 'hobby' of farming ought to show profit. His manual is full of hard-nosed advice on the practicalities of owning land: 'Sell off the old oxen, the blemished cattle and sheep, wool, hides, old wagons, old tools, old slaves, sick slaves and whatever else is superfluous' (Cato, *On Agriculture*, 57). There is no hint of sentiment here, items of no further use include human beings. Unskilled farm slaves were completely dispensable and many were kept permanently chained (slave chains have been discovered on Roman sites in Britain). They had no legal rights but were just part of the property to be used and abused as the owner thought fit. In his book on Roman slavery, Keith Bradley also quotes Cato (*On Agriculture* 59, Bradley 1994, p. 89) on the economical clothing of slaves. Farmhands should be allocated tunic, blanket or cloak and wooden clogs every other year and recycling the harder-wearing garment was a recommended option. Another farming handbook by Columella recommends how chain-gang slaves could be housed and gives a brief insight into the bleakness of their lives: 'For those in chains let there be an underground prison [*ergastulum* in the Latin], as wholesome as possible and getting light by means of many narrow windows which are built too high from the ground to be reached with a hand' (Columella, *On Agriculture* 1.6.2).

You might contrast their lot with the affection and friendship felt for Tiro, Cicero's secretary, who was freed after years of loyal service (the extract in Chapter 2). The household slave with skills to offer might be integrated into the life of a Roman family. The agricultural worker was a depersonalized element in the process of production. Not surprisingly, rural slaves were known for making desperate bids for freedom. They joined Spartacus' rebel army in droves as it marched through Italy, defeating trained troops under experienced commanders. This was a terrifying period for the Romans and when the slaves were finally defeated by Crassus in 71 BCE the reprisals were savage. Thousands of slaves were crucified along the length of the Appian Way.

Not all estate owners used chain-gangs on their land. Pliny the Younger, who lived under several emperors from the latter half of the first century CE and survived into the reign of Trajan in the second century CE, states that he, and other landowners in the area of his estate, did not have chained slaves on their property. As in all work, whether manual or skilled, and whether town or country based, slaves and free labourers could toil side by side. However, given the fluctuations of farm working it made sense to employ slaves on tasks that needed doing all year round (shepherds, overseers) and to hire in labour for harvest time and other seasonal activities. Having slaves to do everything could be to show off abundant wealth and conspicuous consumption. Connections were bound to be made between better treatment and more efficient production. Attitudes to slaves were changing too, so that, by Pliny's time, it was not just a question of economic imperatives which dictated more humane treatment and enabled the slaves to work harder and live longer.

View from a poet

The poet Tibullus was a fairly close contemporary of the three poets discussed in Chapter 2. He was a member of the equestrian class, the second rank in the social order. They were very often businessmen (in 'vulgar' trade) but, like the top stratum, they tended to invest most of their capital in land. Tibullus made a profession out of his poetry, which suggests he was a man of independent means. He did not hold political office but he did win some military awards (accompanying his patron Messalla Corvinus on active service abroad.) Tibullus, like Horace, regarded country life as both a retreat from urban pressures and a time of productive labour and productive leisure. What picture of rural life does he paint in the following verses? Note Tibullus' different standpoint when reading his poem.

Let another man pile up for himself gleaming gold and own many acres of ploughed land and let his unending labour make him fear the neighbouring enemy and the trumpets of war put his sleep to flight! May my poverty lead me through a life of ease as long as my hearth burns with a continual light. As a farmer, I will sow the soft vines at the right time and sturdy fruit trees with a skilful hand. Never may hope desert me but provide a plentiful harvest and rich musk in full vats.

Tibullus 1.1.1–10

Discussion

Tibullus' ideal life is not rooted in such base concerns as making money. In fact, he seems to view making profit as a threat, a source of envy and attack. His vision of a farmer's life is comfortably limited. Vine sowing and planting fruit trees may have taken some skill but if that was the extent of Tibullus' work on the land, he was no more a farmer than those of us in modern life who have grown a few tomato plants. Note the loose definition of poverty. Tibullus was not poor and, in any case, the truly poor farmer could hardly have enjoyed a life of ease (*vita iners*).

In subsequent lines, Tibullus looks forward to a life which will not involve travel but will be time spent relaxing under the cool shade of trees in high summer. The farming side is the pursuit of a dilettante:

I don't seek again the wealth and income which came to my ancestors from the stored-up grain: a small crop is enough, it is enough if I can rest on my couch and ease my limbs on my own bed. How pleasant it is to lie in bed and listen to the wind blowing while I hold the mistress of my heart in a soft embrace, or when the winter wind brings storms, to fall into a carefree sleep deepened by the drumming of the rain.

Tibullus 1.1.41–4

The sound of a storm blowing would fill the serious farmer with a different emotion, since he could be made destitute by crop damage or loss of property. The introduction of the love interest puts a different slant on the idyllic scene. *Domina is* the word for Tibullus' girlfriend but it is also used to denote someone in a position of power and control. Mistresses like this often kept the biddable poet dancing attendance in the city. Tibullus clearly has others to do the farm work on a regular basis and there is a dose of self-irony in the way he depicts his rustic activities: 'However, let me not be ashamed from time to time to hold the hoe or urge on the slow oxen with the goad. Let me not be reluctant to carry back home a lamb or a kid deserted by its forgetful mother' (1.1.29–32).

Virgil, who wrote poetic manuals about living off the land (the *Georgics*), was much more aware of the demands of subsistence-level farming: 'Jupiter himself decreed that the way of agriculture should not be easy and he was the first to ordain that the fields should be tilled systematically, sharpening mortal wits through hardship, nor did he allow his kingdom to grow sluggish with heavy lethargy' (*Georgics* 1.121–3). Tibullus' emphasis on cultivating the vine does not quite fit with the anti-sluggish model posed by Virgil. In common with Tibullus, however, Virgil had a concept of countryside that transformed its lifestyle into an ideal, presenting rural life as both restorative and intellectually undemanding. Horace 'sold' the countryside to his patron, Maecenas, by presenting it, with its simplicity and the lack of pressure, as a retreat for the ancient equivalent of a stressed-out executive. All this sounds sentimental and of course this was hardly life in the rural raw for Horace or his guests. The poet boasts fine wine and good living.

Horace returned to the homily on the countryside in his fable about the town mouse and his country cousin. In this story (which appears in his *Satires*) the unsophisticated rural mouse finds eating at the loaded tables of his relative a dangerous experience; the 'civilized' town riches are ephemeral and always liable to be snatched away. There is a high price to pay for urban luxury:

This is the scene: the town host has made his country cousin comfy; the guest lounges on the brightly coloured coverlet while his urbane cousin has hoisted up his garments and bustles about serving one course after another. The host acts the part of a house-born slave, does all the duties, even to the preliminary tasting of everything he has on offer. The rural mouse reclines and revels in the new experience. He is slipping into the role of pampered guest amid all this good cheer, when suddenly, a violent noise of doors thrown open catapults them both from their couches and they run in fear and trembling through the length of the hall. The barking of Molossian hounds reverberates

> around the lofty residence and the mice are even more convulsed
> with fear. Then the country mouse speaks. 'I can do without a life
> like this. I shall say my goodbyes. My wood and my hollow, safe from
> unexpected attack, will more than compensate me for the modesty
> of my produce.'

Horace, *Satire* 2.6.106–17

Tibullus, like Horace, has a minor obsession with the quiet life and rural simplicity. Their descriptions of country living are seductively sympathetic. The driest piece of Latin prose, extracts from farming manuals, can yield similarly absorbing evidence on how the Romans reconstructed their rural identity. The countryside was a place where satisfaction and self-awareness could be gained along with the strength and stamina needed to face a life of responsibilities away from the agricultural world. Many of the Roman religious festivals were relics of the ancient agricultural tradition, for instance the Parilia and the Suovetaurilia, so called because it required the sacrifice of a pig (*sus*), a sheep (*ovis*) and a bull (*taurus*).

Tibullus seems to be firmly convinced that his success in farming was largely due to his dutiful attitude to the gods. No rural deity was short-changed in sacrifices:

> For I am reverent, whether it is a lone tree trunk in the field or an old
> stone at the crossroads which has its wreath of garlands. Whatever
> harvest the new season provides me, the first fruits are placed in front
> of the god of the farmer. Golden Ceres, may you have the crown of
> corn ears which hangs in front of your temple doors, and may the red-
> painted guardian be placed in the orchards, so that Priapus scares the
> birds with his cruel sickle. You Lares also, who are the guardians of an
> estate once prosperous but now poor, take the gifts due to you.

Tibullus 1.1.11–20

Insight

It is difficult to get a handle on Tibullus. He seems to present more than one self-image to his readership and some commentators suggest he has a kind of personality disorder, with his darting from one theme to another and demonstrating contradictory perceptions and values. However, interesting work is being done by Open University doctoral student Rebecca Cann, who is approaching Tibullus as a master craftsman 'mapping the shifting hopes and self-perceptions of the Roman psyche during a period of instability and flux.'

Behind the familiar Roman gods such as Jupiter, Mars and Apollo, with their large temples and public rituals, lurked a whole host of less-defined divinities. There was a strongly held belief that there was a divine agency in all the important life processes and that these agents were forces to be reckoned with, and appeased, for humankind to survive and be successful. These were more down-to-earth deities than the larger abstraction like Peace. Division of labour is probably the best way to describe the set-up. Tibullus' 'lone tree trunk' or 'old stone' may represent the boundary markers of his land. The first-fruit offerings are made to the goddess of the crops, Ceres (our word 'cereal' comes from her name). Ceres received public status because of the constant and civic importance of a good grain supply. Vesta, the goddess of the hearth, is another deity who made the transition into the public life of the state. Her fire and cult were supervised by the Vestal Virgins in Rome. Priapus, who guarded the orchards, received his offering of fruit. There are a number of surviving figurines and statues that represent him, most of them explicit about his upfront fertility. Priapus' genitalia were always paraded as larger than life, for he was the icon of productive sexuality.

There was a city shrine to the Lares in Rome, at the summit of the Sacred Way. The Lares were guardians of the house but also guardians of the household of the nation. In the individual Roman house they were statuettes placed in the Lararium, the shrine in the main hall, or *atrium*. They were involved in all aspects of family life from the mundane, small daily offerings of wine to important rites of passage such as a coming of age, when the good luck charm (*bulla*) and toys which the child no longer needed were dedicated to the Lares.

The rural spirits, or *numina*, were present in every aspect of activity, each with a narrow sphere of influence. Every stream and tree had its presiding and protecting deity. The farmer ploughing his field had to acknowledge the *numen* (singular form of *numina*) of that field but also the spirit of the plough. In childbirth the family had to sacrifice to Wailer (the spirit of the infant's first cry), Cradler, Bedder, Breastfeeder and so forth. This, for us, rather alien practice inspired the joke from Sir Frank Adcock (quoted by L.P. Wilkinson in *The Roman Experience*, 1975, p. 205) that 'If the Romans had had bicycles, they would have had a goddess, Punctura.' The comment is quite a nice illustration of the apotropaic element in Roman beliefs. Warding off the bad outcome was a big part of the ceremonies.

The agricultural community could not function without a constant source of fire, good crops and fertile livestock. Tibullus claims that he has treated the local deities with respect and reverence. As he has fulfilled his part of the bargain, with the correct rituals and observances, the gods have supported his enterprise. The beauty of this contractual arrangement is that the gods are not to blame if things go wrong. In that case, someone has failed to carry out the correct ritual or simply carried the ritual out incorrectly.

> Take a look at Cato's advice. What impression of Roman ritual does it give you?

When thinning a grove of trees you should observe the following Roman ritual:

> Sacrifice a pig as a propitiatory offering and utter the following prayer. 'Whether you are a god or goddess to whom this grove is sacred, as it is your right to receive as sacrifice a pig, as a propitiatory offering for causing a disturbance of this sacred place, and therefore for these reasons whether I or someone I have appointed carries out the sacrifice, let it be performed correctly. To this end, in sacrificing this pig, I pray in good faith that you will be benevolent and well disposed to me, my home and my family, and my children. For these reasons therefore, be gracious enough to accept the sacrifice of this pig as a propitiatory offering.' If you wish to plough the cleared land in the grove, offer a second sacrifice in the same way but add the words 'for the sake of doing this work'.
>
> Cato, *On Agriculture* 139

Discussion

Fussy is a word that comes to mind, along with 'repetitive' and even the reaction 'overkill'. Acts of appeasement seem to have been a tedious affair. If you attach the ritual to the contractual nature of the human–divine relationship, it makes a lot more sense. The language is legal to cover every eventuality (a bit like the 'party of the first part'). The specific deity of this grove is unknown so the address has to be to both sexes. If the farmer says 'god' and the resident spirit turns out to be female then the prayer may be ignored.

The formula 'it is proper' marks the farmer's awareness that it is his duty to carry out this ritual and the proviso on the correct performance of the ritual means that he accepts responsibility should he default on the contract. The head of the household (i.e. the father (*paterfamilias*)) normally carried out these rituals or, failing that, his official appointee. The prayer, in this case, draws to a close with an itemized list of beneficiaries. The word family (*familia*) includes relatives and slaves. The farmer makes a special and separate plea for his children, for they were the continuation of the family line and a way of prolonging its name and status. In Chapter 5 you will finding out how vulnerable young children were in the ancient world.

Case studies: two country villas

We leave the countryside with a brief, but revealing, tour of two interesting rural homes. This is a thinly disguised exercise in plan reading but the intention is to take the mystique away from the process.

BOSCOREALE – A WORKING FARM

Boscoreale was situated just outside Pompeii. Its ruins survive and it appears to have thrived in the time of Cicero. As farmhouses go, this was at the upper end of the market but was primarily a working business rather than a gentleman's residence. There is archaeological evidence of an upper storey and this may have accommodated the leisured members of the household. However, we cannot say for certain how it looked or how it was used.

Look at the ground-floor plan and consider why rooms might have been arranged as they were. How does layout help efficiency in the production process?

Discussion

You might have found working through this a tall order. One major feature you might have noticed is the compactness of the site. The places for the producing and refining of the two main crops, wine and corn, are within easy reach for convenience and protection. Threshing floors and the storage of fermenting wines needed large areas. As is the case today, there were vineyards on the slopes of the volcano, Vesuvius, at this time. Campania was famous for fine wines. The villa has its own oil and grape press and a flour mill. The bakery, baths and toilet are all grouped around the kitchen so that they are all close to the common heat and water supplies. Fresh water was not far

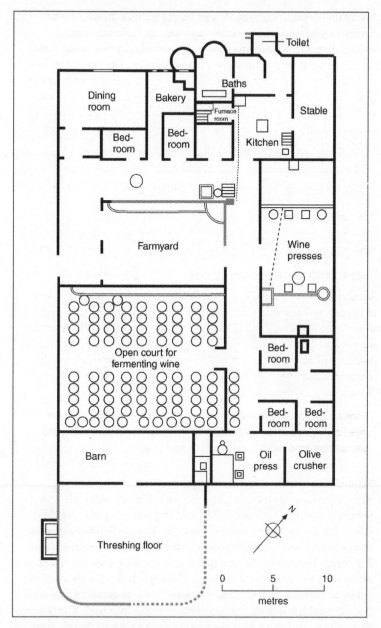

Plan of a working farm villa at Boscoreale

away, in the courtyard, but water for the baths may have been stored in lead tanks which have been discovered in the courtyard. Once used for the baths, the water could have been flushed through the toilets.

Notice how close the stable was to the kitchen. Even more unexpected to the modern eye, the only access to the stable was through the kitchen. There is no sign of an entrance in the outside wall. The stable housed animals such as donkeys which were used to turn the oil and grape presses, so the proximity may have been a convenient design. This also illustrates how careful one has to be in not assuming that certain rooms had exactly the same functions then as they would now. Take the kitchen, for example (*culina*). In Roman life it could have been a workshop or meeting place as well as a place for preparing food.

Most rich establishments and larger townhouses would have used the *atrium*, a substantial entrance hall, for gathering together members of the family and also for receiving friends, guests, clients and dependants who came to pay their respects at an agreed hour. It was very much the public face of the household, and ancestral busts, family trees, trophies and badges of office would be put on display there. The architect Vitruvius, writing at the time of Augustus, points out how necessary an elaborate *atrium* was for those with obligations to receive and to keep up appearances. The working villa at Boscoreale does not appear to have an *atrium* so presumably there was not the same social pressure in a country estate of this nature. An alternative explanation is that the owners – and this villa was probably adapted for different purposes over time – might have conducted business, or had political careers, which would have required an *atrium* area, in suitable accommodation in nearby Pompeii.

LEISURE AT LAURENTUM – PLINY'S VILLA

Pliny did have working estates and he took a keen interest in good management and in the wellbeing of his tenant farmers. In some of his letters he complains, in a jocular fashion, about the intrusion of these farmers wanting him to settle disputes, or give them his help, when he is really trying to have a break from his duties in Rome. This villa is very much designed for relaxation and seclusion. It brings a different set of problems from Boscoreale because, although Pliny gives us a detailed description of it and we know where it was, the actual site has never been discovered. (He talks about the villa in the seventeenth letter of Book 2. All Pliny's letters are available in the Penguin translation.)

The plan shown below is a reconstruction from the written evidence. Pliny had a real eye for detail but he was also showing off about his cultured and sophisticated lifestyle in a rural environment. Pliny's account of his villa could be modernized into any interview from the home of the well-off, with money from birth, business or stardom. These usually come with a photograph of a large residence and its tasteful interiors. We can duplicate this to a certain extent with the plan reconstruction but in spite of Pliny's blow-by-blow account of the layout of his mansion, there are several different interpretations of his words and not every reconstruction looks the same.

Pliny introduces the topic with a recommendation of the site. It is only 27 kilometres (17 miles) from Rome (not a bad commuting distance if you think back to Horace's comment about how quickly you could travel if you wanted to; see Chapter 2), but it is in the country and by the sea. It was a distinct advantage to have those cool sea breezes during the hot Italian summer. If you look at the plan now, you will see that Pliny had one of his dining rooms (*triclinium*, a place for reclining on couches as you ate), his gymnasium and a garden all overlooking the sea.

Pliny has an extension (X marks the spot on the plan) where he could obtain a rare commodity in any Roman house: secluded privacy. In this carefully designed, self-contained suite of rooms he could study and write, undisturbed by the voices of the slaves, and he could shut out the sound of the wind and the sea. He remarks that he is

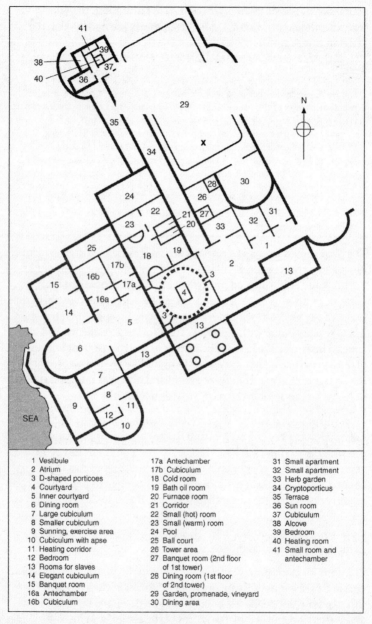

1 Vestibule	17a Antechamber	31 Small apartment
2 Atrium	17b Cubiculum	32 Small apartment
3 D-shaped porticoes	18 Cold room	33 Herb garden
4 Courtyard	19 Bath oil room	34 Cryptoporticus
5 Inner courtyard	20 Furnace room	35 Terrace
6 Dining room	21 Corridor	36 Sun room
7 Large cubiculum	22 Small (hot) room	37 Cubiculum
8 Smaller cubiculum	23 Small (warm) room	38 Alcove
9 Sunning, exercise area	24 Pool	39 Bedroom
10 Cubiculum with apse	25 Ball court	40 Heating room
11 Heating corridor	26 Tower area	41 Small room and
12 Bedroom	27 Banquet room (2nd floor	antechamber
13 Rooms for slaves	of 1st tower)	
14 Elegant cubiculum	28 Dining room (1st floor	
15 Banquet room	of 2nd tower)	
16a Antechamber	29 Garden, promenade, vineyard	
16b Cubiculum	30 Dining area	

Pliny's villa at Laurentum (a possible reconstruction)

68

particularly glad of this retreat during the Saturnalia, the midwinter festival, which was when a (noisy) good time was had by all. (Remember from Chapter 2 that, for the Romans, Saturn was the god of jollity.) Slaves and masters sometimes reversed roles for the time of this celebration so a certain amount of controlled anarchy must have taken place. Pliny's arrangement meant that he could carry on with his cerebral pursuits and his household could enjoy themselves without either interfering with the pleasure of the other.

Pliny also benefited from the presence of an *atrium*. He did receive visitors at his villa but he could keep the *hoi polloi*, those tenant farmers for instance, in the reception area. If he chose, more intimate acquaintances and distinguished callers could be brought into, and suitably impressed by, the unusually shaped courtyard. The courtyard (walled gardens were a popular feature borrowed from Greek house-building traditions) could be a conversation piece as it consisted of two D-shaped porticoes protected from bad weather by some arrangement of windows and a roof overhang. The large open areas of the villa were given over to a garden where Pliny grew mulberry and fig trees, evergreen shrubs and herbs. The proud owner describes his garden in sensuous terms and the whole locality comes across as an aesthetic invention. Latin had a phrase, *locus amoenus*, which conjures up a beautiful or pleasant place. Such ideal spots might, however, be already inhabited by some supernatural creature and be best left undisturbed.

There is everything here that a man tired and stressed by life in the city could dream of: exercise areas, a bath suite, a ball court. The number of *cubicula* (again *cubiculum*, singular, can be misleadingly translated as bedroom; that was not its exclusive function) may, at first, seem surprising but, although the basic meaning of *cubiculum* is a room for lying down, it seems to have been used variously, as an intimate reception area, a sort of boudoir, as a study or even as a storage room. Just as we use rooms differently at different times of the day and at different phases in our ownership, the Romans too employed their domestic space flexibly. Pliny the Younger waxed lyrical about other extensive dwellings he possessed and might even have named them after literary genres (perhaps to remind the reader that they were primarily places for relaxation and intellectual pleasures). For instance, he characterizes his villas at Lake Como as follows:

One is built on the rocks with a view over the lake, like the houses at Baiae, while the other stands at the water's edge in a similarly Baian design. For this reason I have called the first Tragedy because it appears to be elevated on actors' boots and the second Comedy because it wears low shoes.

Pliny, *Letters* 9.7

Conclusion

This has been a mere taste of some facets of the Roman countryside, idyllic imaginings from Tibullus, practical realities in Cato and the rural retreat of professional politicians. Although touching on the pragmatic attitudes we find towards countryside connections, I have deliberately marginalized vital but complex questions about the existence or otherwise of a 'macro' economic relationship between Italy and the capital city, Rome. I hope that this chapter has given some sense of what rural life and idylls meant to those Romans who have left us their thoughts on the countryside in Italy. The regard for country life draws us deeper into the Roman psyche. You have started to grapple with the challenge of 'reading' architecture, from the monumental and propagandist, the *Ara Pacis*, to the site plans and remains of Roman villas. Nothing is more exciting than integrating the evidence and coming up with some conclusions about life as it was lived, or dreamed about, in the rural environment.

POINTS TO REMEMBER...

1 Monuments like the *Ara Pacis* and Trajan's Column could be as eloquent a statement about the Roman imperial self-image as an elaborate piece of poetry extolling the virtues of the conquering nation and its defining characteristics.

2 Peace, Honour, Virtue and Concord were divine forms, as was the embodiment of Italia or Roma herself, represented as a female deity worthy of worship and yet in need of constant protection.

3 Leading citizens were not just senators or magistrates; they also performed priestly offices. This might suggest that religion was solely at the service of the state (and the poet Ovid penned the line 'expedit esse deos' – 'it is expedient there are gods' – going on to say that therefore we believe they exist), but it is also true that public policy needed sanctioning by tradition and precedent in law, all of which operated in a divine frame of reference.

4 Roman prose writers display a practical attitude to husbandry: ownership and good management of the land guaranteed the wealth of the aristocracy and, indeed, of the mercantile classes who invested in working estates.

5 Slaves and free labour made up the workforce of the larger estates which had replaced many smallholdings during the expansion of Rome's empire across the Mediterranean (with the conscription of the yeoman farmers) but did not entirely supplant them. Toiling in the fields was the lot of many slaves and they had very different and much shorter lives than house servants.

6 The poets tend to romanticize the rustic beginnings of the Roman race and to suggest that in the countryside they could enjoy (light) labour and leisure on their own terms. The rural villa served as a place of retreat, renewal and as a focus for poetic introspection about wealth, poverty and the pursuit of happiness.

7 Horace's tale of the town and country mouse embedded in a gently ironic satire about life in the city and the benefits of owning a well-situated farm has stood alone as a moral fable ever since. Alexander Pope, for example, used it to comment on the humiliation of the patronage system in Georgian England.

8   Early Roman rural spirits (*numina*) did not disappear on the adoption and adaption of the Greek gods of Olympus but they were not divine personalities as much as 'immanent' essences of just about all aspects of nature. Even sophisticated poets like Tibullus were in the habit of appeasing these forces and conducting time-honoured rituals, invoking them at planting and harvest in particular.

9   Pliny the Younger has left us a number of detailed descriptions of life in the countryside during later imperial regimes. He managed to survive the more tyrannical rule of Domitian and balance his civil service duties at Rome with intellectual distractions (if not uninterrupted free time) at his enviable range of coastal and inland villas.

10 As ever, we need to analyse and synthesize archaeological and literary evidence as well as the visual images and inscriptions on monuments and epitaphs to gain a comprehensive picture of rural life. This chapter has at least identified the territory but further exploration is recommended.

4

Point of departure

Although I'm upset that an old friend is leaving I applaud the fact that he is intending to settle down in depopulated Cumae and to grant the Sibyl, its resident prophetess, at least one fellow citizen. It is the gateway to Baiae and a lovely retreat on a pleasant coast. I would choose its nearby barren island Prochyta in preference to our crime centre at Rome, the Subura, for how can we view any place wretched and isolated in comparison with the perils of the city? I mean the ever-present fear of fires, the constant collapse of buildings, the thousand dangers of the urban jungle, and not least the poets reciting in the month of August!

> [Quamvis digressu veteris confusus amici
> laudo tamen, vacuis quod sedem figere Cumis
> destinet atque unum civem donare Sibyllae.
> ianua Baiarum est et gratum litus amoeni
> secessus. ego vel Prochytam praepono Suburae;
> nam quid tam miserum, tam solum vidimus, ut non
> deterius credas horrere incendia, lapsus
> tectorum adsiduos ac mille pericula saevae
> urbis et Augusto recitantes mense poetas?]

Juvenal, *Satires* 3.1–9

Our exploration of the seamier sides of Rome will focus on a poem written in the early second century CE. Before the poet's friend, Umbricius, departs from the city for the quiet of the countryside, he strikes a rhetorical pose (his style of speech is bombastic) and delivers 300 lines or so listing the evils of Rome. In Chapter 3 you read about the Roman representation of the Italian countryside. The writers displayed ambivalent attitudes but a significant tendency was one of sentimentalization. In Juvenal's poem, Umbricius' decision to leave Rome seems to do an admirable job of reinforcing the rural ideal.

A close-up on this satire will demonstrate how ancient Rome could assault the senses. I shall also guide you around some of the strategies of the satirist. You should start seeing beneath the surface of the city and of the literary text as Umbricius is not a mere mouthpiece of Juvenal but also part of the parody in the poem.

Because I have used Satire 3 as a focus and frame for this chapter, I shall be working through some key passages and elaborating upon their topical allusions. The second task entails a deliberate straying from the text of the satire, so that one can become acquainted with significant features of the Roman world. This may feel like a whistle-stop tour of the poem but Juvenal's complete works are available in paperback so you can, in the future, read the satire through and appreciate its cumulative and climactic effects.

I have found that the detailed commentaries accompanying the Latin text of Juvenal (there are several available) can be invaluable for background information and, although initially complex, they can be accessible to the beginner. User-friendly notes, which translate all their Latin or Greek references, for instance, frequently tell a story of their own about big issues in Roman society. Commentaries are worth consulting if you are inspired to launch into independent study after reading this book, but be warned: they can be expensive. In this book I have selected information from them to extend your vision of imperial Rome.

Decimus Junius Juvenalis: a profile

Juvenal was born in Aquinum in Italy in the 50s or 60s of the first century CE. He came to Rome to study rhetoric and became a friend of the Spanish poet Martial. He seems to have known Britain at first hand, perhaps from being on active military service, and he was possibly also in Egypt. Unfortunately, most of the above is conjecture based on evidence from a book of Lives which was written hundreds of years later. We are on relatively safe ground in assuming that Juvenal lived through the reign of the Emperor Domitian who is portrayed by the ancient historians as an autocratic and punitive ruler.

Juvenal was writing when he was much older, in the more liberal reigns of Trajan and Hadrian (his *Satires* probably span the years from 110 to 130 CE).

An added complication is Juvenal's tendency to refer, in his poems, to episodes and figures from previous generations – for instance Satire 1, lines 147–71, where Juvenal makes a programmatic statement about using famous names of the late Republican period to represent contemporary vices. In this way historical characters become almost mythological, although the poet says pointedly that it is safest in satire to attack the dead. So searching through the poetry for clues about the man and his times is not a straightforward business.

Satire: the rules of the game

Consider the word 'satire'. What comes under its heading nowadays?

Discussion

Did you find you were thinking of various forms of comedy and doing a few subdivisions in your head? Comedians past and present are in the business of making fun of anything and everything. Sometimes self-irony is the mainstay of the act. The comedian's own inadequacies as a person or in a social situation are subjected to sardonic scrutiny or the description of their humiliation is simple slapstick; either way, this trend for self-analysis in comedy usually involves several side-swipes at the broader cultural environment, implying that the comedian has a sense of proportion that his society has lost.

Maybe you felt that satire implied having a political axe to grind or at least denoted 'attitude' in one respect or another. In that case, a good example of an upfront satirical magazine would be *Private Eye* on the UK market. *Private Eye* traditionally combines the 'send-up' of pretensions, personal foibles of individuals and of group behaviour with what I would call political exposures. It has in the past highlighted corruption in government, in political parties, in administration and in business.

For the Romans, there was a specific genre of satire which conformed to certain traditions and had a particular poetic form. Satire, or *satura*, its Latin name, was verse written in the traditional metre of the epic, the dactylic hexameter. Roman satire was a literary form invented by the Roman writers. There is no Greek equivalent, although, of course, you will find satiric comedy in the plays of the fifth-century BCE Athenian Aristophanes, and you will also encounter satiric tone and parodies in other types of Roman literature. The satiric genre adopted by Juvenal was a uniquely Roman one. It covered a wide range of material and allowed individual poets to strike whatever pose they felt was appropriate to their material. The subject matter was as varied as that found in modern-day satire. One of the meanings of the Latin word *satura* is 'miscellany'. It is associated with the mixed dish, or *mezcla*, and with a rich and plentiful stuffing, made up of many ingredients.

The 'father' of Roman satire, Lucilius, was writing around 130 BCE. Only portions of his work survive but he seems to have made full-frontal attacks on posturing and arrogance. His was a far angrier voice than the one Horace was later to adopt. Consider Horace's journey described in Chapter 2. That was satire in the form established by Lucilius, but Horace's semi-documentary style drew from his own experiences, allowing the reader to have a laugh at his expense. (Remember his restless night at Beneventum!)

Lucilius gained the reputation of being rather a raging bull against individuals and their faults. In the ancient world, explicit insults, libels and graphic portrayals of named individuals did not attract libel or slander suits. Verbal assaults could be vicious but it was part of a tradition of parody and aggressive rhetoric, especially in the public life and politics of Republican Rome. Some of Cicero's court cases and his speeches, both for the prosecution and for the defence, provide a flavour of ancient character assassination.

Persius, writing satire in the first century CE, declared his intention to visualize all Romans with asses' ears. No aspect of Roman society escapes his censure, which he delivers in the guise of the angry young man. His influence on Juvenal must have been significant. Juvenal's declaration of intent in his opening satire informs the readers that 'it is difficult *not* to write satire'. The reality around him compels him to produce his angry poetry, such is the force of his passionate disdain. (The Latin phrase is *saeva indignatio*).

Insight

I have since thought over this statement from Juvenal in his first Satire – that 'saeva indignatio facit versum' (by which he means that a fierce sense of injury or insult produces his poetry). In my contribution to an Open University course called *Culture, Identity and Power in the Roman Empire* (Block Two) which ran from 2000 to 2010, I suggested Juvenal was making a melodramatic gesture, raising himself up to the heights of righteous indignation in order to write satiric poetry. In that case, *indignatio* appears as his muse or like an abstract deity who will inspire him, in the tradition perhaps of poets who called upon Apollo or Cupid as spurs to creativity.

Look who's talking

Satire 3 is full of vignettes of urban existence reproduced through the jaundiced eye of the character Umbricius. Travelling through Umbricius' invective on the city, it is apparent just how useful scholars of the Roman world have found Juvenal in reconstructing life in the capital. I had not intended to select it or to use it so extensively when I set out to write this chapter, but the poem is, in many ways, an unavoidable source, as well as an entertaining read.

In her essay on 'City and Country in Roman Satire', Susanna Morton-Braund lists some of the echoes of other voices in Juvenal, namely his poetic predecessors, Lucilius and Horace. In the time-honoured tradition of *imitatio* Juvenal alludes to and reworks those authors' pictures of city life, 'the bustle, competitiveness, cheating and crime'. The point is that this is as much a *literary* city as a real physical location.

> *This is not to say, of course, that none of these details is drawn from real life; but the realization that certain details may be included and others excluded under the influence of literary tradition must affect our use of such details as evidence for everyday life.*
>
> Braund, 1989, p. 37

The poet takes us on a different kind of tour from the ones you enjoyed in Chapter 2 and the message here is to proceed with caution. Here is the seamy side of Rome, its slums, its noise, its smells and its collective aggression. The opening lines catapulted you into a familiar polarity: town versus country.

> Look back at the quote and see how Juvenal builds up his indictment of Rome. What is the scenario? Does the map of Italy tell you anything about Umbricius' destination? Does anything strike you as contradictory in Juvenal's depiction of the country and the city?

Discussion

The city is falling apart according to the poet, but what about the anticlimax of 'poets reciting in August'? In the first lines of the opening satire of Book 1, Juvenal had despaired of ever escaping the hordes of orators and poets whom he meets declaiming behind every colonnade. But surely this is hardly a hazard equal to the life-threatening ones just mentioned in Satire 3. The first rule of reading Juvenal is to see the joke before you look for the moral.

It is important to be aware of the technique of 'interrogating the source'. Juvenal needs careful watching or reading because he enjoys demolishing his own case for the prosecution just when you think he has won it hands down. So the skills one develops of looking under the surface for less obvious agendas will be needed from the beginning. For instance, the idea that Umbricius will be about the only person living at Cumae (giving the Sibyl a citizen) almost immediately makes him look rather comical.

It's interesting, too, that the first time we meet negative words like 'wretched' and 'isolated' they are applied to the offshore island where Umbricius is taking his refuge. Later, these same adjectives (*miserum*, *solum*) or words like them are used to describe life in Rome. Maybe this is just to emphasize how inhospitable the city, in spite of all its amenities, could become but it is possible that Juvenal is putting down an ironic marker about life outside Rome.

Cumae stands on the Bay of Naples and was the oldest Greek colony in Italy. A substantial piece of the southern Italian peninsula was known as Magna Graecia because so many Greek settlers had established towns there, long before Rome became the power centre of Italy. Cumae had become a backwater, outshone by Puteoli, which the early Cumaeans had themselves founded. Puteoli had an excellent harbour and became a popular place for wealthy Romans to visit and to build holiday retreats.

Within spitting distance of Cumae was Baiae, a seaside resort which Martial 'could not praise too highly' (*Epigrams* 11.80). According to Horace, a hundred years before Martial and Juvenal, many of the villas were pushing out to sea: 'You are building houses and eagerly extending the shoreline of the sea that thunders around Baiae. The crowded coastline is not enough!' (*Odes* 2.18.20–22). We could mischievously note that Baiae is not so different from Rome if it has undergone a building frenzy of this nature. So far, we have heard the poet's preferences for country life but he hands over to Umbricius to make the detailed case against the city. During the course of the poem, Juvenal's friend dramatizes the dangers of life in the 'high-rise' flats and more than justifies Juvenal's trailer, the opening lines, about badly built tenements and urban ghettoes in Rome.

> We live in a city which is for the most part teetering on undersize beams. For this is how the landlord props up the crumbling walls, by papering over the cracks. He urges us to sleep without a care in the world, but collapse is imminent.
>
> Juvenal, *Satires* 3.193–6

The *insulae*, or tenements, were notorious. *Insulae* remains found in Ostia and Pompeii indicate a variety of heights and standards. Some could be quite attractive with a garden incorporated into the complex. The apartments could house shops and small businesses. One apartment block could contain a wide variety of accommodation, though. Even in Rome a first-floor flat (the modern Italian *piano nobile*) might be quite an upmarket residence but, as you moved higher up the building, your expectations and status became correspondingly lower. What was more, you were vulnerable to a sudden conflagration.

> It's got to be a better life anywhere where there are no fires, nights without fear. Picture it, someone is shouting for water, the next minute he's rescuing his bits and pieces. In the meantime the smoke has reached the third floor and you are blissfully unaware.'
>
> Juvenal, *Satires* 3.197–9

Even without the fires, sleep was impossible if you lived off any of the thoroughfares. *Insulae* really were 'islands', the literal meaning of the Latin word, being surrounded on all sides by streets, and providing a sharp contrast with life in the suburbs on the Palatine Hill or on the banks of the Tiber. To make matters worse for those renting in the nexus of roads, wheeled traffic had been banned from the city during the day by Julius Caesar. This meant that the wagons rolled in during the night. Lodgings closed the doors on sleep.

0   15
metres

Elevation and plan of insulae at Ostia

> Only the rich get any rest in this city. The 'route' of the trouble? It's the rattle of the wagon winding its way through the narrow streets, the curses of the herdsmen who have been held up.
>
> Juvenal, *Satires* 3.234–7

Daytime offered no respite. Umbricius' Rome was a noisy, crowded, claustrophobic, sprawling city:

> The surging crowd in front stops us in our tracks. The mass behind have been funnelled into our backs. One man prods me with his elbow and another with a sharp pole. Worse still, one fellow strikes me on the head with a crossbeam and a second wields a barrel. My legs are layered with mud. In next to no time, I am kicked from every direction and all the feet outsize. A soldier's hobnailed boot lands squarely on my toes.
>
> Juvenal, *Satires* 3.243–8

Let's pause for a moment and bring in Martial, a contemporary and friend of Juvenal. Martial praised the Emperor Domitian for his clearance programme in the city. It seems that the street sellers and their stalls had colonized the main thoroughfares:

> The casual trader had taken over
> Our whole city, no longer ours.
> His boldness knew no bounds
> But Domitian, our hero, commanded
> That the streets be cleared.
> And what was lately a track
> Became a boulevard.
> No more wine vessels hitched up
> To the pillar of a portico.
> No judges forced to flounder
> In the muddy middle of the road.
> No indiscriminating razor
> Unleashed on a closely packed crowd.
> No smoky fast-food stalls
> Monopolizing every road.
> Barber, barman, cook and butcher

> Stick to their pitches now
> Lately one large open-air market,
> Rome is Rome once more.
>
> Martial, Epigrams 7.61

MORE FROM THE MOUTH OF UMBRICIUS

Umbricius' negative feelings about Rome are not confined to the physical discomforts. In fact, I have plunged you into the middle of the poem in this last discussion. Tied up with the speaker's feelings of being a victim, being vulnerable to material disasters and having too submissive a body language to make his way in the crowds, is the issue – which the poet tackled first – of social mobility. Umbricius has already revealed that he cannot 'play the game' to get on in Roman society generally.

Look through the Latin of this passage first and work out a few English derivatives from words like *librum*, *laudare*, a*strorum*, *ignoro*, etc.

> What am I to do at Rome? I don't know how to dissimulate. I can't praise a book if it's bad nor can I ask for a copy. I am all at sea with the stars and their movements! I don't want to predict the death of someone's father, by means of astrology, even if I knew what I was looking for; I am not the sort to go scrutinizing frogs' entrails.
>
> > [quid Romae faciam? mentiri nescio; librum
> > si malus est, nequeo laudare et poscere; motus
> > astrorum ignoro; funus promittere patris
> > nec volo nec possum; ranarum viscera numquam
> > inspexi.]
>
> Juvenal, Satires 3.41–5

You have already met the notion that star groups could be identified with mythological beings (the mention of Hercules and the Nemean lion in Ovid). People of the ancient world assumed that the movements of celestial bodies were connected to terrestrial events, that there were cosmic patterns which could be followed and individual destinies were bound up with these. The casting of horoscopes was popular throughout society and the 'science' of

the stars was always a growth industry. Juvenal made it a target in
other poems:

> But for real reliability, it's the Chaldaeans from Egypt every time.
> Whatever the Chaldaean astrologer says, the gullible swallow as if
> relayed straight from the oracular fountain of Ammon [the Egyptian
> god regarded as a version of Greek Zeus and the Roman Jupiter], not
> surprising since the Delphic oracle has lost its voice and the human
> race is prey to an uncertain future.
>
> Juvenal, *Satires* 6.553–6

Astrology, however addictive, aroused suspicions. Astrologers were
both persecuted and expelled from the city at regular intervals.
Umbricius' picture of unscrupulous practitioners is a distasteful one.
For a fee they would promise the death of a relation to a greedy heir.
Speculating on the lifespan of the ruler or any of his family would invite
immediate reprisals. Astrologers featured in a number of treason trials
under the emperors and Tiberius, himself an eager user of horoscopes,
expelled them wholesale. He pardoned those who begged for
forgiveness but they had to guarantee an end to all predictions of death.

Delving into the insides of frogs also suggests Roman techniques
for foretelling the future. Interpreting the signs by inspecting animal
entrails was a legitimate practice in religious rituals and something
the Romans had inherited from the Etruscans (the early settlers of
Tuscany whose kings had once ruled in Rome). Known as extispicy,
this practice is perhaps more understandable if you think back to
ancient assumptions about universal structural harmony. Vital
organs, like the liver of a sacrificial animal, were imagined as a micro-
configuration of the cosmic patterns, hence their careful division into
parts for divination and interpretation.

Umbricius is, of course, proud that he is so disempowered and
unknowledgeable in all these areas. (Latin negatives build up –
nescio, nequeo, non possum, non volo, ignoro (I don't know, I can't,
I am not able, I don't want to, I am ignorant of).) In any case, none
of the occupations mentioned is a respectable profession, whatever
cachet they have all achieved in the Rome of Umbricius' day. The
whole passage has a definite air of mock humility at his shortcomings
in so many areas and it continues in that vein.

> There are those who know how to be the go-betweens, carrying
> messages and presents back and forth between bride and adulterer.
> Not me, and no one will be a thief with my assistance; which means
> that I am no earthly use on the staff of a provincial governor.
>
> Juvenal, *Satires* 3.45–6

Prophecies and potions – this should give you a flavour of Umbricius'
fish-out-of-water feeling in the Rome of his day. Supernatural evils
aside, he is also a sad spectator of wholesale corruption and of the
sharp practices of racketeers. He is a stranger to this environment
where everyone is on the make and skill in subterfuge is a *sine qua non*
(the Latin phrase for a prerequisite; literally, 'without which not') for
any prestigious position. He implies that going out to take charge of a
province was a golden opportunity to make money out of vulnerable
provincials. You needed a canny and acquisitive staff to support you
in this. Umbricius would not in any way fit the 'job description'.

The speaker produces a flattering self-portrait. Umbricius is too good
and upright to survive in the city of Rome. He has already exhibited
utter contempt for those social climbers who have reached the top
by trade, by contracts for public works or by putting on a good
gladiator show. You could conclude that Umbricius is a snob and a
very self-important one into the bargain.

The enemy within

> But fellow citizens, I cannot put up with Greece here in Rome. To be
> accurate, what per cent of the dregs are genuinely Greek? For a long
> time now the Syrian Orontes has been emptying out into the Tiber.
> This eastern river carries with it the native language, the lifestyles,
> along with flutes, bizarrely configured harps, foreign tambourines and
> girls primed to prostitute themselves around the racecourse.
>
> > [...non possum ferre, Quirites,
> > Graecam urbem. quamvis quota portio faecis Achaei?
> > iam pridem Syrus in Tiberim defluxit Orontes
> > et linguam et mores et cum tibicine chordas
> > obliquas nec non gentilia tympana secum
> > vexit et ad circum iussas prostare puellas]
>
> Juvenal, *Satires* 3.60–65

The capital city in his day is truly, irrevocably and, from Umbricius' point of view, horribly cosmopolitan. The only way to be Roman is to leave Rome. Returning to the issue of identity raised in Chapter 2, Umbricius' sense of disorientation and his complaint that he is a stranger in his own society, is highlighted by his description of an immigrant city. Virgil reinforced the reality and familiarity of Rome in his day by superimposing it on an imaginary past peopled by foreign exiles. Juvenal's character, Umbricius, targets the very same races as subverters of Romanness.

The vivid metaphor about the Syrian river, Orontes (close by the great city of Antioch), pouring its peoples into the city of Rome suggests a dilution of Roman identity. Many Greeks had settled in Syria and there was an assumption that much of the Asia Minor coast remained essentially Greek in character. Umbricius hates the Greeks – that's how the tirade begins – but, worse still, the city is being invaded by 'Greek' elements who have themselves been influenced and orientalized by racial mixing.

> Off you go if you fancy a foreign whore with a decorated turban. O Romulus, that peasant stock of yours puts on evening wear and sports decorative accessories around a neck smeared with oily foundation.
>
> > [Ite, quibus grata est picta lupa barbara mitra,
> > rusticus ille tuus sumit trechedipna, Quirine,
> > et ceromatico fert niceteria collo.]
>
> Juvenal, *Satires* 3.66–8

Umbricius chooses the Latin word *Quirites* to designate genuine Romans descended from Romulus (Romulus is addressed by his alternative name, Quirinus, a local god with whom he became associated). It's as if the term 'Roman, has lost its force. In the passage, words of native origin jockey for position with long Greek words like *trechedipna, niceteria, ceromatico*.

The message has the perennial ring of paranoia: 'our language is being distorted along with our customs'. Umbricius goes on to say that the Romans have adopted an outlandish lifestyle – the list covers taste in music, in dinner parties, in sport and in sex. Citizens of Rome would no longer be recognized by their beloved founder, Romulus. This influx of immigrants from Asia Minor are the 'degenerate offshoots' of the Greeks as far as Umbricius is concerned.

Remember Horace's *Graecia Capta* quote? In the Rome of the second century CE the city appears to have been colonized all over again but, this time, by means of sordid pursuits and pleasures rather than the adoption of noble or liberal arts. The ambivalent attitude to the Greeks had a long history. Long before the time of the emperors, in the days of the Republic, Roman high society was divided over the influx and influence of Greek culture. Fierce debates raged about the dissipating effects of luxury and easy living, the use of leisure for aesthetic hedonism and the subversion of Roman austerity by the seductive appearance of Greek art and literature.

Insight

Dr Tony Keen has reminded me that one of the leading figures in the Hellenization of Roman culture in the second century CE was none other than the emperor himself, Publius Aelius Hadrianus (Hadrian even sported the Greek-style beard associated with a refined philosopher). Is Juvenal capturing a mood as the people of Rome put the young Hadrian down with the word *Graeculus*? The first book of satires may have been roughly contemporary or well into Hadrian's accession, and possibly in this case the satirist felt he could risk breaking his rule about confining his targets to figures in the distant past.

Because the belief that Rome had gained the world but lost its 'soul' (or spirit) was a regularly articulated one, I feel that Umbricius' accusations against foreign influences end up as a parody of prejudices past and present. I would say that it is typical of a xenophobe, like Umbricius, to show a considerable amount of confusion and to be guilty of a fair number of inaccuracies about his own cultural identity as well as about the true nature of the threatening 'other'.

I shall be exploring aspects of Roman life that the foreigners seemed so aptly to adopt, and be drawing a few conclusions about what really disturbs Umbricius in his observations of city life. No society likes looking in a harshly lit mirror.

YOUR IMPRESSIONS

Read on and see what Umbricius says about the 'pure' Greek character. The Greeks come in for a real pasting. Why do you think Umbricius finds their behaviour so intolerable? What do you learn about their professional roles in Rome? Last, but certainly not least, work out what allusions you would like to have explained, and why.

> As for the genuine Greek, he has come armed to us with a whole set of characters: secondary school teacher, college professor, surveyor, painter, masseur, diviner, tightrope walker, magician, our hungry little Greekling knows the lot. Say the word and he will fly skyward. And why not? It was not a Moor nor a Slav, not even a Thracian who put on wings but the man born in the centre of Athens, Daedalus.
>
> Juvenal, *Satires* 3.76–80

Discussion

Greek versatility is the principal issue at stake. We hear of many slaves who reached positions of trust and whose background, cultural and educational, suited them to learned professions. As freed slaves or freeborn settlers in the city, they could turn their hands and brains to skilled work and they could teach at any level in the three-tier education system. Umbricius suggests that Greeks also made good masseurs, tightrope walkers and magicians.

This passage is full of Greek terms for the various occupations, even when there is a Latin equivalent available. Some of the talents paraded were associated with the more specifically oriental or outlandish and the poet does not miss a chance to drive this home. This is probably why Umbricius reminds his reader that it was not a Moor nor a Slav nor even a Thracian but an Athenian who invented flying. Thrace was regarded in ancient times as outside of the Greek world, even though it shared its mainland, and the original inhabitants had a reputation for savagery and sorcery.

The ancient reader was expected to pick up the allusions. The man born in the centre of Athens was Daedalus. The legend of Daedalus and Icarus has proved a lasting one. Daedalus made a tragic attempt to escape with his young son from the island of Crete where Minos, the king, had confined them. Carefully constructed wings were held together with wax and when Icarus foolishly flew too near the sun, the wings melted and he plummeted to his death in the ocean. The story traditionally celebrated the great craftsmanship and ingenuity of Athenian Daedalus but also the dangers of aspiring to flight. Umbricius uses it to point out that you can put nothing past the Greeks when they are aiming to impress. Roman poets were particularly good at giving a new slant to old myths.

As you read on, apply the same principles, references to be explained but also attitudes you can detect which spur you on to more searching questions.

Can I avoid these men with their flashy clothes? One of their number signs his name before me and makes himself comfortable on the couch, a guest of honour at dinner. Yet he arrived at Rome propelled by the same wind that brought the plums and figs. It cuts no ice that I was a child in these hills, that I drank in the air of the Aventine sky and was nourished on Sabine olives.

[horum ego non fugiam conchylia?
me prior ille signabit fultusque toro meliore recumbet,
advectus Romam quo pruna et cottana vento?
usque adeo nihil est quod nostra infantia caelum
hausit Aventini baca nutrita Sabina?]

Juvenal, *Satires* 3.81–5

The 'flashy clothes' were bright purple, presumably the sort of garish colour that would inspire jokes nowadays about onlookers needing sunglasses. Under Julius Caesar and Augustus, Roman senators were entitled to wear purple only on certain official occasions. Can we infer from this passage that the colour has been devalued or that this is foreign mimicry of a good old Roman tradition? This scene is full of references to status and social climbing. It was customary to organize witnesses to important documents and to order the seals or signatures according to their prestige. Umbricius may have been called to witness a will, a marriage contract, or the freeing of a slave (manumission was the technical term). To his chagrin he is second to the foreign upstart in status and seniority.

The final humiliation comes with the seating arrangements. Romans reclined on couches around three sides of a square table or on a semi-circular settee with the food set out on a round table – this last arrangement probably being the more common one in Juvenal's time. Whatever the shape of the couches, the guest of honour was ostentatiously placed in the most convenient spot for eating, drinking and conversing with the host. It's clear that Umbricius is passed over and downgraded again at dinner. It gives you, I think, some sense of the public nature of Roman society and the importance of the social ritual in affirming an individual's place in the hierarchies.

Of course, the irony of this situation is that the man to whom Umbricius comes such a poor second has been 'blown in' with damsons and figs from Syria. He is one of the foreign imports, himself a little luxury item, who now precedes a native Italian, nurtured on the Sabine olive. The food motif is quite prominent in the passage. Umbricius' allusion to the ancient and austere Sabine diet reinforces his self-image as the *echt* Roman (the genuine article). The Aventine Hill could not be a more centrally Roman place to be bred and born. And there's more:

> They are the geniuses of flattery and praise the conversation of an ignorant acquaintance, the appearance of an ugly one.
>
> Juvenal, *Satires* 3.86–7

> They are a race of actors. Laugh and a Greek is convulsed with mirth. He weeps if he sees a friend in tears, but he *feels* nothing. If you order a fire to be lit in winter, he puts on his winter woollens. You say 'I am hot', he breaks into a sweat. So you see, I don't stand a chance. He is ahead of the game and, day and night, he can capture the right expression whoever he is with.
>
> Juvenal, *Satires* 3.100–105

It's fairly clear that Umbricius is jealous of Greek success in social climbing and that he bitterly resents the initiative that has promoted them. The portrayal of the Greeks as adept in the art of imitation, being good actors is one aspect of this special talent, condemns them as shallow and cipher-like in their emotions. Our word, hypocrisy, derives from the Greek stage, and this seems to sum up the Greek as far as Umbricius is concerned.

By Juvenal's time foreigners, particularly freedmen (whose talents as civil servants had become indispensable to the emperor Claudius in the previous century) were rising through the ranks to positions of power and taking a prominent place in society with their ostentatious displays of wealth. A sinister note creeps into Umbricius' harangue. The unprincipled Greek will alienate the regular client from the entourage of influential men. He'll slander his rivals and at the same time liberally distribute sexual favours to 'get a hold over people'. This is how the immigrant elements push out the native Roman or Italian stock:

> What place is there here for a genuine Roman when some Protogenes or Diphilus or Hermarchus lords it over us? They never share an influential friend; it's not in their (nasty) nature. Then it only takes a

There is more than a hint in the grumbles of Umbricius that the
Greeks had no compunction about behaving in an overtly servile
manner in order to please. The predominant word in this passage is
amicus (friend), but the false flattery suggests that the 'hungry little
Greek' is hoping to ingratiate himself with people who can do him
some good. This laid bare what many native Romans liked to conceal
about the nature of the client–patron relationship. The Greek threw
himself into the part of patron's pet and that, presumably, made
life difficult for those clients who wished to retain some dignity and
delicacy about their equally subordinate position.

Umbricius is incensed that such posturing makes friends and influences
important people at Rome. It is interesting that the Greeks have
latched on to or even locked into some very Roman social structures,
institutions and customs and practices. A major reason for their success
story is their ability to make good clients, or hangers-on. I have alluded
to Roman systems of patronage before and this seems a good place to
give a little more detail.

Technically and officially, the only clients in ancient Rome were
freed slaves who were legally bound to support their former owners
in public and private life. A very common demonstration of loyalty
was the early morning visit to one's patron's house. This courtesy
was known as *salutatio*, or greeting. Clients might then accompany
the patron to the law courts or the senate, a clear declaration of his
status and influence to the outside world. In return – for the theory
was that the wealthy and highly placed had obligations, too – the
clients expected to receive some recognition of services, in the form
of help and promotion in their careers, the compliment of a dinner
invitation, or, possibly, a parcel of food or the equivalent in money of
a day's provisions. This handout was called *sportula*.

From early on in Roman republican history, the different financial
circumstances of its citizens led to free men and women in the lower
and less-advantaged strata relying on the goodwill and patronage of
the aristocratic and upper-middle-class sections of society. Even this
is a simplification, though, as the wealthy and well-born could fall

on hard times and be reduced to relying on their better-off contacts and connections. This sort of support nexus might be portrayed as a friendship circle. Interestingly, if you think back to the relationship between Horace and Maecenas, the poet much preferred to be considered an *amicus*, a friend of the emperor's minister although he clearly owed his comfortable lifestyle to Maecenas' generosity and his patronage.

> Even the slave of a foreign tycoon in the top income bracket can afford high-class whores. He surrenders the equivalent of an officer's pay for a couple of leg-overs. But if an haute-coutured tart takes your fancy, you hold back and hesitate over 'handing' down miss 'wide eyed and innocent' from her expensive chair.
>
> Juvenal, *Satires* 3.132–6

For all Umbricius' attempts to monopolize the moral high ground, Juvenal does not let him escape from the satirical eye. When the disaffected friend of the poet bewails the high cost of prostitutes, it becomes clear that he would be perfectly happy to enjoy all the 'entertainments' of the city but he no longer has the means. For Umbricius – and this is where we are allowed to see further into the Roman psyche – the immorality of the situation is in the social demise of those of decent birth and indigenous origins. Umbricius himself is given the statement that being financially embarrassed makes one ridiculous. Gone are the days when breeding and background produced privileges. The vulgarity of wealth is all that matters:

> That's positively the worst thing about being strapped for cash. It makes a man a joke. 'Who do you think you are? Get up and get out from those reserved seats. Your income disqualifies you. Make way for the offspring of pimps and prostitutes. Let the auctioneer's slick son clap away at the front along with all the trainers' and gladiators' well-turned-out boys.'
>
> [nil habet infelix paupertas durius in se
> quam quod ridiculos homines facit. 'exeat' inquit,
> 'si pudor est, et de pulvino surgat equestri,
> cuius res legi non sufficit, et sedeant hic
> lenonum pueri quocumque ex fornice nati,
> hic plaudat nitidus praeconis filius inter
> pinnirapi cultos iuvenes iuvenesque lanistae.']
>
> Juvenal, *Satires* 3.152–8

There's a good example of the way the language works here because the Latin word *paupertas* cannot really be translated as 'poverty'. Think back to 'pauper Evander' in the Virgil passage of Chapter 2. A similar point was made there. *Paupertas* is a state much closer to 'of small or moderate means', and did not necessarily, in Roman times, denote living below the breadline. So, basically, status is what is at stake here and making an impression in a city where keeping up appearances was extremely important.

No wonder Umbricius appears to crave living away from the social as well as the physical pressures of city life. Trawling through the poem with its almost Hogarthian (Hogarth painted the London life of the eighteenth century in the raw) and episodic picture of Rome, it is easy to become caught up in its condemnatory spiral. On the other hand, the scenes from country life come across as comic vignettes of rustic manners, highlighting Umbricius' sophisticated urban perspective:

> Come on, let's be realistic, throughout most of Italy no one wears the toga until he is a corpse. Even on public festival days, the 'grand' occasion when a familiar old farce is put on in the grass dell of a theatre, and the country child sits trembling in his mother's lap at the sight of the spooky white mask, even then, everyone dresses the same, wherever they sit.
>
> Juvenal, *Satires* 3.171–7

This is rough rural bliss. Wearing the toga was a wearisome chore, but it was expected in many social and certainly public situations. You have heard how Augustus legislated about the toga as dress code, however oppressive the Mediterranean heat. On the other hand, entertainment at the rustic theatre sounds pretty amateurish and not for the cultured palate. Many cities throughout the empire could, by this time, boast at least one stone theatre, but not in Umbricius' rustic vision.

Rome was spectacular in more ways than one for its places of entertainment. In his tenth Satire (line 81) Juvenal uttered a line which has gone down in history, the one about bread and circuses (*panem et circenses*) to keep the mob happy. From this perspective it looks as though there were distinct advantages to living in Rome, but you should not run away with the idea that everyone in the city was busy making bread at the state's expense.

Let's consider what the 'pull' of Rome might have been and why upwards of a million people, including slaves, lived in this overcrowded and stressful city. What sort of amenities and perks were on offer? It's worth an excursus to broaden one's view of city life and give an alternative to the jaundiced eye of Umbricius.

The 'bread'

According to Geoffrey Rickman who, in 1980, made a study of the corn supply of ancient Rome, oats, rye and millets were not established crops, maize was unknown, and rice and sorghum rare. Barley, the easiest crop to grow in the Mediterranean area, had a number of practical disadvantages. Ancient agricultural technology found de-hulling the grain a time-consuming challenge, so barley was ground down along with the husk and eaten as toasted cakes or porridge. This was heavy stuff, known as *polenta*. You will still hear the expression 'as slow as polenta' in modern Italy. Barley was also a bulky commodity to transport and ultimately had less nutritional value than wheat. A decent loaf (like the good bread Horace enjoyed on his journey to Brindisi) was best made out of 'naked' wheat (i.e. with a husk that could be easily removed on the threshing floor). The Romans relied heavily on a variety of the spelt wheat strain called *Triticum vulgare*, which was grown in the Campanian and Tuscan districts of Italy.

The corn dole, a monthly ration of about five *modii*, just over a bushel of grain, had become an institution under the emperors. It was regularized by Augustus, not as a charitable hand-out to the truly poor and destitute, but as a privilege restricted to those designated as *plebs frumentaria* (people receiving the grain). In any case, the monthly ration might have supported an individual, but not a family. Average cereal consumption over the year has been calculated at 40 *modii* per person; some historians believe that 150,000 citizens were entitled to this supplement. The French Classical scholar Paul Veyne argues (in his book of 1976; English title: *Bread and Circuses*) that the hand-out was rather a 'to them that hath shall be given' situation, as those who benefited did so precisely because they were 'respectable', with other means of survival. Augustus tells us in his own record of achievements (*Res Gestae* 15) that he gave 60 denarii apiece, a one-off gift, to those of the plebs in receipt of public grain.

This promotion of an image could cut both ways. The privilege of receiving grain could be passed down to one's heirs and there are examples of epitaphs which proudly proclaim that the deceased was a recipient in the grain scheme. In other words, the supply of grain was tied up with the public relations exercises designed by the emperor to enhance his role as protector, provider and patron (that word again) of city and citizens. Under the emperors price fixing of corn and general subsidies were also the responsibility of the state and a much-needed fail-safe mechanism to keep Rome fed and food riots at bay:

> There was the occasion when the droughts caused grain shortages. The mob barred the emperor Claudius' way in the Forum and he was cursed and pelted so hard with stale bread he only just managed to gain the safety of the palace by means of a side-door.
>
> Suetonius, *Life of Claudius* 18

Some sections of society (e.g. the emperor's urban military unit, the Praetorian Guard) had a permanent right to low-priced grain. In times of crisis or famine, the rest of the population could also buy cheap. The emperor had the means and wealth to sustain all this because Augustus had taken possession of Egypt, one of the chief provincial granaries, as his own estate. The import of grain was a vital operation and one which had to go smoothly. Veyne focuses on the state's (i.e. the emperor's) tight control of the market and the fact that the *Cura Annonae* (Ministry of Grain, Annona being the goddess of the corn supply) was a key branch of the imperial government.

What problems might the emperors and their officials face in the import operation? One problem was getting the grain in the first place, as Rome had to rely on extra supplies to supplement whatever Italy could produce. Collecting any kind of tribute from the provinces required efficiency and often coercion. Veyne (p. 243) laconically concludes that 'the state alone had the necessary network of informers in the provinces and with it also many means of persuasion'.

The logistics of transportation, delivery and storage caused headaches for a succession of rulers. There were some truly gigantic freighters made in Alexandria but, whatever the size of the cargo ships, they all had to negotiate hazardous sea journeys and then offload as close to the city of Rome as possible. Claudius and Trajan developed the harbour at Ostia but, as a river port, it was as liable to silt up as the Tiber had been. For the last 35 kilometres (22 miles) the ships needed tugs to tow them to the Emporium district of Rome. Things could and regularly did go wrong. For instance, in 62 CE (in the reign of Nero) 200 ships were sunk in a storm virtually on the delivery doorstep, the Ostian harbour. A fire at the docks in Rome put paid to another 100 ships full of grain.

Storage became sophisticated and elaborate as the emperors took more responsibility for feeding Rome. Rickman describes a staff run on military lines and a large labour force. The biggest granaries were not merely purpose-built to keep the grain at an appropriate temperature and the porters moving quickly and efficiently along a system of ramps; they were, by the second century CE, fine architectural structures constructed of highly prized, brick-faced concrete. They could function as temples with their own tutelary deity. We know of some with mosaic floors, elaborate doors and even hypocausts. They must have been part of a familiar urban skyline for the inhabitants of the city and a testament to its imperial prosperity.

The 'circuses'

Subsidies and the patron's gift, whoever he was, definitely came with strings. Entertainment was free and open to all the citizens of Rome. Fronto, friend and tutor of the emperor, Marcus Aurelius (second century CE), echoed Juvenal's sentiments and brought home this point forcefully:

> The Roman people are obsessed by the food supply and the spectacles. In their eyes, the provision of sport and entertainment are as much a proof of good government as is the serious business of state. Most damage is done when weighty matters are neglected, but the wrath of the people is greater if you short-change them in their leisure pursuits. The group designated as *plebs frumentaria* are appeased by the occasional gifts. These come to them as named individuals, but the shows are eagerly and aggressively lobbied for because they keep everyone happy.
>
> Fronto, *Principia Historiae*, ed. Naber, p. 210, translated from the Latin

Circenses were the chariot races which took place in the Circus Maximus. By far the most famous and impressive of the tracks in Rome, it was also the oldest. The structure was expanded and enhanced with monuments from the years of the late Republic. Pliny the Younger, a contemporary of Juvenal, claimed that Trajan had provided 5,000 extra stone seats for the spectators, bringing the total capacity to around 260,000. Its dimensions have been calculated at 650 by 125 metres (2,133 by 410 feet) and it boasted three arcades with marble façades. Underneath the arches milled the merchants, the takeaway food traders, the astrologers and prostitutes, all the familiar faces from Satire 3.

Try to imagine what the experience and the ambience of the races might be like. The chariot scene in the film *Ben Hur* surely captures some of the spirit of the contests. Remember, too, that the *Ludi Circenses* (Entertainments at the Circus) included acrobatic horsemanship, displays and parades.

Carcopino (1937, pp. 234–43), in his detailed reconstructions of Roman life, evokes the excitement of the occasions. Bearing in mind that he has produced an historical narrative primarily from poetic sources like Juvenal, Carcopino collates literary facts that should as a rule of thumb be treated with circumspection. We can safely say that the spectators at such events had divided themselves into Circus factions and were the fiercely loyal and partisan supporters of the four chariot clubs – Whites, Reds, Blues and Greens. It seems that all the social and political tensions of the city could be played out in this environment. It was also a bookies' paradise with a wager on every race. Augustus' right-hand man and general, Agrippa, devised a way of diverting the disappointment of the losers, by raining down filled purses, food parcels and raffle tickets with a chance of winning as much as a ship, a house or a farm – not bad consolation prizes.

The races were part of state-provided entertainment associated with religious festival days and were therefore a regular occurrence with set and sacred rituals in honour of the Roman gods and in the expectation of supernatural support for the city and the empire. These religious holidays had proliferated as emperors added on celebrations for significant events at home and overseas, from imperial birthdays to conquests abroad; in short, anything that might need divine sanction and favour, or when a thanksgiving was due to the gods.

The notorious spectator sport, from our twentieth-century perspective, was what went on in the Colosseum, the central amphitheatre of Rome, from the first century CE. Gladiator combats and the contests between humans and wild beasts, the elaborate executions of those judged to be the enemies of Rome, this has been the lifeblood of cinema in its recreation of both the glory and the decadence that was Rome. Artistic licence has put Christian martyrs in the Colosseum from the time of Nero, although it was not constructed until about 15 years later. Mary Beard and Keith Hopkins, in an excellent and spirited account of the Colosseum, note (2005, pp. 103–6) the paucity of evidence for the regular martyrdom of Christians in the arena at Rome, although they were surely a feature during periods of persecution. Apart from a letter of St Ignatius (a bishop of Antioch early in the second century CE) who was condemned to the beasts at the Colosseum, the most harrowing accounts of this style of summary execution are found in the Acts of Martyrs (accounts of Christian martyrdoms of varying authenticity compiled from early Christian times). The provincial amphitheatres, especially Carthage, are the setting for these allegedly eyewitness accounts. They read like a hymn to suffering, a joyous embrace of pain and bodily dismemberment as a means to eternal salvation.

Insight

In 1999 Ridley Scott's *Gladiator* went on general release to critical claim and proved enormously popular at the box office. Open University students reading about the Colosseum in the course *Introduction to the Humanities* started animated online discussions about the costumes, the sets and the sociological and historical aspects of the movie. Robert Rosenstone would probably argue that, in spite of the liberties taken with historical realities (from battles to belief systems), Scott and his all-star cast and production team did recreate some of the horror and fear of facing death in the arena (witness the earlier scene in the smaller amphitheatre at Zucchabar). This and other bloodier moments in the movie did resonate with me when, a couple of years later, I visited the well-preserved arena at Italica (near Seville) and stood under the bright Spanish sun by the doorway to death in the sand.

Tenacious traditions have grown up around the Colosseum. Painting, literature and film have immortalized the building as a symbol of suffering innocents, courageous martyrs and savagely voyeuristic spectators. It was resurrected as a monumental and imperial structure, for overtly political purposes, by Mussolini to announce the twentieth-century ambitions of Italy as a player on the world stage.

Look at the Colosseum in the following photograph. Can you think of any modern stadium it has influenced?

Interior of the Colosseum

Discussion

The designs, decorative and functional, of the Colosseum continue to influence construction techniques today. You might have been struck by similarities in concept to modern sports stadia or civic complexes commissioned to make 'grand gestures'. Building materials might change but the use of space for access and crowd control have yet to be improved upon; 50,000 people regularly flocked to the Colosseum. It was planned on the grand scale and combined the functional with the decorative so that it made a definite statement about the place of the games (*ludi*) in Roman society. Many cities throughout the empire built amphitheatres modelled on the Colosseum (in fact, the provincial arenas were where most of the public martyrdoms of Christians took place). All the exotic conquests of empire – animals, barbarian prisoners of war, and so on – were put on display and elaborate shows were devised to dispatch them. I would certainly not be the first person to point out that the Colosseum brought the empire to Rome and paraded its possessions in triumph.

The Colosseum was a place of punishment and execution. Like the circus, it had its rituals and religious character, but it was not institutionalized and state run in the same way as the *ludi*. The games in the amphitheatre had started life as funeral displays, *munera*, a way in which important figures could be publicly commemorated by their family or friends. The gladiator contests demonstrated fighting skills and defiance in the face of death, so they were seen as quite appropriate for Roman funeral rites.

The contests were also extremely useful to the living and their political ambitions. *Munera* grew in scale and become highly promotional of their various sponsors. It was one of the many public relations exercises that Augustus kept firmly in the imperial family once he came to power, so much so that the games became the emperor's gift to the capital. Elsewhere, city patrons and appointed magistrates were expected to provide this sort of entertainment at their own expense.

Thomas Wiedemann in his book *Emperors and Gladiators* (Routledge 1992), and in his article for the Classical magazine, *Omnibus*, teases out significant ancient attitudes to the displays of the arena. The rulers of Rome and its empire were able to reassure the public that threats from any quarter, barbarians, 'deviants' and the natural world, were being dealt with. Combat to the death was a regular feature, as was the slaughter of criminals with little attempt at an equally matched contest. On special occasions, savage myths would be enacted in the arena with the condemned forced to act out a part to the death. The poet Martial wrote a set of poems, *De Spectaculis*, to celebrate the inaugural games when the Colosseum was finished. The emperor Titus is praised and elevated to almost godlike status for providing such miraculous displays for his people.

The organizers of the shows strived for variety and innovation. Juvenal mentions female gladiators in Satire 6, as does Martial in his poetry. Much later in the history of the empire, when the capital had shifted to Constantinople, senators and chief administrators of Rome were still putting on big shows to impress the people. Symmachus, in the fourth century CE, wrote bitterly of a disaster he experienced. His crocodiles arrived half-starved and his prisoners, 30 Saxon pirates, unsportingly committed suicide in the cells beneath the Colosseum, thus depriving the spectators of gladiator combats. 'How typical of that obstinate race,' he comments in one of his letters.

There must have been an element of social solidarity for, although, as in the theatres, seating was rigidly hierarchical according to income and status, everyone could share in and enjoy the benefits of empire on the days of the shows and everyone could join in the decision about the life or death of a defeated gladiator (i.e. give the thumbs up or thumbs down). This involvement of the people of Rome in the official punishments of condemned criminals, the fact that they could exercise mercy along with the emperor and the state, must have given the urban plebs a sense of power, as well as an identity as citizens.

As the financing of the shows tended to be the special preserve of the ruler or his family, this gift of participation was also linked with the exercise of power and patronage. Juvenal's emphasis is on the people's passivity and he contrasts the clamour for bread and circuses with the old days when the citizens were supposed to confirm the legitimacy of the leaders through their various assemblies. Juvenal's claim that the people used to bestow authority on the men of state and on the army generals is another myth of an idealized Roman past which was discussed in Chapters 2 and 3.

People power was never a concept with much credence in Rome. In the days of the Republic there was a great deal of bribing and bludgeoning of the voters by the candidates and all these candidates were, in any case, self-selected from the families of the rich and the relatively famous. Under the emperors, from the time that Augustus had, to all intents and purposes, disbanded the assemblies as voting bodies, the citizens of Rome continued to express themselves, their dissatisfactions and their desires, through other time-honoured avenues. I mentioned the attack on Claudius and the occasional riot if grain supplies failed and prices were not controlled. The races and the games, where the emperor was so often on show, were also good places for angry demonstrations. Emperors could and did read subversive signs into the support of the crowd for a particular chariot colour or a popular gladiator, especially if the people pointedly opposed an imperial favourite:

On one occasion when the people cheered the wrong team, the emperor Caligula cried out angrily: 'I wish all you Romans had only one neck for the severing.'

Suetonius, *Life of Gaius Caligula* 30

You may or may not have found this perspective of city life an antidote to Umbricius' negative view of the capital. Juvenal more than hints that his friend's disillusion stems from becoming one of the anonymous masses, but there was something to be said for staying at the centre of things in the imperial capital, whatever your social status. The attractions of Rome are as implicit in the poem as the bad vibrations. In Juvenal's eleventh satire (Book 3) the poet has invited a friend to a pleasant rural-style meal at his place in the city but the location only becomes clear at the end of the poem. The relish with which he describes the sorts of urban treats he will *not* be providing must, one feels, be done for badness. Umbricius may be on the move but Juvenal is left behind to revel in his friend's feelings of repulsion towards Rome and to keep up the good work with the satire. Juvenal himself had no intention of leaving Rome. These are the words addressed to Juvenal by Martial in his short poem in praise of rustic simplicity:

O Juvenal, while you are in all likelihood wandering ill at ease in the noisy Subura or trailing around the hill of goddess Diana, while you perspire in your toga and flap it about for a bit of a breeze, worn out by doing the round of the rich on the Caelian Hill, I, in the meantime, am recalled, after many Decembers, to my Bilbulis, proud in gold and iron [Bambola, in Spain, and Martial's birthplace]. She has welcomed me and turned me into a farmer.

Martial, *Epigrams* 12.18.1–8

Does this verse prove that Juvenal suffered the same discomforts as Umbricius or is Martial entering into the literary spirit of Satire 3?

Next stop

I suggested at the beginning of this chapter that you might like to read more of Juvenal. There are 322 lines in Satire 3, making it the longest poem in the first book. Juvenal appears complete in the Penguin edition *The Sixteen Satires*. Juvenal's Satire 10 was reworked by Samuel Johnson in the eighteenth century. Johnson entitled his poem 'The Vanity of Human Wishes'. Johnson also produced a version of Satire 3, applying the condemnation of the city to the London of his day. In the poem, quoted below, Johnson's friend is off to the Hebrides to live the quiet life.

Over the centuries, Juvenal's poem has frequently been received as a sentorious survey of corrupt urban existence. Juvenal himself gained a reputation as a moralist and Roman satirists were praised for 'lashing the vices of the town'. But life and literature are rarely that simple. Samuel Johnson could energetically promote the Scottish Highlands, denigrate the city and yet pronounce that 'the man who is tired of London is tired of life'. I leave you with the opening two stanzas of Johnson's 'London'. For your interest, too, I have also added an extract from a twentieth-century version of Juvenal by John Holloway. Written in 1968, this poem operates in a cultural milieu that has also dated significantly, in three decades, as opposed to the 260 years that separate us from Johnson.

You might like to pursue either or both of these two pieces of poetic *imitatio* and to pose a few critical questions of your own, for example: Do they capture some of the Juvenalian spirit? How reliable would Holloway be as a witness to life in the London of the 1960s?

London

A Poem in imitation of the Third Satire of Juvenal

Though grief and fondness in my breast rebel
When injured Thales bids the town farewell,
Yet still my calmer thoughts his choice commend;
Resolved, at length, from vice and London far,
To breathe in distant fields a purer air,
And fix'd on Cambria's solitary shore,
Give to St David one true Briton more

For who would leave, unbribed, Hibernia's land,
Or change the rocks of Scotland for the Strand?
There none are swept by sudden fate away,
But all who hunger spares, with age decay:
Here malice, rapine, accident, conspire,
And now a rabble rages, now a fire;
Their ambush here relentless ruffians lay,
And here the fell attorney prowls for prey;
Here falling houses thunder on your head,
And here a female atheist talks you dead.

Samuel Johnson, 1738

London, Greater London (After Juvenal's Satire III)

Well, it really hurts to think of him going away.
But he's made the right decision: that's got to be faced.
For what could be worse than – well, yes, the horrors of London
(Culminating in the Festival of Poetry)? ... His station waggon
Was crammed the day he went. I joined him as far as Richmond,
Though the publishers have moved up west, and the Royal Car Parks,
And the spacious villa Estates in the Green Belt.
This is what he said: 'It's unlivable-in:
Gets worse every day; so I'm off, before I'm senile.
Agreed, it's a real break – but what's the good?
How can I cope with London? When a book's bad,
I just can't say it was "deeply moving" and "I wonder
If you'd care to inscribe my copy ...?" I haven't read Jung.
Don't know any abortionists. Can't play bingo.'

In some parts of the country, perhaps, folk don't ride
In a car, till the hearse knocks at the door. Even now
Have gymkhanas and village fêtes, and the children don't call
Westerns vieille vague. Men's clothes don't run after the fashion,
And the cops don't drive white Jags. But where we are
It's the affluent society to the gusset (Extended play,
Extended payments, Creative Fares and everybody Conforming Upwards).

John Holloway, 1968

POINTS TO REMEMBER...

1 Satire as an extended verse form was a Roman literary invention and different poets strike distinct poses and tones in their works. Horace (see Chapter 2) developed a learned and yet relaxed style of self-irony along with his observations on the human condition.

2 Juvenal states his intention to bring an epic grandeur to satire to match its epic metre. Although it is unwise to use his poetry as social history, it is perhaps too glib to see him as simply role playing the angry observer of the seamier side of Roman life, and consequently compromising his criticisms. Recent books on satire and Susanna Braund's excellent commentaries and articles on Juvenal are well worth reading for a balanced view.

3 Rome was most definitely a city of contrasts from palaces to high-rise tenements. The vivid picture Juvenal's Umbricius paints of its squalor, noise, hazards and criminal classes has become an influential template for negative snapshots of urban life from Samuel Johnson onwards.

4 Rome's multiculturalism is caricatured by Juvenal's Umbricius in a bombastically racist way but Juvenal himself is not a respecter of persons, in that he viciously lampoons men, women, citizens, foreigners, rulers and plebs throughout his *Satires*. Umbricius comes across as part buffoon and part hypocrite.

5 Juvenal probably did have some personal grievances about the costs in dignity that came with staying in Rome and finding an audience for his poetry. He, too, had to try to gain favour and patronage at Rome.

6 Satire 3 is one of several sources we have for the patronage system in Roman society. Juvenal's frustrations are echoed by Martial in his *Epigrams* (for instance how to divide the day between the duties of a client, paying court to the emperor and enjoying the parks and pleasurable pastimes the city offered) and by Pliny the Younger in his criticism of a patron who gives cheaper wine to his lowlier acquaintances.

7 'Bread and circuses' is a convenient way to characterize the control emperors exercised over the people of Rome in a kind of rule by consensus. However, the hand-outs and the ancient pleasure palaces were both quite complex sociological phenomena.

8 The masses in attendance at the races and the games and those reliant on the corn dole used these regular events to express discontent and to invade the social spaces of the wealthier classes. There is much more to probe here about life and leisure in the city. Jerry Toner's *Leisure and Ancient Rome* is a key text in this area.

9 Even contemporary commentators on Rome in all its physical and social aspects are in the business of dramatization and entertainment. Greek and Roman historians were also quite capable of composing speeches and reconstructing events to drive a point home about corruption or to support their interpretation of general trends and individual motivations (see the comments in Chapters 1 and 2).

10 I hope by this point you might feel confident enough to ask some pertinent questions about not just movies reliving the Roman experience but also about current television documentaries that give such plausible accounts of the past. They might introduce a Roman voice (with an actor speaking as Juvenal or Pliny the Younger) plus a dramatic reconstruction, but they may not give you much context about their sources.

Meeting the people: Roman relationships

> When the report reached me of the death of your daughter Tullia, I was indeed deeply and grievously sorry, and I felt that the blow had struck us both. Had I been in Rome, I should have been with you and shown you my grief in person. And yet that is a melancholy and bitter sort of comfort. Those who should offer it, relations and friends, are themselves no less afflicted. They cannot make the attempt without many tears, and rather seem themselves in need of comfort from others than to be doing their friendly office for others. Nonetheless, I have resolved to set briefly before you the reflections that come to my mind in this hour, not that I suppose you are unaware of them, but perhaps your grief makes them harder to perceive.
>
> Servius Sulpicius to Cicero, *Letters to Friends* 4.5

This short extract from Sulpicius' letter of condolence, also quoted at the start of this book, was written in sympathy on the death of Cicero's daughter, Tullia, who died a month after giving birth. The reason for including it in the early stages of this encounter with Roman civilization was to allow us to get in touch with familiar feelings. The loss of a child (although Tullia was a grown woman of 30 when she died) was and is a tragedy not easily borne by affectionate parents. Cicero's grief is easy for us to understand. Romans had high hopes for their children just as we usually do and they regarded them as an investment in the future, potentially a credit to their families and a support to parents who were lucky enough to live to an old age.

Reading on in this letter from Sulpicius will help unravel what is specifically Roman from those expressions of a general and universal nature. Cicero and the death of his daughter have been chosen as the anchor text for the opening of this chapter. Expanding on this case study will enable us to cover some of the essential relationships we encounter in the Roman family, bearing in mind that the Latin word *familia* encompasses all those in the control of the father, the *paterfamilias* (i.e. children, grandchildren, slaves and *sometimes* wives), a point to which I shall return.

This chapter will encourage you to look critically at evidence we have for patterns of life and death, feelings within families and among friends, and attitudes towards women, children and slaves.

The man and his medium

First, Cicero needs to be put in his place on the timeline and given a brief curriculum vitae, literally 'the course of one's life', yet another Latin phrase in common use today. Marcus Tullius Cicero was born in 106 BCE and was beheaded in 43 BCE. He was a prominent victim of the Second Triumvirate, the power-sharing alliance of Antony, Octavian and Lepidus who issued proscriptions against past and potential opponents in the influential classes. Proscriptions were grim advertisements, public declarations naming political enemies and tantamount to a death sentence for those 'damned with a spot' (Antony's sinister phrase in Shakespeare's *Julius Caesar*, Act IV, Scene 1).

Cicero was a skilful orator and his performance at a number of political trials had advanced his public career and helped promote him to the highest office, that of Consul, in 63 BCE. It was this combination of talents and his position as an elder statesman that made his later sustained and published attacks on Mark Antony so authoritative. Antony mutilated Cicero's corpse and had his head and hands pinned up in the forum because these had been his most offensive weapons.

As a successful 'new man' (*novus homo*), Cicero had experienced the resentment of the nobility throughout his career but he was extremely eager to be identified with their interests and to be counted an honorary member of the aristocratic class of Rome. He was the first in his family to break into this political preserve, having become a consul with no prestigious aristocratic name to help him along.

He was deeply and publicly proud of his achievement and exaggerated his contribution to the safety of the Republic during a number of crises in the 60s BCE. Cicero's struggle to 'arrive' on the political scene explains much about the man. He has come down to posterity with some detailed documentation of his life which gives us almost painful insights into his weaknesses and neuroses. Much of his considerable literary output has survived, speeches (knocked into a literary shape for publication after their delivery in the law courts or the senate), ethical and philosophical treatises and some rather indifferent poetry. In addition to these formal works there are 931 letters which were not written for general consumption but which were collected, collated and published by Cicero's freed slave Tiro.

Also in this chapter we will be meeting another prolific letter writer, Pliny the Younger, who himself sorted, selected and polished his correspondence with an eye on publication. His subject matter is equally personal and his expressions of grief and affection are heartfelt at times, but you will notice a difference in style and tone after Cicero's invariably spontaneous exchanges with friends and family.

Insight

No Classicist has an uncomplicated relationship with Marcus Tullius Cicero. Scholars have condemned him for decisions and actions that he celebrated as courageous, decisive and principled. He is not always an attractive figure personally or, from a left historical perspective, ideologically. Michael Parenti (2003, p. 86) quotes Friedrich Engels who called Cicero 'the most contemptible scoundrel in history'. For Parenti, even in an historical period that was a school for scoundrels, Cicero is perhaps somewhat unfairly singled out for doing what came naturally to so many: being a self-enriching, slave-holding slum landlord.

Take a letter: propriety, paper and postal services

There were handbooks on letter writing and schoolboys were taught the art with these as models but it is difficult to date the teaching material to a particular period. Philosophers, like Seneca for example, who virtually ruled Rome for the emperor Nero in the 60s CE, produced ethical treatises masquerading under the title of epistles. A collection of letters to a friend or friends might, deliberately, double as a series of learned and sententious observations about life and all its little ironies or they might belong to categories such as advice, reproach or consolation.

It looks as if the Vindolanda birthday invitation which was included in the introduction to Chapter 1 was written in three different hands and the middle paragraph, the earnest 'please come' request, was probably the wife's personal touch. It is not as elegantly expressed in the Latin as the opening and so suggests that the invitation proper was written by a literate scribe or was, perhaps, the work of the husband. The Vindolanda letters survive on wooden tablets. They do not have a beeswax finish but are such thin slivers of timber – leaf letters in fact – that they could be inscribed with pen and ink. Elite men like Cicero and Pliny, or their slave scribes, would have used the papyrus roll or pages made out of reeds from the Nile delta, for their writing material.

Augustus organized a postal service, the *Cursus Publicus*, but the couriers, usually army men, were on diplomatic dispatches for the emperor and it was a high-speed exclusive business, with pre-arranged transport and an up-to-date itinerary of stopping stations (these could be selected inns and hostels). For example, when Nero was emperor, Galba was the commander in Spain, promoted by his troops as a candidate to replace Nero. Evidently Galba and his troops heard from Rome of Nero's death within seven days, which demonstrates what could be done at times of crisis. Presumably such speedy delivery of news necessitated night-and-day travel. In the normal run of things, letters and news would take a lot longer. In Cicero's day, it really was pot luck. Prolific letter writers either relied on travellers who might be heading for somewhere near to the destination or gave slaves the job of long-distance postmen. Slaves they may have been, but Cicero seems to have had the run-around from these couriers and to have been at the mercy of their convenience:

> Your couriers are out of order. They hassle me for a letter but they do not bring any. They don't allow me a moment to jot something down but they come in, with their hats on, to inform me that their companions are waiting at the gate.
>
> Cicero, *Letters to Friends* 15.17

The attitude of the messengers suggests that travelling was safer in numbers. Perhaps they were fidgety about setting out late and on their own. The efficiency of this ad hoc system was highly variable. Cicero managed to send and receive letters within the peninsula of Italy in anything from one to four days. Certain sea routes were quite speedy – for example letters to and from North Africa could arrive within a few days – but Cicero's correspondence with his son in Athens (he was finishing off his education there) was unavoidably patchy, with delays in delivery ranging from three to seven weeks.

The letters provide a slice or cross-section of Cicero's life but they are also a valuable historical source of information for the people and politics of the late Republic. Private though the letters are, this does not alter the fact that a man of Cicero's importance could not help but be a public personality. Even in his most intimate moments his cares and concerns are bound up with his political and social status and his relationship to other influential figures of his day. For this reason his letters read like an epistolary novel and they force us to focus on an important aspect of Roman high society, namely the constant interpenetration of family matters and public considerations. Setting Cicero's letters, those he sent and those he received, into their social context will hone your skills of source analysis.

Read the further extracts from Sulpicius' letter translated below. You read a little of this letter of consolation from the senator Sulpicius Severus to Cicero in the introduction. Is this what a close friend should say and do you think Cicero was comforted or convinced by his arguments?

Why should your own private trouble affect you so much? Think how unkindly fate has already treated us, robbing us of things that should be as dear to men as their children – country, reputation, position, our whole career. Could this addition of this one drop add anything to our cup of woe? What mind schooled in such adversity should not be steeled by now to take anything less hardly?

Discussion
Did you feel less in tune with Sulpicius when he tried to put Tullia's death in perspective? The opening of his letter seems genuine and warm enough but he then adopts the air of the acute observer uttering truisms, facts universally acknowledged, about the state of bereavement (e.g. collective grief is cumulative and the levels of hysteria rise rapidly when close family and friends gather together for mutual consolation). Sulpicius was a Roman jurist of some renown and you just may have gained an impression, in the ensuing

consolation, of a legal mind making a case for emotional damage limitation; but is that an uncharitable way of interpreting Sulpicius' intentions?

The rationalizing of grief and the curbing of strong emotions were tenets of the Greek philosophical school Stoicism. Cicero felt some affinity towards this philosophy. It had already been adapted by educated Roman men to function as a practical guide for rational living in their particular circumstances. Cicero made a significant contribution to the process. Being steadfast in the face of adversity was a Stoical stance and one to be recommended for those who chose to pursue public careers in the late Republic. Both Cicero and Sulpicius, who was also a staunch supporter of the Republican system of government, had plenty of practice in weathering the political tragedies of the age, principally the 'death' of the Republic. Sulpicius points out that devotion to country, and achieving the goal of personal success during the course of one's contribution to that country, were becoming things of the past. In the light of these casualties, the loss of Tullia was just 'one more drop in the cup of woe'.

> Or can it be for her sake that you are mourning? How often must the idea have occurred to you, as it has to me, that in these times people have not had a bad fate who have been allowed painlessly to exchange life for death! For what great incentive to living could she have in such an age, what possession or prospect or solace? To have a married life with some distinguished young man? You were welcome, no doubt, in virtue of your position, to choose any son-in-law you liked from the youth of today, if you could find one to whom you would confidentially entrust any child of yours.

Sulpicius is obviously preoccupied with current affairs in Rome and the empire. This is hardly surprising as he had been born into the senatorial class and was an active administrator during the Republic. He is writing to Cicero from the province of Greece (Achaia) where he was governor at the time. Sulpicius is so disillusioned with the state of the Republic that he sees no future for posterity. Tullia had been married three times but Sulpicius suggests that there was a limited supply of eligible and worthwhile men. She was fortunate in that she had made three prestigious matches with eminent husbands and had seen her father appointed to key posts in the running of Rome.

So that she might have children, and the joy of seeing their success? Children who would be able to maintain freely the inheritance their father left them, and to stand in due course for each office, with freedom of action in public life and in promoting the interests of their friends? There is not one of these promises that has not been snatched away before it was fulfilled. To lose one's child, you will say, is a calamity. I agree; but to have to endure all this may well be worse.

Tullia left no children but that, too, was seen as a blessing in disguise as there would be little guarantee for them regarding their protected rights of inheritance, nor would they enjoy careers without harassment. Clearly, things had changed for the worse during her lifetime and her departure could be viewed as timely; she was leaving 'a vale of tears'. The 'isn't she better off out of it' argument strikes a chord whenever the world seems an ugly place to live in and there is little opportunity for individual fulfilment.

As you read through the last extract from Sulpicius' letter, consider Tullia's role as a well-born woman in the time of the late Republic. Can you draw any conclusions about her from this letter or about the way women were regarded in this society?

Lately, at one and the same time, many outstanding men perished, the government of the Roman people suffered a crippling loss, and all our overseas possessions were shaken: are you then so distressed for the loss of one little life of one wee woman?

Sulpicius goes on to say that Tullia was only mortal and would have died a few years later anyway.

If she had not died now, she would have had to die a few years later, since she was born mortal.

[Modo uno tempore tot viri clarissimi interierunt, de imperio populi Romani tanta deminutio facta est, omnes provinciae conquassatae sunt; in unius mulierculae animula si iactura facta est, tanto opere commoveris?]

Then take your mind off these things and turn to thoughts worthy of your role: that she lived while life had anything to give her; that she lived as long as we were still free people; that she saw you, her father, hold office as praetor, consul and augur; that she was married to young men of the foremost rank; that she experienced almost every happiness; and that when the Republic was falling, she departed this life. What possible quarrel could you or she have with fortune on that score?

Insight

Roman attitudes to death and to grieving and commemoration are expertly surveyed and analysed by Val Hope in her 2007 sourcebook, *Death in Ancient Rome*. Her pertinent and measured remarks include what emotions were expected and accepted, how we should view formulaic and public demonstrations of sorrow and how often conventional limits to grief were transgressed.

Discussion

Let's concentrate on this last passage initially and see what conclusions can be drawn about general attitudes towards women of Tullia's class. Sulpicius' emphasis on Tullia's marriage and children, alongside his comments on the prestige of her father's career, suggests that women mostly basked in reflected glory and were identified by their relations with the important men in their lives. Girls could be betrothed as children and married as young as 12 years old. Their husbands tended to be older, at least in their early twenties, and to be embarking on an administrative or a military career. Tullia's first husband died at 40 years old leaving her a teenage widow. In matters of property women were supposed to defer to appointed guardians (*tutores*) if they had lost both father and husband.

The *tutor* was seen as a means of protecting a woman's interests; he was someone who could advise against an unwise investment, for instance. The measure of women's independence in financial and business transactions depended on the conscientiousness or co-operativeness (perhaps we should say connivance) of these guardians. In theory, women were not liable for repayment of debts and so could not stand security in business ventures. In practice, the law was flexible enough to allow the *praetor*, a senior city magistrate, to intervene and uphold a creditor's claim against a woman who was judged to have acted in full knowledge of the consequences.

Augustus' legislation, which was designed to strengthen the institution of the citizen family, allowed the upper-class Roman mother (*matrona*) to dispense with a guardian completely if she had three or more children living, and the freedwoman gained a similar privilege once she had produced four children. The attitude towards women did shift and Roman legislation reflected changing realities, but there was a continuous and underlying assumption that the female sex could be easily led astray by cunning operators and betrayed by their own gullibility and extravagance.

The reason for including a short piece of the original Latin in the second paragraph of the extract was to highlight two words used to describe Tullia. *Mulierculae* and *animula* are both diminutive forms of the Latin words, *mulier* for 'woman' and *anima* for 'life' or the 'breath of life'. In English an equivalent would be 'let' on the end of a word (e.g. piglet), or we might get the same effect with a phrase like 'my little darling'. As in modern languages, Latin diminutives can incorporate a sarcastic note. They can be dismissive as well as affectionate and the phrase 'the little life of a wee woman' emphasizes Tullia's weakness as well as her smallness in the scheme of things.

Pliny the Younger, who was a high-level administrator under the regimes of Domitian, Nerva and Trajan and on the last lap of his career became governor of the troublesome province of Bithynia Pontus (on the Black Sea), wrote in the following vein about his much younger wife, Calpurnia. She was probably about 15 when Pliny married her. He was 40 and had been married twice before.

She combines high intelligence with excellent practical skills of housekeeping. The fact that she loves me is a sign of her virtue. An arousal of enthusiasm for literature has been born out of her affection for me. She keeps books I have written to read over and over, even to memorize them. When she realizes that I am going to plead in court, she becomes anxious and when I am done, she is overjoyed. She posts messengers who tell her about the impact I have, the applause I receive and what the verdict is. This is a wife who sits behind a curtain close by whenever I am reciting and hears the praise of my work with the most eager ears. On top of all this, she has set my verses to music and sings to the accompaniment of the lyre, a skill she has learned not by formal tuition but prompted by love, the best teacher.

Pliny, *Letters* 4.19

The negative side to Calpurnia's youth, impressionability and general lack of experience is revealed in later letters when Pliny writes sadly, but also slightly irritably, about his wife's miscarriage. News of this event was sent to Calpurnia's grandfather and aunt, who seem to have brought her up, and Pliny informs the aunt that Calpurnia had not realized she was pregnant. He is relieved that she has come through the experience safely and that he believed this to be a consolation for those grieving over the loss of 'a descendant to come' for Calpurnia's family line (*Letters* 11.8 and 9). Pliny's hopes for a future full-term pregnancy were not fulfilled. Calpurnia did not conceive again and Pliny left no children on his death.

The picture of Tullia which emerges from Sulpicius' letter of condolence reveals the prevalent male attitude to the place of women in the upper echelons of Roman society. He acknowledges and shares Cicero's sense of loss but he tempers this with an evaluation of her significance in a man's world. This does not deny her emotional and personal importance within the family but it does simultaneously reduce her stature in the public arena and in the historical sweep of the Republic's destiny. Sulpicius is counselling moderation in grief and, perhaps short on tact, points out that Tullia was only a frail and dispensable woman. Important men, guardians of the empire, whom the state of Rome will sorely miss, are a more legitimate cause for mourning.

Cicero's speedy response to Sulpicius survives and he accepts all the points about regaining a sense of priority. He does, simultaneously, pursue the commemoration of Tullia with vigour and concern and we have other testimony which tells us that he was estranged from his second and much younger wife because she showed no genuine grief at Tullia's death and was put out by her husband's strong sense of bereavement. Cicero seems to have been obsessive about commemorating his daughter in an elaborate way. The immortalization of Tullia's memory was important to Cicero. He agonized over the suitability of the site and style of a shrine, rather than a tombstone, and how best to serve his daughter's departed spirit:

> I intend to honour her memory to the highest degree in this extremely cultured age, with every kind of memorial based on the wealth of artistic achievement from Greece and Rome.
>
> Cicero, *Letters to Atticus* 12.18

> This is certainly a pleasant place, right on the sea and within sight of both Anzio and Circeii; but it must count with me that many changes of ownership may occur in the countless years to come. I must find a way of securing that the site remains consecrated ground as long as an empire survives. I don't need a large income now, and can be content with quite a little. Sometimes I think of buying some gardens across the Tiber instead, for the very reason that I can think of nowhere more frequented; but which gardens I should buy is a matter for discussions when we meet, provided only that the shrine must be completed this summer. But I leave it up to you to settle about the columns with Apella of Chios.
>
> Cicero, *Letters to Atticus* 12.19 (from Astura, near Anzio, 14 March 45 BCE)

In a later letter to Atticus (3 May, 12.36) Cicero explains that he does not want a tomb but a monumental shrine. There was a law against extravagant funerals and mausoleums, whereas a shrine might evade the strictures on expenditure. No physical evidence of a shrine to Tullia survives and it may never have been built in spite of all this literary evidence for careful preparations and negotiations with designers and sculptors.

Insight

The written word can prove less fragile than a tombstone. Tullia lives on in the letters of Cicero. Horace believed that his poetry would make him immortal and he had no need for an epitaph carved in robust material ('exegi monumentum aere perennius' – I have constructed a monument more lasting than bronze). Pliny the Younger wrote in some distress about the terrible state of Verginius Rufus' tomb and how much the Roman state owed to his military campaigns.

The father figure

Roman law and tradition had given the father of the family total jurisdiction over all of its members. In theory, the head of the family (*paterfamilias*) had the power of life and death over his household. How often did fathers exercise their legal rights over all those in their power? The decision to raise the new-born baby was his; he actually picked up the child placed at his feet in acknowledgement of his parenthood and responsibility. The right of life and death was a permanent one while the father lived, but there were obligations attached to the exercise of authority and the Roman concept of *pietas* regulated relationships between parents and children.

Pietas, like a number of Roman words, carries a complex cultural nexus with it and cannot be translated into a simple English equivalent. This particular word and its cognates figure significantly in Virgil's portrayal of Aeneas. Virgil's hero is called *pius Aeneas* and most translators struggle to find the *mot juste*. *Pietas* encompasses all the appropriate feelings and correct behaviour one owes to family, friends, fatherland and the gods of the fatherland. 'Sense of duty' comes pretty close to the concept, but the Romans were no fools and realized that loyalties (and duties) have a nasty habit of conflicting.

The elder Seneca, father of the famous philosopher already mentioned, collected up typical test exercises used in lessons for teenage boys. These *controversiae*, as they were called, required the pupil to argue either side of a case in which one or both parties claimed dereliction of duty or the breaking of a sworn promise. The scenarios are sometimes bizarre and unbelievable, yet the moral dilemmas and the legal repercussions are far from fantastic because they focus on the hierarchy of obligations which made up the fabric of Roman society.

It may have struck you that the debate over the extent of a father's control, in reality, ought to take into account how many fathers were still living when their sons reached manhood. Analysis of the few statistics we can produce from the ancient evidence has changed the once common picture of grown men still deferring to their father in matters of finance and private and public activity. The assumption is that most sons would be independent by the time they were married themselves (around their mid-twenties) for the simple reason that their fathers would die in their mid to late forties.

This conclusion is not undisputed because it in turn assumes a consistency in material circumstances that rarely applies to any society over a span of 700 years. Plagues, wars and, in the case of the late Republic, proscriptions always skew statistics. Life expectancy at birth does not necessarily tell us how long people actually lived, especially once they had made it through the dangerous years of early childhood, the hazards of giving birth or serving in the army. The age of eligibility for the Roman consulship was 41. Octavian broke the rule by being elected when he was in his twenties but in the normal run of things there was, presumably, a tranche of elder statesmen available to take office.

Nor should shorter average lives lead to presumptions about earlier senility. Cicero could refer to himself as *adulescens* (literally, young man) on becoming consul at 43 because, technically, this distinguished him from the *senex* (old man) stage of life. Even if the deductions are roughly accurate and two-thirds of men over 25 years old no longer had a father living, being 40- or even 50-plus was in no way an entering of the twilight years for the Roman politicians and leaders.

Tullia was obviously a firm favourite with her father, but Cicero was actually equally besotted with his small son Marcus. Other letters reveal that Cicero was involved, too, with the upbringing of his brother's son, young Quintus, whom Cicero admired for his lively mind but whose independent spirit he felt should be curbed. Cicero seems to have supervised a great deal of his nephew's higher education, for young Quintus accompanied his uncle and cousin Marcus on educational tours to the provinces and Cicero appointed the tutors who would complete the boys' training in literature and rhetoric; the art of speaking persuasively was an important skill. It had catapulted Cicero to fame and continued to be a badge of status and success throughout the history of the empire.

The concern for his nephew was an affectionate and caring one in spite of the exasperations he felt at the boy's wilfulness. Cicero was worried by Quintus' reaction to his parents' proposed divorce: 'He wept as he lamented over it to me.' Cicero urged positive intervention upon Quintus who succeeded in reconciling his father and mother for a while. Bradley (1991, pp. 181–2) uses Cicero's family closeness to demonstrate how the spirit of an extended family might operate among the Romans. Cicero is a caring uncle with a developed sense of duty towards Quintus, his nephew. Cicero also talks warmly of one of his own uncles who took an interest in him and his brother. They looked forward to his regular visits and learned a great deal from him. Impressions of Roman family life have changed radically in recent years. Large numbers of co-resident households probably did not exist but family ties beyond the nucleus of father, mother and children did.

A life less ordinary – what more can we learn?

Tullia is an enlightening study because she apparently showed a measure of independence in choosing her second husband. The father, in this case, Cicero, was the centre and authority of the household who in theory made all the decisions about the conduct of those in his family. The *paterfamilias* selected partners for his sons and daughters, taking into consideration political and economic circumstances and how the marriage might serve the family's best interests. For the upper classes, marriage and divorce were strategies in the wheeling and dealing of public life, career advancement and the signalling up of expedient friendships or, equally significantly, current and inherited enmities on the political scene.

All three of Tullia's marriages were recognized in law for the purposes of transmitting property and continuing the family line. Tullia's first husband died and she divorced the second and third. Marriage and divorce could be painless processes on the practical level because both were private declarations and not state registered procedures. The law only stepped in (and then it had to be invoked by interested parties) when a dowry dispute occurred on divorce and separation. Tullia's last marriage seems to have incurred knotty problems of this nature. Several of Cicero's letters show great anxiety about Tullia's financial affairs. If her husband started divorce proceedings, she would be entitled to the return of her dowry. If Tullia made the first move, she would have to prove a case about his misconduct to get anything back (*Letters to Atticus* 9.18, 23, 24).

While Cicero was away governing Cyprus, his wife, Terentia, and Tullia started marriage negotiations with Publius Cornelius Dolabella, an ambitious aristocrat with a reputation for loose living. Cicero's anxious letters to his close friend Atticus give the distinct impression that he, Cicero, was actively suppressing qualms about the match but that he was not going to gainsay his wife and daughter. Perhaps Dolabella's aristocratic connections were a big enough plus for Cicero to be persuaded, and the marriage went ahead. Dolabella's political career progressed well while he had the support of Julius Caesar.

This one incident – and there are examples of similar situations – shows that a combination of circumstances, an absent father, a strong-willed wife and a beloved and possibly indulged daughter, could produce an alliance accompanied by reservations from the head of the household and warning noises on the part of trusted friends and advisers. When the marriage failed, Cicero blamed himself on a number of counts and, as you have probably gathered from the business about the dowry, he felt distinctly outmanoeuvred by Dolabella with regard to financial settlements and Tullia's security.

There is no room to go into the dowry laws in detail but it is interesting to note that an author of the second century CE, one Aulus Gellius, in his mixed bag of observations, anecdotes and interesting facts, *Attic Nights*, mentions a treatise *On Dowries* by none other than Servius Sulpicius.

You could conclude that Roman women of means were relatively independent and not without influence over their own lives. They could own, inherit and control property. They could also enjoy a full social life and entertain alongside their husbands. Calpurnia might have modestly sat apart while Pliny recited his works but Roman women were certainly not debarred from dinner parties nor excluded from public life. There does not seem to have been the same separation or seclusion of women that one finds in Greek society. Of course, both in Greek and Roman society we have to draw distinctions between women of leisure and those who worked in the fields, shops and taverns and who were thus constantly out and about and in the public eye.

Tullia's and Terentia's selection of Dolabella may not have been an unusual business. Anyway, it seems that Roman fathers did not always monopolize the decision about prospective partners and impose wives and husbands against the wishes of their immediate family circle. Friends could be consulted and involved, as you have seen with Cicero. A strong dislike from either of the two intendeds might be taken into account. If you read the following extracts from Pliny's letter, you should receive a fairly unambiguous message about desirable qualities in a husband. The last line demonstrates Pliny's sensitivity to the young bride's situation, but again only in its own historical context. The modern reader might interpret it less charitably.

Minicius Acilianus is energetic and hardworking, but also very modest. He has held high offices, quaestor, tribune and praetor, and performed them to satisfaction. (So there is no need to budget for election expenses.) He has the demeanour of a gentleman, a healthy complexion and is generally a fine-looking fellow with the bearing of one of senatorial rank. These are important factors, for attractiveness is some return, we might say, for the surrendering of the girl's chastity.

Pliny, *Letters* 1.4 (a recommendation to a friend in search of a suitable husband for his niece)

This young man, who was so warmly recommended in this avuncular fashion, was actually close to Pliny's age. We get some inkling of the advantages a marriage might bring: for example, money and influence provided by the wife's family in the pursuit of high office. There were fewer political alliances in the days of the emperor, but marriages invariably had a practical motivation, whatever the social group involved. The noble look of Pliny's candidate for marriage is both an inducement to the bride and a way of advertising the innate value of the groom who is as good as he looks.

Pomp and circumstance

Wedding ceremonies and celebrations, familiar features of 'the big day' in the modern world, were also part of Roman tradition. We have artistic representations, on tombstones or grand sarcophagi, and literary descriptions of the procession of the bride to the house of her husband. A number of books on Roman civilization will give you detailed compilations of a 'typical' marriage ceremony and it is interesting and intriguing to draw parallels between then and now, to speculate on the ancient origins of our own wedding traditions.

Read the extract from a marriage poem celebrating the union of two aristocratic young people. What kind of rituals can you identify here?

O Hymen, marriage maker
Mount Helicon your hill
Urania your mother,
You seize the virgin girl
and take her to her husband
we sing your praises still.
The thrilling day excites you
to sing the wedding chant,
and clarion clear the singing
Now pound the earth with dance
now take the pine torch smouldering
and shake it, to advance.
Now lads lift up your torches
the flame-coloured veil is near
Go sing your parts for Hymen
O Hymen, hail, is here.
The feisty Fescen banter

> unmuzzled for the day
> the slave boy now thrown over
> leads the lads in play
> Yes, throw the nuts, pet lover
> scatter them abroad
> take pleasure in the service
> of Talassius, Hymen lord,
> for you have lazed in leisure
> played the partner and the bawd.
>
> Catullus, Poem 61

Discussion

You probably picked out the presence of a god as master of ceremonies, something about wedding clothes and colours, a procession with torches, singing and dancing and nut throwing.

The marriage god Hymen was a key deity to be revered and the presence of divine spirits who would protect the couple in all their endeavours was assumed, so these *numina* needed appeasing and involving. From that point of view the day had to be carefully chosen. There were appropriate dates (*dies fasti*) and ill-omened ones to be avoided (*dies nefasti*). Cicero had to put off an engagement ceremony between Tullia and her first betrothed, Furius Crassipes, because some days were inauspicious according to the religious calendar. This principle applied to public business as well as private matters. The place of the gods and the proper conduct of any event which needed their goodwill should not be confused with modern religious notions of making sacred vows before god. In Roman times, no priest was required to sanction the union. The extent of a verbal commitment was an optional declaration by the bride: *ubi Gaius, ego Gaia* (Where you are Gaius, I am Gaia); the sentiment roughly translates as 'I'll stay by your side at all times'. Traditionally, bride and groom clasped right hands, a gesture depicted quite frequently on monuments to denote a citizen marriage.

Young boys belted out crude songs ('the feisty Fescen banter') which livened the occasion up as well as marking the day as a sexual rite of passage. The bride wore a flame-coloured veil and might undergo a mock kidnap from her mother's arms. Sometimes her hair was parted with a gladiator's sword, another potent symbol of her physical surrender within marriage. The boys in the Catullus poem are scattering nuts, rather like the custom with confetti. The favoured slave has to vacate his place in his young master's bed. (Towards the end of this chapter something will be said about the situation of the household slave.) In the rest of the poem Catullus puts quite a heavy emphasis on mutual fidelity and the production of an heir who will be the spitting image of his father.

You should be wary of visualizing every Roman marriage with all the ingredients listed above. You have heard how the upper classes, in particular, could have a succession of partners, frequently in the interests of political and economic expediency. Marriage arrangements could be made in the context of a much simpler social occasion. The more elaborate aspects may have been regarded as old-fashioned fuss and inappropriate to someone like Tullia embarking on a second or third marriage. In any case, we really cannot say for certain how widespread or how formulaic the ceremonies actually were or what local colour and additional rituals might have varied the occasions throughout the empire and among different social groups.

Good companions

By Tullia's time it was common practice for the new wife to remain in the *familia* of her father. Naturally, the wife would take up residence in her husband's household but she would, in most cases, continue to belong to her natal family in the legal and formal sense. The point was made earlier that wives did not necessarily fall within the orbit of their husbands' authority. The Romans themselves believed that in their early history the majority of brides had passed into the power of their husbands or their fathers-in-law, for if the husband's father was still living, sons, daughters and daughters-in-law would be answerable to him. The first written laws of Rome, known as the Twelve Tables and memorized by the Roman schoolboy, declared the woman's automatic subordination to a husband in whose house she had lived continuously for a year. The development of the simple strategy of spending a few nights apart prevented this particular process of the husband taking legal possession of his wife.

The woman who wished to marry *cum manu*, acknowledging her subordination to her husband, could declare this ritually by taking part in an ancient ceremony, *confarreatio*, which involved a sharing of a sacred emmer wheat cake with the bridegroom. Or a formal sale (*coemptio*) could be conducted at any time after the marriage, which was a formal declaration that the wife was now *cum manu*. She passed into the total control of her husband, who was henceforward *in loco parentis*, in the place of a (male) parent. This *cum manu* wife had the right to inherit from her husband and to share with any children the property he bequeathed on his death.

Tullia seems to have married *sine manu* (without subordination) in every case. In other words, she never left her father's guardianship and protection. She would have retained the right to inherit from him if he had predeceased her. It was expected that sons and daughters would share any legacy equally, as there was no pattern of primogeniture (i.e. the eldest son receiving the lion's share of the property and assets) in the Roman system. Women like Tullia who married *sine manu*, the majority by the late Republic, did not automatically receive any inheritance on the death of their husbands.

The children in the *sine manu* marriage could not, in theory, rely on a legacy from their mother if she died intestate, because she and any property and income she possessed were independent of the husband's family. This is not the whole story. Roman law recognized changes in custom and practice and eventually a mother's will which did exclude children could be challenged in the courts by disappointed offspring. Murdia, a Roman mother of the first century CE, was praised for specifically naming her children as heirs and avoiding the charge of making an unduteous will (one which did not fulfil family obligations).

EULOGY TO MURDIA

She made all her sons heirs in equal proportion, and she gave her daughter a share as a legacy. Her maternal love was expressed by her concern for her children and the equal shares she gave each of them. Recalling the memory of my father (her first husband) and advised by that and her own sense of what was right, she left me a legacy chargeable on the estate.

Corpus Inscriptionum Latinarum (Compilation of Latin Inscriptions) 6.10230

It is also true that if the mother's background was a prestigious one, boasting some illustrious ancestors for instance, sons in particular might find it useful to promote the maternal side and even to adopt the mother's family name, extending the *tria nomina* (three names) which signified citizenship and the paternal line. (See Appendix on Roman names.) Generally, on the breakup of a marriage the children were the responsibility of the father and it was the wife who left the marital home and returned to her own family, unless a new husband was already on the horizon. A subsequent marriage might require a woman to take on children from a previous union. Julia (the daughter of Julius Caesar) was a great deal younger than Pompey when they married, 16 years to his 46 years, so she became the stepmother of 'children' of the same generation as herself. We can guess, and occasionally read, about possible tensions between husbands and wives and how they manifested themselves. The poet Martial, whom you met in Chapter 4, suggested, tongue in cheek, how one recipe for marital disaster might be avoided:

> You ask why I won't marry a rich woman?
> I don't plan to have a husband for a wife!
> Priscus, a woman should obey her husband in all things.
> That's how you achieve equality, and the only way a woman and man can be the same!
>
> Martial, *Epigrams* 8.12

Concordia, or harmony, in the household was not a concept of equal partnership but of co-operation and role demarcation. Augustus, as you have seen in Chapter 3, promoted the picture of old-fashioned domestic bliss. His wife Livia may or may not have had a significant influence in affairs of state but the public image was of a woman supervising her daughters-in-law in weaving and carrying out other domestic chores. When you look later at a list of Livia's household's slaves, you may wish to adjust this picture of the élite Roman women doing the spinning and other household tasks.

The ideal of the chaste and obedient wife was not confined to the high-born of Roman society. It is interesting to compare a glowing commemoration on a tombstone which acknowledges a wife's loyalty in simple terms and a more elaborate funeral oration which survives from the late Republic. First the more modest epigraph:

> Lucius Aurelius Hermia (Freedman of Lucius), a butcher from the Viminal Hill. 'This is my only wife, who died before me, was chaste in body, loved me, and owned my loving heart. We were true to each other and our love was equal. She was never distracted from her duty by greed.'

Philematium has a 'cute' diminutive meaning 'little kiss'. Both the husband, Hermia, and his wife, as freed slaves, have incorporated the name of their former owner, Aurelius, into their own, a standard practice, in deference to the man who has freed them, but also as part of the *tria nomina*, the three names which indicated that they were now of citizen status.

A common claim was that the marriage was *sine querela*, without complaint. One lengthy and published funeral oration listed the virtues of a wife, Turia (don't confuse her with Cicero's Tullia) who had supported her husband when he was forced into exile; she had protected his property, suffered abuse and rough treatment by his powerful enemies and, after all this proof of her fidelity and devotion, suggested divorce because she was infertile. The husband tells of his horrified refusal to be parted from her even though childlessness was technically a legitimate excuse for the husband to end the marriage. The funeral elegy to Turia makes fascinating reading but it is one of those sources that is quite problematic. We cannot even identify or place the couple for certain and some scholars feel that this eulogy does have a slightly manufactured air. The full Turia text is published in E. Wistrand, *The So-called* Laudatio Turiae: *Introduction, Text, Translation, Commentary*, 1976.

Pliny – as you probably are realizing, a rich source for family values in the second century CE – mentions one Fannia with admiration and affection. There are some similarities between Fannia and Turia.

As you read this letter, make a mental list of Fannia's qualities. What behaviour and what activities are praised by Pliny the Younger?

I am so worried about Fannia's illness. She became sick while tending to Junia, one of the Vestal Virgins, and this was a duty she volunteered for, Junia being a relative, and the Pontiffs confirmed her in it. (If sickness compels a Vestal Virgin to leave the hall of the Goddess Vesta, she is put in the care of a married woman.) So Fannia was attending conscientiously to her task as carer when she became ill. [*A description of Fannia's failing health follows: the prognosis was not good.*]

My anxiety is aggravated by my grief, a terrible grief that such a wonderful woman will be lost to the sight of her country. Her like will not be seen again, not her measure of purity and integrity, her nobility and faithful heart. Loyalty sent her twice into exile, following her husband. [Next comes the story of her standing up to the senate on a question of censorship – this was the time of the infamous Domitian, the overtly autocratic emperor.] She has great quantities of friendliness and charm, the rare gift of inspiring affection as well as respect. Where will we find another to hold up as a role model to our own wives, whose courage could teach even the male sex? This is a woman to be admired alongside the heroines of our history even while she lives among us. For me, though she leaves descendants, the very foundations of her house are shaking and it is on the verge of total collapse. Can the deeds of her descendants ever be enough to guarantee that she does not perish, the last of her line?

Pliny, *Letters* 7.19

Discussion

Apart from the side issues which do not concern us at this point (e.g. interesting facts about life and sickness as a Vestal Virgin), the eulogy of Fannia focuses on a familiar female role (even today, we could say), that of the carer. To be fair to Pliny, he also highlights Fannia's bravery in tough times and her refusal to be cowed at a hearing about a politically sensitive book, the life of her husband, Helvidius. (She had supplied Helvidius' diaries to the biographer.) As well as being a noble adjunct to her husband, Pliny suggests that her charm and heroism buttress, not merely ornament, her house.

Harriet Flower (1996) has written on ancestor masks as symbols of aristocratic power. Their presence at the funerals of the prestigious demonstrated the importance of lineage and family traditions of office holding and commanding armies. Pliny is making the point (and he does it in other letters when he praises young men as a credit to their family name) that unless the noble behaviour is sustained, the prestige of the line will fail. By Pliny's day most of the old aristocratic families had died out. The emperor Augustus had, in any case, discouraged displays of aristocratic status at home and abroad. In life and in death, Fannia is a shining example of a woman who set her own standards without the props of the past.

Cicero provides us with a scene from married life that was not intended for public consumption. The following extract shows his concerns about Pomponia's treatment of her husband, Quintus, Cicero's brother:

> As soon as we arrived, Quintus very courteously said, 'Pomponia, you ask the ladies in and I'll invite the men.' From my observation, nothing could have been more agreeable in the way he asked and his expression, and no exception could be taken at his words. But she replied in front of us, 'I am a guest here myself!' Then Quintus whispered to me, 'You see! This is what I put up with every day.' I rest my case. In my opinion, my brother was doing his best to keep the peace and your sister was as being as awkward as she could. And I am passing over a lot of things that irritated me even more than they upset Quintus.
>
> Cicero, *Letters to Atticus* 5.1

Although this seems a slightly comical scene with a modern ring – Pomponia is portrayed by Cicero as taking umbrage over nothing and sulking – there is quite a history to this partnership. Pomponia was some years older than Quintus and was in her late thirties in this, her first marriage, an unusual situation when you think back to the norm quoted earlier in this chapter. Pomponia was bound to be a deal less biddable than Pliny's Calpurnia, who had so much to learn about life and marriage.

Keith Bradley traces the ups and downs of Pomponia and Quintus' married life in the last chapter of his book, *Discovering the Roman Family*. Using Cicero as his case study, Bradley considers the emotions involved in relationships between siblings, parents and children and the feelings towards members of the extended family. An interesting aspect of the Pomponia/Quintus saga is the responsibility both Cicero and Atticus took, on a number of occasions, to patch things up. In other letters, Cicero suggests that Quintus has behaved insensitively. The marriage limped on for some 20 years before the couple parted.

There is plenty of evidence for educated and accomplished women who won some grudging admiration from writers of the time, although less trouble was taken to educate upper-class girls beyond the marriageable age of 14. A few love poems survive which are ascribed to one Sulpicia and these are a rare extant example of female creativity. Sulpicia might have been the daughter of the very Sulpicius whose letter started off our discussion about relationships within the family, in which case she would have been a contemporary or even an acquaintance of Cicero's Tullia. Sulpicia's poems were attributed to Tibullus and included in his corpus until 1838. They are of particular interest because otherwise the male perception of women in love predominates in Latin elegiac poetry. Alison Sharrock and Maria Wyke have both written on the image of the Roman mistress or girlfriend (*puella*) as literary constructs. One of the Clodii sisters (aka Catullus' Lesbia) established her own coterie (a writers' circle cum book club) and held her own in discussions about literature and philosophy.

There was an undercurrent of uneasiness about these women, especially during the Republic. Several forceful females were cited in court cases for corruption and treason and gave orators such as Cicero a field day. All the same, he relished the attractions of Sempronia (the wife of the consul in 77 BCE, she was implicated in Catiline's conspiracy to overthrow the consular government) who was both physically seductive and impressive intellectually. Roman women could plead their own legal cases, although they were not expected to make an exhibition of themselves in the law courts. Afrania, a senator's wife, became notorious for her love of advocacy and her 'shamelessness' is reported by Valerius Maximus, *Memorable Words and Deeds* 8.3.2.

However accomplished, these women had stepped over the boundaries of modesty and, more threatening, into the public and political arena, the male preserve. The ideal of an unassailable *matrona* (citizen wife) with her husband's and children's best interests at heart might have turned out in many instances to be a sad male fantasy, but many women surely subscribed to models of appropriate female behaviour. There's not much point in describing the realities of male-dominated societies and then denying that these material circumstances affected the attitudes of the female population. Sulpicia's poems are about love and marriage, not politics nor a public career. Citizen women, however well born, had no official clout in political life, no voting assembly and no possibility of holding office.

Imperial women, on the other hand, could influence events and emperors. Male Roman authors, historians and biographers portrayed these women as exceptional and dangerous. The problem was the special position they held close to the seat of power. In normal circumstances, wives and mothers were respected for their central role in the home and it was expected they would be involved in decisions about the family albeit, technically, at their husband's discretion. Boundaries between the imperial family and the administration of the empire could become blurred, however, so that a 'meddling' wife had an impact beyond the private domestic sphere. The appeal of 'bad women' lives on. The empress Livia who was married to Augustus suffered from a fair amount of demonization by the modern author Robert Graves in *I, Claudius*.

Another woman of spirit was Agrippina (the Elder), the wife of Germanicus. (Germanicus was the heir and nephew of the emperor Tiberius.) Augustus had approved of wives accompanying their husbands to provinces they had been allotted to govern. In theory, the wives were a stabilizing factor and this tied in with Augustus' ideas about encouraging family values. Agrippina was in the habit of travelling with her husband on his military campaigns. She took the children along as well, and it was in the army camp that her small son Gaius was nicknamed Caligula and made a mascot by the troops. As an adult, he was less charming; some of the stories told about him depict him as the most sadistic of the emperors. His mother, Agrippina, comes across as 'pushy' in the pages of historians such as Tacitus but also popular and carrying the sympathy vote when Germanicus died in the east. (Tiberius evidently alienated the people by not showing enough public grief at this royal tragedy.) As a widow, and eager to remarry, Agrippina was a disturbing player in imperial politics from Tiberius' point of view. Not known for his lightness of touch, he had Agrippina exiled for treason and she died in suspicious circumstances on a remote island.

Agrippina the Younger, her daughter and the emperor Nero's mother, was something of a notorious legend in her own lifetime. Agrippina married her uncle Claudius while he was emperor and she was later implicated by rumour in his death. She put two loyal men at the imperial helm when her adolescent son became ruler of the empire. One of these men was Seneca whom she had persuaded Claudius to recall from exile on Corsica. She was a force to be reckoned with over the span of two reigns and eventually antagonized her son into planning her murder. It took Nero several attempts to assassinate her, passing over the notion of poison because she had fortified herself with various antidotes. He then commandeered a shipwright to devise a collapsible boat, pretended to be reconciled with his mother, and sent her off to the festival at Baiae. The boat disintegrated at sea but Agrippina gamely swam ashore. She was beaten to death with cudgels shortly after, in her home. She was aged 44. The whole episode was a bizarre human drama told with relish by Tacitus (*Annals* 14.7–10). Allegedly, she asked her assassins to strike the womb that had spawned the monster, Nero.

Insight

There were wealthy women throughout the Roman empire and not just by virtue of high birth. Wives and widows might make money in manufacture, running workshops and factories. There are no definitive answers about the influence of educated élite women on the ruling class of Rome and upon the running of the provinces but there is a growing scholarly trend that questions a hitherto narrow definition of political activity in the Roman empire. Women certainly networked even if they could not hold public office and, as we have seen, they did not necessarily put up with being pawns in the marriage alliance game.

From birth to earth

Citizen women had a central place as producers of legitimate children. Tullia had two sons but neither survived infancy. The second child did not outlive his mother by many months. Cicero mentions a 'puny creature' who was the result of a seven-month pregnancy in May of 49 BCE, four years earlier. Tullia's experience was pretty typical. Infant mortality was high and pregnancy and childbirth a risky business all around. Children were not named nor their arrival into the world formally celebrated until they had survived eight days and then it was a touch-and-go business throughout their early years. It was customary not to mourn the death of an infant under one year old and Cicero is matter of fact about the sickly state of Tullia's first child, whom he refers to in a detached way. He is mainly relieved that his daughter had a good delivery. His affection and concern for Tullia is attested throughout his letters, as is his attachment to both his own children when they were small. Note the affectionate use of the diminutive Tulliola for Tullia.

> Here in exile, how I long for my daughter, Tulliola, the most loving, modest and clever daughter a man ever had, the image of my face, my speech and my mind. And my sweet and charming little boy. I had to be an unfeeling brute and thrust him from my arms. Too knowing for his age, my poor child realised what was happening.
>
> Cicero, *Letters to Quintus* 3.3

When it came to Tullia's baby, his grandson, Cicero was being realistic rather than callous. The death of a child might come as less of a surprise to the Roman parent but in many cases being prepared would not have lessened the sense of tragedy. In spite of expressions of disapproval about publicly mourning the child who died in its first year, a bereaved father, serving with the army in York, could be moved to mark his daughter's brief life:

> **Inscription**
>
> To the spirits of the dead and in memory of Simplicia Florentina
> a most innocent soul
> who lived ten months
> Felicius Simplex her father
> a soldier of the Sixth Legion had this made
>
> *RIB* 1.690

It is frustrating but sometimes inevitable to conclude that Roman perceptions of childhood are multi-vocal and contradictory. A father had the right to expose an unwanted child. (In urban areas this did not necessarily mean abandoning a baby to the elements. For instance, there was apparently a recognized spot in the city of Rome where slave dealers collected up any of these human commodities.) Parents' participation in their children's upbringing was generally less intense than is the custom of modern nuclear families. The rich could choose the extent of their involvement as the whole *familia* of slaves could be called upon and there was hired help available, too.

The historian Tacitus spoke disapprovingly of the tendency among the upper classes to hand over sons and daughters to wet-nurses. Mothers who were intimately involved in the raising of their children often did so in a disciplinary capacity. Maternal feelings existed but were filtered through traditions of a firm upbringing and strict parenting. Sons in well-to-do families were to be groomed for service to society, both military and political. Suzanne Dixon (*The Roman Family*, p. 131) points out that 'both parents were expected to give their children moral training and oversee their formal education'.

Delegating the nurture of children was not confined to the rich. Keith Bradley's book (1991) has a fascinating chapter on all the different carers who could be involved in the upbringing of children from a variety of backgrounds. The communal living space of tenement apartments and the co-residency that existed in these places would facilitate farming out and sharing the tasks of childcare. In the élite house or in the small craft business, slave women might be released from breastfeeding their own babies, so that they could quickly return to a long and unbroken day's work. It was not uncommon for the freeborn children of a household to share a wet-nurse with slave children. They grew up as *collactei* and sometimes continued to acknowledge this bonding into adulthood.

A tentative conclusion

One way of negotiating the range of practices and approaches concerning children that the evidence suggests is to engage with the total experience of producing and losing children in the ancient world. The Romans probably felt that the baby and the small child were living on borrowed time. It might seem bizarre to apply that concept to the young as well as the old but reaching five or even ten years old was an achievement in a world where health hazards were legion and gynaecology and paediatrics at a basic level. For this reason, the child must have been characterized as vulnerable and, at the same time as being valued, also viewed as potentially dispensable. This might explain the mixture of callousness and sentimentality about childhood as a phase which emanates from the evidence:

Her most unhappy parents, Faenomenus and Helpis, set up the dedication to Anteis Chrysostom – sweet prattler and chatterbox – who lived three years, five months and three days, our dearly beloved, well-behaved daughter, with her piping voice. Porcius Maximus and Porcia Charita and Porcia Helias and Sardonyx and Menophilus who tended her to the day of her death also commemorate her.

Corpus Inscriptionum Latinarum 6.34421

Tablets of stone?

Not just how but whether we can safely use commemorative patterns to reconstruct Roman families is a moot point. As ever, all the available evidence has to be put on the table. Roman epitaph frequently mentions the bereaved and their relationship to the deceased. A pattern emerges of heirs who had an obligation to set up the monument. Drawing attention to commemorators in this way had not been such a common practice among the Greeks or contemporaneous cultures. For this reason, historians have matched up the Roman habit of commemoration with Roman views on the significance of life and death. The tombstone doubled up as an advertisement of pertinent facts about the living as well as the dead.

Alongside the literature of the upper classes and their views of family life, there is a large body of evidence in the form of funerary inscriptions. The value of the inscription is its socially inclusive nature. During the course of this chapter you have encountered the grief of a soldier serving in Britain, the blameless life of a butcher's wife and the lament of an adult circle beyond the biological parents for a small child. We can only guess at the diverse circumstances surrounding the individuals and their loss. Some parents might leave a formulaic commemoration or a few studied phrases while others had to write something much more immediate and from the heart.

Tombstones tell us about a broad social spectrum, and the range of information they might contain about the deceased and their family, friends and heirs have encouraged historians to make some educated guesses about demographic trends. Demographic studies cover a number of issues: speculations on life expectancy, infant mortality, social mobility and types of household residency. The language and architecture of the funerary monument make statements about life as well as death throughout the Roman world. Recurring terms of endearment and variations upon expressions of sorrow indicate a decorum of emotions which crossed class and social boundaries in the commemoration of the dead.

Inscriptions are a fascinating and controversial area of scholarship – hence the challenges we constantly confront, one being the usual problem of gaps in the evidence. To date, about 185,000 funerary inscriptions have been recorded from the whole timespan of the Roman empire. Unfortunately, they do not form a representative or steady stream of evidence for Rome's 700-year hegemony. The epigraphical habit, as it has been called, the custom of marking death with an elaborate or a modest monument, ebbed and flowed during the existence of the empire.

It's not just a problem of chronology; some regions have a richer supply of surviving tombstones than others. A bewildering intermesh of factors means that treating inscriptions as 'hard data' (the demographic angle) has its dangers, but they do tell us more about the lives and aspirations of those lower down on the social scale who otherwise would only appear to us through the filter of upper-class assumptions. Slaves find a place on family tombstones and freed slaves proudly proclaim lives of upward mobility through the epitaphs and carved reliefs on their grave monuments.

Relating to slaves and slavery

My dear Marcus, I am truly grateful about what you have done about Tiro, judging his former condition to be beneath him and preferring us to have him as a friend rather than a slave. Believe me I jumped for joy when I read your letter and his.

From Quintus Cicero to Marcus Cicero, *Letters to Friends* 16.16

Oh do you see how the child is torn away even as he clings to me with dying arms, holding on to my life-giving heart and soul. He is not of my seed, nor does he bear my name. I was not his father but look at my tears, you who are bereaved, and my bruised cheeks and believe my sounds of lament, because I too am bereft.

I did not buy him as a chirpy charmer, off a ship from Pharos, as a little darling fluent in the chit-chat of his native Nile. I did not fall in love with a precocious wit and quick tongue. This boy was mine, all mine. I caught sight of him as he lay on the ground, and I composed the birth song which welcomed him on his day of anointing. I enrolled him into life as he grasped it breathing new air in the gulps of his shaky cries. Your parents could not bestow more upon you, for I gave you a second birth and freedom, my little one, at the moment of your suckling, even though you chuckled, quite unappreciative of the gift.

Statius, *Silvae* 5.5.8–13, 66–75

It is a slave, yes a slave, whom you mourn, Ursus. This is the way Fortune blindly hands out and makes a lottery of the names of things. She is indifferent to our hearts. This slave was dutiful, his love and loyalty deserved these tears and his sense of inner freedom was greater than the liberty bestowed by an ancestral line. Don't economize on grief and don't be ashamed of it.

> [...famulum – quia rerum nomina caeca
> sic miscet Fortuna manu nec pectora novit –
> sed famulus gemis, Urse, pium, sed amore fideque
> has meritum lacrimas, cui maior stemmate iuncto
> libertas ex mente fuit. ne comprime fletus,
> ne pudeat...]
>
> Statius, Silvae 2.6.8–13

All three pieces of 'evidence' above have been deliberately chosen for the feelings of common humanity they convey and their warmth and affection for those fortune has made slaves, although they are fit for freedom for a number of reasons. However, as with the grief of Cicero and Sulpicius, they do not tell the whole story. Tiro, whom you might remember from the sample of Roman 'voices' in the introduction, had a long wait before his talents and loyalty were rewarded.

The Statius poems are of a later date than the Cicero letters. Publius Papinius Statius was from Naples, born in the 40s CE and living about 50 years. He was a talented court poet under Domitian, writing epics and shorter poems with a wide range of subjects and themes. In the first poem we hear how Statius' adopted son was freed at birth by his owner, and this reminds us of one important source of slaves, their procreation within the household. These slaves were called *vernae*, which distinguishes them from slaves bought on the open market, as the booty of war or supplied by pirates.

In the second poem we are presented with a friend's, Ursus', faithful slave who died with no change in his servile condition but whose passing was marked with a poem of praise and an acknowledgement of his inner, 'spiritual', freedom. The Latin of this verse was included to highlight some keywords; do you recognize *Fortuna*, Fortune, Fate or Kismet; *pium* (*pius*), dutiful, and *libertas*, freedom, liberty? It certainly seems as if this slave was mourned over as one of the family. Pliny the Younger wrote of his own liberality and humanity in allowing sick slaves to make wills and bequeath any belongings they had (*Letters* 8.16). After all, he says, the house is its own state and community. Rather typical of Pliny, you might say, to advertise his own kindness and gentility, when he had the chance.

Think about these representations of relationships between slaves and owners. Why is this evidence of limited value as it stands? What other testimony would you like to hear about slavery?

Discussion

It would be naive to assume that all slaves were loyal and loved and that all owners were caring and needed no convincing about the fair treatment of fellow humans who had simply drawn the short straw in life's lottery. Cicero's generosity towards Tiro can be counterbalanced by other evidence from the letters. Cicero could be vindictive and indifferent to uneducated or disloyal slaves who tried to flee his service.

Using a rather florid poet as evidence of fine feelings towards slaves is risky. Statius is mannered and it is his part of his poetic role to sublimate grief and produce a lament for a special occasion. I have omitted all the mythological references and parallels he indulges in. These individualized slaves stand out among millions of men and women who were just part of the inventory for many owners on large estates.

You may have studied the history of slavery and know something about the slave trade in Europe and America. You probably asked yourself about the wide variety of treatment meted out to slaves, depending on where they worked and for whom. You have been given a glimpse of the harsh conditions of rural slaves and the way in which the landowners calculated their productive capacity and cost of keeping, along with their animals and within the context of profit and loss on a large estate. Keith Bradley (*Slavery and Society*, pp. 178–9) reminds us, without flannel, of the indignity and violence of the slave's experience:

> *The bare record of fact shows that Roman slaves, like those in the Americas, were bought and sold like animals, were punished indiscriminately and violated sexually: they were compelled to labour as their masters dictated, were allowed no legal existence, and they were goaded into compliance through cajolery and intimidation. They were ultimate victims of exploitation.*

Bradley explores strategies of survival and resistance that the slaves developed and the way in which their owners articulated exasperation, and their low expectations of servile efficiency and behaviour in general. The lazy, sly and manipulative slave was a recognized type in literature and life, a different model from Cicero's Tiro or Ursus' nameless paragon of virtue and devotion. Although this last section will be dealing with urban slaves and their place in the household, you should be alert to the fact that the town/country polarity is not a straightforward one.

Ovid, the urban and urbane poet you met in Chapter 2, wrote a jokey poem about concealing an affair with a slave girl from his lover, Corinna, who was the girl's mistress. He loudly protests his innocence and points out that the slave, Cypassis, would not be an attractive proposition.

> What an unprecedented crime to charge me with! And Cypassis, your skilful make-up maid, is accused of contaminating her mistress's bed. By the grace of the gods, if I lusted to do wrong, it would not be with a girl soiled in service and ill-fated into the bargain. What free man would want a sexual encounter with a slave girl or to close his arms around a back all cut up with the whip.
>
> Ovid, *Amores* 2.8

Suffering in service could at times be as acute in the performance of menial tasks about the house as in the hard labour of the fields. Cypassis was a good hairdresser, but the slave girl who was incompetent in coiffuring a demanding mistress could be beaten on the spot, in the anger and frustration of the moment. Cypassis is forced to continue the dangerous affair with the poet, otherwise he will confess all to Corinna. In that case, the consequences for the slave hardly bear thinking about. Ovid's love poems are, in all probability, set in a fictional scenario, but there has to be a believability factor and the attitudes towards slaves come across loud and clear. Strictly speaking, Ovid has no right to 'damage' or take liberties with someone else's slave; there were legal penalties for this, but Cypassis could hardly have started proceedings.

As the Ovid poem demonstrated, slaves were at the mercy of the tantrums and whims of their owners. For this reason Seneca the Younger (Emperor Nero's mentor and adviser in the first years of his rule), in one of his philosophical works, *De Ira* (On Anger), pointed out the negative side of slavery, not from the point of view of the slave but on the grounds of practicality (the slave would try to escape or to take revenge) and also because it encouraged indulgence in extreme emotions. The existence of a punching board who had little if any recourse to reprisals, who could not fight back, meant that the bad-tempered man or woman need not make any effort to control their emotions:

> Plato [a fifth/fourth-century BCE Athenian, follower of the philosopher Socrates and founder of his own philosophical school] refrained from exercising total power over his household and once when he was excessively angry about some wrongdoing, he said, 'Speusippus, you

> beat this wretched slave [*servulum*], for I am angry.' This was his reason for not giving into anger, when another would, for the same reason, have given in completely; 'I am angry and I shall go over the top. I shall enjoy doing it too. The slave should not be in the power of one who has no power over himself.' Should someone wish to entrust vengeance to an angry man when Plato himself delegated this authority? Do not allow yourself such power while you are angry. Why? Because then you wish to legitimize everything.
>
> Seneca, *On Anger* 3.12

Seneca pointed out that those who could not control their passions were in a sort of slavery themselves. The sinning slave was a contemptible creature who deserved punishment. The use of the diminutive of *servus*, *servulum*, in the passage reinforces the slave's worthlessness and inconsequentiality and also suggests Plato's irritation. On the other hand, Seneca can be scathing about 'metaphorical' slavery to appetite and self-indulgence, a condition he has witnessed among the well-born and intelligent. He suggests that no one has the right to feel superior to their slaves. They share your house and have the right to expect courteous behaviour. He makes these points in his *Letters from a Stoic* (Letter 47) along with the observation that many of the Romans were descended from slaves and their own families might one day be reduced to slavery again. In many ways, Seneca's arguments for treating slaves well anticipates Christian attitudes. Neither the Stoical school of philosophy nor the Christian religion advocated abolishing slavery but legislation about the treatment of slaves did increasingly emphasize humane treatment.

None of this undercuts Bradley's summary about slavery as a condition. It indicates how much it was embedded in the fabric of Roman civilization. Roman society was organized, on the commercial level, with slave and free labour working side by side (slaves could be contracted out for long hours in craft shops and small-scale pottery factories). The role of slavery in the economy is best understood in the context of the forces and relations of production that operated in the ancient world (the Marxist approach, which still takes some beating). The elite family structure was of course bound up with the existence and presence of slaves. Even the modest shop-owner was likely to own a few.

I rather lament having neither the space nor the expertise to tease out even a few fundamental issues and challenges we face in trying to understand the Roman economy. There are plenty of works to grapple with on this topic. Lively and only partially resolved debates continue on the levels of exploitation of enslaved and free labour, the rate of economic growth in the imperial period, and the nature and impact of large scale trade and mass production. There seems to be a consensus that 'business life throughout the history of the Greco-Roman world remained wholly individualistic' (Richard Saller, 2002, p. 256). Nor is it easy to gauge per capita consumption. A predominantly poor peasantry, swathes of urban populations living at subsistence level (however publicly grand and prosperous big cities might look) and slaves as producers and consumers present a complicated picture for the economic historians.

Livia's household (preserved as tomb inscriptions)

Look at the range of tasks, below, that the household slave could perform. Can you draw a few basic conclusions from this list? And are there some unexpected omissions?

aquarius	*(water carrier)*
arcarius	*(treasurer)*
argentarius	*(silversmith)*
ab argento	*(slave in charge of silver)*
atriensis	*(steward)*
aurifex	*(goldsmith)*
calciator	*(cobbler)*
capsarius	*(folder of clothes)*
colorator	*(furniture polisher)*
cubicularius	*(chamberlain)*
supra cubicularios	*(supervisor of chamberlains)*
delicium	*(pet child)*
dispensator	*(steward)*
faber	*(craftsman)*
insularius	*(keeper of the apartment block)*
lanipedus	*(wool weigher)*
lector	*(reader)*
libraria	*(clerk)*
a manu	*(secretary)*

margaritarius	*(pearl setter)*
medicus	*(doctor)*
supra medicos	*(supervisor of doctors)*
mensor	*(surveyor)*
nutrix	*(wet-nurse)*
opsonator	*(caterer)*
obstetrix	*(midwife)*
ab ornamentis	*(servant in charge of ceremonial dress)*
ornatrix	*(dresser)*
ostiarius	*(doorkeeper)*
paedagogus	*(companion for schoolchildren)*
a pedibus	*(supervisor of footmen)*
pedisequus and	
pedisequua	*(male and female attendants)*
pictor	*(painter)*
pistor	*(baker)*
ad possessiones	*(financial administrator)*
a purpuris	*(servant in charge of purple garments)*
rogator	*(issuer of invitations?)*
a sacrario	*(servant in charge of shrine)*
sarcinatrix	*(clothes mender)*
a sede	*(chair attendant?)*
strator	*(saddler)*
structor	*(builder)*
ab supellectile	*(servant in charge of furniture)*
tabularius	*(record keeper)*
a tabulis	*(servant in charge of pictures)*
unctrix	*(masseuse)*
ad unguenta	*(servant in charge of perfumed oils)*
ad valetudinem	*(sickbay orderly)*
a veste	*(servant in charge of clothes)*

Discussion

Livia was the empress so the size of her household is not that typical. The services she needed may well have been standard for the rich, though. Cooks and launderers are missed off. Without these, the list still emphasizes the number of slaves in the large houses and the range of skills they could offer. They were put in responsible and important jobs. The only profession from which they were for ever debarred was military service, although they were present in the army camps as the personal slaves of soldiers.

Another thing worth observing is the differentiation of jobs. They could be divided and subdivided so that a status and hierarchy was developed, even in servile tasks. Bradley calls it a chain of command and he believes that the Roman eye for detail and for demarcation shows up in the way the jobs were organized and designated. Flory (1978), who has done work on inscriptions put up by freed slaves, concluded that bonding of slaves within the *familia* resulted in some lasting ties on the basis of tasks in common. Once they were freed and had struck out on their own, they continued to commemorate each other as erstwhile 'work colleagues' and fellow slaves (*conservi*). As the freed slave automatically became a Roman citizen, he or she felt no embarrassment about their former state. On the contrary, they advertised their altered condition at every available opportunity.

A house the size of Livia's looks like a hive of industry. In the later imperial households a servile career structure emerges, for the talented and educated slaves were involved in the administration of the empire. They may have taken positions of high trust on gaining their freedom. The emperor Claudius' freedmen were intensely disliked by senators because they supplanted upper-class administrators.

Did you wonder about the actual arrangement of domestic space around all these people in service? Excavations of Roman houses do not necessarily give us the answers. Think back to the discussion in Chapter 3 and the varying ways in which we could 'read' the plan or the site. Pliny's villa had special slave quarters but this was not always the case. Slaves might share sleeping areas and the amount of daily toing and froing around the house which must have taken place adds to an impression of limited privacy on all sides in the typical slave household. Like households with live-in servants – and they are by no means a thing of the past – families with slaves were largely families without secrets. In court cases, evidence was extracted from slaves by torture, however willing the unfortunate witnesses were to speak out. It was considered a method of ensuring truthfulness and it was not until the Antonine emperors in the second century CE that slave children under 12 were exempted from this form of interrogation. This piece of information is perhaps one last and apt antidote to the sentimental picture the extracts at the beginning of this section conveyed about slavery.

This has been rather a random harvest of Roman relationships and the way in which the Roman *familia* functioned in life and death. You are probably leaving this chapter with a number of questions. Some of the areas will be revisited in the conclusion – the changing face of empire. In the meantime you could check out for yourself what new insights you have gained about the Roman way. Most importantly, would you now ask different questions or frame your questions differently when you next come across evidence of marriage, children and slaves in the Roman world?

POINTS TO REMEMBER...

1 Cicero's letters are a rich source for Roman relationships but also give us tantalizing glimpses of the volatile politics at the end of the Republican era. Along with his surviving speeches (a one-sided documentation of his legal career and his time in high office), the letters show us a man whose principles and courage ebbed and flowed in adversity.

2 Cicero's letters from exile and from his period governing Cyprus demonstrate a surprisingly steady pace of communications and his reliance on family, friends and allies to keep up his profile in Rome. Letter writing in general provides us with a whole range of insights into life in the empire at home and abroad.

3 The death of Cicero's daughter, Tullia, allows us to empathize with her grieving father and family but, while participating in a universal response to loss, we can identify some distinctly Roman attitudes to death. High mortality was a given in this period and Cicero's sense of bereavement is very bound up with and accentuated by his anguish at the death of the Republic. Tullia was in many ways his distraction and consolation, an 'angel in the home'.

4 Tullia's brief life prompts questions about the role of women in the Roman Empire although we are very much confined to the perception of male authors in our investigations. On the other hand, Cicero and a later and equally inveterate letter writer, Pliny, can be used as indicators of social realities as well as treated with care when parading positive and negative female role models.

5 Marriage among the elite classes in the time of Cicero was generally pragmatically motivated and politically functional. First marriages were likely to be festive, drawing upon ancient rituals and colourful customs. They were public occasions but not legal contracts as we would understand them, and so divorce could be by mutual agreement.

6 It was rare in the Late Republic for a wife to pass into the jurisdiction of her husband (*cum manu*), so technically she was not counted as part of his *familia* although she ran the household (*domus*).

7 Pliny the Younger wrote letters with an eye on publication and, indeed, polished his collection to showcase his wide range of knowledge, his many aesthetic and cultural interests, his wisdom in day-to-day matters and his success, status and material possessions.

8 Epitaphs and commemorative writing celebrate loyal and biddable wives but also praise women who were heroic advocates and activists on behalf of persecuted husbands. Other energetic females related to the key political players in Rome (and later those of the imperial family), who interfered in male spheres of government, were viewed by male writers as dangerous and aberrant.

9 Young children were mourned but parents were expected to 'move on' as mortality was high and the early years full of health hazards. Epitaphs can be touching, with sentiments that speak to us across the centuries. The frequency, location and chronology of these and other inscriptions are an important but by no means straightforward aspect of demographic studies.

10 Like women and children, slaves tend to be a silenced as much as a silent majority whose treatment varied on the domestic front and could be brutal and short on farmlands, down mines and in all projects requiring hard labour. They were fundamental to the Roman economy but there is work still to be done on how slaves and free labour co-existed in large and small-scale production.

6

Going abroad

By the end of this chapter, you should feel familiar with a number of facets of Romanness. Your study will have taken you through a variety of sources straight from the Roman world. You will have been exposed to inscriptions, monuments and literature and explored methods of integrating as well as interpreting the evidence. What we cannot retrieve is the very verbal and oral nature of the Roman world, nor the number of local languages and customs which went unrecorded. The gaps and uncertainties in what remains of the Roman world should not discourage anyone from visiting, revisiting and re-evaluating what we do have. With the advances in archaeology there is always hope of more.

This chapter has been designed to help you develop a conceptual framework for all the evidence. Modern historians and students of Roman civilization need to construct a clearer overall picture than one made up, mosaic-like, of a number of vignettes of Roman life. That is why I shall be generalizing about the Roman experience across the empire. You need not accept all of my conclusions but I feel it is important that general conclusions are drawn about the past.

You have come to the final stage of your journey through Roman civilization and the moment when life beyond Rome and Italy becomes part of the picture. Italy was the first Roman province and the beginning of the Romans' empire building. The Romans themselves liked to portray this as a purely defensive expansion, a response to having their interests challenged. Horace's journey through Italy revealed, if only by allusion to other settlers and their cultures, the diverse character of the land around the city and the not always smooth path to power that Rome had pursued from its agricultural beginnings. Certain cultures and languages in

Italy survived in spite of being relatively 'local' to Rome (e.g. Oscan, Samnite).

The south of Italy was, from the early days, a Hellenized area, known as *Magna Graecia*. *Pax Romana*, a concept discussed earlier (Chapter 2, in relation to the *Ara Pacis*), defined the places that the Romans had pacified and signified their overall dominion, so it cannot be neatly related to modern notions of peace in an equal partnership of nations.

It is a real challenge for any guide to give you a sense of the shape and compass of the world beyond Rome the city, places bound by notions of Romanness and well within Rome's administrative sphere. Terms like 'the Roman empire' and 'Roman civilization' suggest a comforting uniformity but one aim of this book has been to delve beneath the surface of common definitions and assumptions. When we start to extend our search for Roman identity outside Rome and Italy, we find a combination of the familiar and the foreign. A look at the following map should tell you something about the extent of what was technically Roman territory by the time of Augustus, and it had expanded further by the time of Trajan in the early part of the second century CE.

Military might

A study of the Roman army, like so many aspects of Roman civilization, is a book in itself. Fighting ability had been the key, not just to the success of Rome as an agricultural community but also to its survival in the early days. The courage of the soldier was closely linked to the tenacious character of the peasant farmer. Fighting farmers and the harsh conditions of the early settlements in the centre of Italy became a powerful part of Roman mythology, the stuff of legend and the core of the Romans' identity as conquerors and colonizers.

Once Rome had an established empire to run, the recruitment of the army and its composition had to change radically. The gaining and retaining of her many provinces had long since required foreign auxiliaries to be part of the mobile military machine. However, the idea and the ideal of the ethnic Roman military character persisted. This and Rome's special relationship to the powerful gods in the pantheon explained and justified her domination, as far as many contemporary commentators were concerned.

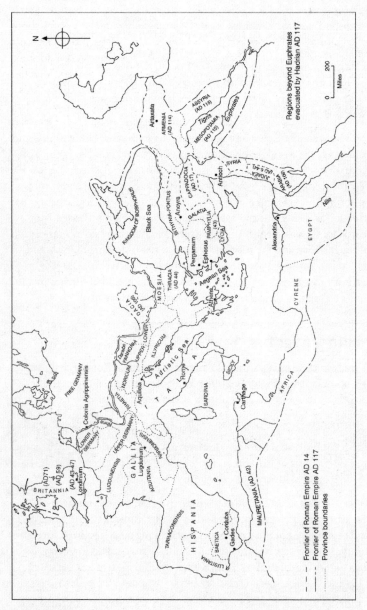

The Roman empire

The soldier/statesman leading his armies into battle, with the gods on his side, was a tenacious image. Just for a moment, I would like to transport you forward historically – principally to make a point about the cultural continuum but, partly, too, to acclimatize you to the much wider timespan of this chapter. Claudian, a poet from Alexandria in the fourth century CE, wrote in glowing terms of his patron, Stilicho, Regent in the western half of the empire. When we read Claudian's accomplished Latin verse, it is as if culturally time has stood still. Here is Stilicho preparing to do battle against the Hun at the river Hebrus in Thrace (modern Macedonia and the Southern area of Bulgaria).

> Fearless against these forces, you, Stilicho, made for the waters of foaming Hebrus, and before the trumpets brayed the battle signal, you prayed thus: 'O Mars, wherever you are, whether you are relaxing on the cloud-capped mountains of Haemus, or you are to be found on Rhodope white with frost, or Mount Athos, channelled out by the Persian fleet, or perhaps you are at Pangaeus, impenetrable with its dark holm oaks, gird on your armour and at my side defend your Thracians. If glory for us is the result, you will be honoured with an oak tree adorned with battle spoils.'
>
> Father Mars heard the prayer and rose up from the snowy peaks of Haemus and shouted for servants at the double. 'Bring my helmet, Bellona, and Fear, fasten the wheels of my chariot. Terror, harness my swift horses. Everyone, speed to the tasks in hand. Take heed, my Stilicho is preparing for war and he is the one who habitually enriches me with war trophies and hangs the plumed helmets of his enemies on the tree.'
>
> [audit illa pater scopulisque nivalibus Haemi surgit et hortatur celeres clamore ministros: 'fer galeam, Bellona, mihi nexusque rotarum tende, Pavor. frenet rapidos Formido iugales. festinas urgete manus. meus ecce paratur ad bellum Stilicho, qui me de more tropaeis ditat et hostiles suspendit in arbore cristas.']
>
> Claudian, *In Rufinum* 1.332–46

There's a great deal of interest in this passage. You may have realized that it is written in the epic metre of dactylic hexameter. Indeed, Stilicho is presented as an epic-heroic figure. The prayer formula recalls the eye for detail we met in Cato's recommended words in the country sacrifice (Chapter 2). Stilicho has to cover all the possible addresses where the god may be resident. Luckily, he was right first time. He promises Mars a proper thanks for his hoped-for help and

Mars responds by reminding his helpers, all abstract facets of war which have a real presence as his servants, that Stilicho has frequently honoured and acknowledged him with war trophies.

The really intriguing thing about Claudian's poetic composition is that he is writing in the era of established Christianity. Stilicho is a Christian commander. He is also a barbarian, not a Roman, by birth; his father was a Vandal chieftain. The armies on both sides contained a great many barbarians. In the era of the fourth century CE, large portions of the 'Roman' army were likely to defect and quite often the frontiers east and west were so hard-pressed they had to bribe the encroaching barbarian hordes to go away, or allow them to stay on large parts of Roman territory (and even to administer them). This poem is primarily aimed against the devout Christian Regent, Rufinus, who controlled the East from the capital at Constantinople. He is accused of stirring up the Huns against the Western armies.

These were interesting and very different times from the ones you have been becoming acquainted with. However, the image of a noble and courageous Roman commander with a hotline to the Roman god of war still packed a punch if you wanted to promote your patron and demonize the opposing forces. Many poets of the later centuries, whether pagan or Christian, used the old mythologies and were wedded to Roman cultural traditions. This is a theme I shall return to.

Army life

Part of this chapter will refer to provinces that needed pacifying, so let's begin by setting a different kind of scene and thinking of the army as an integrated part of Roman civilization abroad. Early on in imperial history veteran soldiers had been granted settlements in the provinces, usually as a gift from their individual commander (under Augustus, a common soldier signed up for 20 years and was on the reserve list for another five). Where the veteran communities remained and thrived – Timgad in Africa was a good example – they spoke Latin and developed a Roman lifestyle in their locality. Timgad also boasts wonderful mosaics and the remains of a town on distinctly Roman lines. The spirit and semblance of a Roman town could develop around semi-permanent garrisons across the empire. Vindolanda in the north of England (remember the birthday invitation sent by an army wife) was a fort occupied by auxiliary units and, although much smaller than a fortress (which would house the legionaries), it became a hub of local civilian life.

The existence of a large army camp could stimulate trade and industry in the local communities, as they had a ready market for goods to supplement the soldiers' standard rations. Permanent legions in relatively peaceable provinces had time on their hands and could be employed in the construction of roads, bridges and fortifications. This paints a rather rosy picture of relationships between garrisons and the local population. The army could, of course, be a burden and a collective bully. There are surviving complaints about soldiers carrying out bullying requisitions with no comeback for the aggrieved provincials. Apuleius' novel *The Golden Ass* has the following scene set in Greece in the second century CE. Lucius, the hero and the narrator, has been turned into an ass and he and his master, an impoverished market gardener, have met a legionary soldier on the road:

> The soldier addressed us in haughty and aggressive speech and asked where my master was leading an unladen ass. My owner, barely recovered from the recent tragedy [witnessing a suicide, among other things], and, to make matters worse, not familiar with the Latin language, kept quiet and attempted to keep going. The soldier – this was a man who could not control his violent temperament – took silence as a slight not to be borne, set about my master with a vine stick he was carrying and turfed him off my back.
>
> Apuleius, *The Golden Ass* (*Metamorphoses*) 9.39

The poor gardener tries reasoning with the soldier, who insists on his right to requisition the ass for transporting supplies. He gets nowhere and in desperation attacks the soldier and beats him almost to a pulp. Eventually, the army catches up with Lucius' unfortunate master and he is condemned to death. The ass changes hands once more, but the story makes it clear that he is quite a prized commodity.

Insight

My doctoral thesis (now 27 years old) was an interpretation of the many layers in Apuleius' novel. Since that time research and publications on Greek and Roman prose narratives have grown exponentially. Much has been written on the literary texture of Apuleius' fantasy fiction but a number of scholars favour a socio-historical approach to episodes that depict life from the perspective of the enslaved (animals and humans) and dispossessed.

Living off the land?

Throughout the history of the empire under the emperors, the total number of troops fluctuated between 300,000 and 400,000 legionaries and auxiliaries. Garnsey and Saller, in their book *The Roman Empire: Economy, Society and Culture* (London 1987, pp. 88–97), estimate that the army consumed upwards of 150,000 tonnes of wheat per year. Egyptian papyri from the time of the later empire show soldiers receiving about a kilogram (2.2 lb) of bread rations per day plus about two-thirds of a kilogram of meat, a litre (1.7 pints) of wine and 75 ml (2.5 fl. oz) of oil. We find a mix of methods for supplying the troops. The local population always had to put up with demands for foodstuffs and equipment, but compulsory purchase also operated when the army ran short of basic provisions.

There were postings to remote parts of the empire where it just was not feasible to sustain a legion in this way. Sometimes the garrisons had to make their own cooking pots and weapons. The army also had land attached to its legions to graze cattle if they were in isolated and underdeveloped areas (the Rhineland, for instance). Although the army in Britain was better off for supplies in the south-west (the Gloucester garrison benefited from the pockets of trade and industry around them), the bulk of the troops were in the north and the army had to transport supplies from one end of the island to the other. They also had to look to Gaul for goods and the mainland of Europe for a range of artefacts (Garnsey and Saller, *The Roman Empire*, 1987, p. 91).

In the Roman world, agriculture, and the economy in general, were not as sophisticated as the still-visible signs of Roman life might suggest through the spectacular remains of its wealth, power, culture and 'leisure industry'. Whatever the volume of goods, the trading was not centrally co-ordinated and there was no concept of national, let alone global, economies. There was plenty of fine glass, artistic pottery and metalware circulating and a lively export and import trade in wines, oils and savoury fish sauce. The many surviving amphorae give us some idea of the scale of activity. The amphora was a two-handled container with a pointed base which could hold several gallons of liquid or a substantial weight of dried fish, flour, fruit or nuts. A large hill of broken bits was discovered at Rome. Monte Testaccio is a great heap of amphorae, about 55,000 if you could piece them together. They were the containers which had transported olive oil from Spain. For the archaeologist, dustbins and rubbish tips speak volumes.

Supply and demand

In Chapter 4 you had a glimpse of Rome as the great consuming centre of the empire. Perhaps it is appropriate to end our tour of the provinces with a short visit to Egypt and North Africa, since their grain was so crucial to the stability and survival of the imperial city. The islands of Sicily and Sardinia were also an important part of the production. Historically, the mention of these provinces catapults us back in history for they were very early acquisitions of empire and date back to the series of wars between Rome and Carthage over control of the Mediterranean.

Obviously, other areas in the empire grew and exported grain but Rome relied most heavily on the surplus produced by the provinces above. The emperors also kept tight control over Egypt as their private estate and used the Egyptian grain to help out other areas of empire in a food crisis. The key thing was that the emperor was the one distributing the distress parcels, whether at home or abroad.

This situation was only possible once the principate of Augustus had pacified Egypt and North Africa. It had been a theatre of war during the power struggles between Caesar and Pompey. Julius Caesar's eventual alliance with Queen Cleopatra was not just a romantic attachment but a practical arrangement on both sides. Mark Antony's liaison with Egypt's Macedonian queen proved dangerous and disastrous for him because, in spite of the wealth and influence it might have bought him in the east, it allowed Octavian to present him as a foreign enemy and to de-Romanize his chief rival. Augustus liked to depict the final battle at Actium as having reliable Roman gods ranged against the alien deities of Egypt.

Insight

Virgil's depiction of Actium as having a supernatural dimension, the reliable Roman gods ranged against the alien deities of Egypt, gave the battle an epic flavour (see Insight in Chapter 3). Ironically, the portrayal of this final civil war conflict in the 1963 Mankiewicz film, *Cleopatra* (with Roman soldiers on both sides and Octavian suffering from seasickness below decks), is probably closer to historical reality. Virgil's image of heroic Octavian at the prow of the ship and basking in the light of Apollo is poetic 'spin' and various other accounts suggest a less clear-cut encounter.

A settled province for hundreds of years to come, Egypt yields a large percentage of ancient documents. Not only do we have literature on papyrus which has survived in the deserts but archives of bureaucratic paperwork and potsherds recording transactions as well. An official papyrus document discovered at Oxyrhynchus (a place so rich in papyrus finds that it has its own titled collection, *The Oxyrhynchus Papyri*) is headed 'Instructions for delivering letters to Rufus'. The directions are amusingly pedantic.

From the Moon gate walk as if towards the granaries and, if you will, turn left at the first street behind the Baths, where there is a ???? and go westwards. Go down the steps and up — and turn right and after the precinct of the [temple] on the right there is a seven-storey house and on the top of the gatehouse [a statue of Fortuna?] and opposite a basket-weaving shop. Inquire there or from the concierge and you will be informed.

The Oxyrhynchus Papyri, vol. 34 (London, 1968) no. 2719
(third century CE)

I have spared you the linguistic notes which try to make sense of the *lacunae* (gaps). Considering Rufus is making his way through an Egyptian town, probably in Hermopolis, several of the landmarks have a very Roman ring. The granaries, the baths and what sounds like a tenement demonstrate the influence of Roman town planning throughout the empire.

Another intriguing piece from papyri finds is a Roman soldier's will. The last wishes of Gaius Longinus Castor have been dubbed one of the few examples of pure Roman law found in Egypt. It is a careful itemization of legacies, duly witnessed but also with codicils added in Gaius' hand. The original will had been written in Latin in 189 CE but we have a later Greek translation, perhaps done at the request of one of the heirs. The soldier was a resident of Karanis in Egypt but he was a veteran of the praetorian fleet near Naples. You will see from the commentary on the text that the story behind the will takes some teasing out.

Gaius Longinus Castor, honourably discharged veteran of the praetorian fleet of Misenum, has made a will. I order that Marcella my slavewoman, over 30 years of age, and Kleopatra my slavewoman, over 30 years of age, become free. Let them in equal shares be my heir. [In the event of his slavewomen's deaths, Gaius devolves Marcella's share upon Sarapion, Sokrates and Longus, and Kleopatra's share upon Nilos.]

> Let my slavewoman Sarapias, daughter of Kleopatra my freedwoman, be free; to whom I also give and bequeath: five *arouras* of grainland which I hold in the vicinity of the village of Karanis, in the place called 'Ostrich'. [More land and shares in a house and a palm grove are left to Sarapias.]

The two primary heirs, the slavewomen, are assumed to be common-law wives of the soldier. The information about their ages was vital to their manumission as there were restrictions on the freeing of slaves under this age by means of a will (the Augustan law Lex Aelia Sentina of 4 CE). Soldiers under the rank of centurion were not allowed to have a legal marriage while in service (this was relaxed at the end of the second century CE) but they could marry upon an honourable discharge.

Unfortunately for Gaius, bigamy was not recognized in Roman law and so neither of his families formed a legally recognized unit. Gaius' discharge papers would have stated his right to legitimize a union but they also would have prohibited the legitimizing of bigamous relationships. Assuming that Sarapion, Sokrates, Longus, Nilos and Sarapias were all the soldier's children, the first four boys and the fifth, a girl, were all illegitimate (fatherless in the eyes of the law). The penalty was a 5-per-cent tax on inheritances and this is stated at the end of the will. Gaius may have adopted Egyptian cultural practices but as a Roman citizen he was still subject to Roman law in the matter of his last will and testament.

Papyrologists wading through the mass of administrative matters may not regard Egypt as quite such an exotic place as the vision of Cleopatra and wondrous barges on the Nile conjure up in most minds. We can be thankful, though, that the climate of the country means that age has not withered so much of the papyrus. With this factor and what looks like a propensity in the Roman east to keep files on everything or everything on files, the Egyptian desert continues to yield exciting evidence on the running of this crucial imperial province.

Taking it all in

It is not possible, in one slim book, to do justice to the diversity of life and civilization throughout the Roman empire. We could begin by adding things to the map of Roman territories and renewing acquaintance with some of the figures who passed through the earlier pages. Cicero, for example, was writing those worried letters about Tullia's marriage from Cyprus in the 50s BCE. He was actually responsible for the whole province of Cilicia, taking in a large chunk of the coast between Syria and the rest of Asia Minor. The scenery was beautiful, the land fertile and the climate comfortable. Among its products were *cilicium* (goat's hair cloth), corn, wine, oil and saffron.

In Cicero's time, Pompey had annexed the eastern half of Cilicia for Rome, partly to suppress the piracy and slave hunting of their people over neighbouring coasts. Cyprus was a strategically important island midway between the Cilician and Phoenician coasts. In legend, the island was the birthplace of the goddess Venus, and it remained sacred to her through its history. After their formal subjugation to Rome in 58 BCE the islanders were in the habit of finding upwards of 5 million sesterces a year to bribe the Roman rulers. Five million was a tidy sum; it was the equivalent to about 11 times the property qualification for being an *eques*, a rich Roman knight.

The Cyprians paid the money to keep the governors from billeting troops on the locals. Making the people pay for the keep of the soldiers was a regular fiddle because the governor could then pocket the expenses the Senate provided for the purpose. Presumably, that is why the provincials had to make the gift of money large enough for it to be worth the governor's while. We hear from Cicero that the natives were speechless with amazement when he organized his army to live under canvas without accepting the Cypriots' bribe. Allowing for a measure of exaggeration – Cicero could be a self-congratulatory soul – Cicero's claim that he had difficulty dissuading the grateful islanders from erecting temples, statues and marble chariots in his honour is probably close to the truth.

Cicero must have been a relief after aristocrats like the noble Brutus, the principal assassin of Julius Caesar. Brutus harassed Cicero in haughty letters to collect outstanding interest on loans Brutus had made to the city of Salamis at the extortionate rate of 48 per cent per annum. The previous governor had allowed Scaptius, one of Brutus' debt collectors, to be appointed prefect and to besiege members of the Salamis town assembly in the council chamber. Five of these local councillors starved to death during the blockade. When Cicero arrived, he flatly refused to keep Scaptius in post as prefect. Brutus probably regarded this as a personal slight. In the end, Cicero had to put pressure on the Salaminians and to try, at the same time, to persuade Brutus to compromise on the payback. Cicero did not resolve the situation and he did not hold out much hope that the next governor would either. He wrote to Atticus in 50 BCE 'but what will happen if my successor is Brutus' brother-in-law, Paullus?' (*Letters to Atticus* 6.1).

Cicero was, in addition, supposed to be calling in debts from the king of Cappadocia. Brutus was also one of his creditors but the largest repayment was due to Pompey who, according to Cicero, was much more accommodating (*Letters to Atticus* 6.1). Pompey by this stage in his career was embarrassed by riches and accepted a monthly repayment of the interest, which was all the impecunious king could manage. What Cicero perceived as his duties to the provinces abroad were constantly intermeshed with obligations to contacts at home. Caelius, who was serving a term in Rome as a city magistrate, wrote a rather anxious letter to Cicero reminding him about the panthers he needed for his show at the capital (to supplement panthers he had obtained from Africa). 'For old friendship's sake, Cicero, please get this done,' he pleaded (*Letters to Friends* 8.9).

Pliny the Younger (from 110 CE) was another example of a Roman governor trying to be just and meticulous in his role. He operated under, and deferred to, an emperor at home whom he regularly consulted. His years in Bithynia and Pontus on the south coast of the Black Sea – another, on the face of it, exotic Eastern location – were, like Cicero's time in Cilicia, rather troubled and stressful. The area had been bequeathed to Rome by its last king in 74 BCE. Pompey had added in the western part of Pontus. The pressures in Pliny's province arose from debts of a different kind. Pliny was sent out to deal with municipal bankruptcy, incipient political disorder and an administrative mess.

We have Pliny's correspondence with the emperor Trajan and Trajan's replies. These are famous principally because Pliny is not quite sure how to handle the Christian sects in the province, but for Pliny and Trajan the Christians were only a potential part of a whole host of problems in the main cities. Overenthusiastic building of the usual amenities, aqueducts, baths, gymnasia and theatres had put the town councils in debt and in many cases the projects had been badly planned and not even finished. In one town, Pliny even found slaves serving in the legions, a situation which produced another bout of concerned correspondence with Trajan.

Pliny sometimes comes across as fussy. He certainly sought the emperor's advice and arbitration on a number of issues, particularly in his first year as governor from September 111 CE. However, he seems to have got on efficiently with providing the amenities and resolving the financial crises. Trajan might have been laconic in his replies at times, but Richard Miles (2000, pp. 38–9) argues forcefully that it was good practice for a provincial governor to be in close contact with the emperor on all matters of administration. Pliny rightly recognized the importance of consulting the centre on a range of matters: 'So to a great extent imperial power rested on the successful use and control of the written word' (p. 38). Presumably, by Pliny's death the province was back in business with the familiar features of Roman urban life restored and expanded. After all, provincial emulation of Roman civilization was not to be discouraged even when it had been carried out in a slipshod way:

> My lord, an outstanding feature of the city Amastris (which is well constructed and well laid out generally) is a long street of great beauty. Unfortunately, some kind of stream runs the length of this road and constitutes nothing less than a filthy sewer. It looks and smells horrendous. With your permission I would like to get this filled in and covered. The health and the look of the city will be vastly improved. I will make sure there is no lack of money for this large-scale work and I would like to prioritize it.
>
> Pliny to the Emperor Trajan, *Letters* 10.98

> My dear Pliny, there is every reason to go ahead and cover this water over, if, as you say, it flows through the city of Amastris and is a health hazard as a running stream. I am confident that you will be your usual energetic self in ensuring that funds are found for the enterprise.
>
> Emperor Trajan to Pliny, *Letters* 10.99

Doing as the Romans do

Although other authors you have encountered did not take up important administrative posts, they all illustrate the cosmopolitan nature of the empire and the extent of its cultural as well as its geographical map. Routledge's *Atlas of Classical History* by Michael Grant (fifth edition, 1994) includes a double-page spread locating the origin of

Latin authors and a special inset for Italy. This pictorial placing of the collective cultural talent of the empire brings home the breadth of Roman civilization more clearly than any list or index can do.

The cultural pull of Rome and the power of the Latin language cannot be underestimated. It was the official written language of the West. Horace came from a town in Italy; Ovid and Virgil were also born in Italian districts and yet their strong sense of what it meant to be Roman permeates their poetry. Do you remember other authors like Seneca and Martial? They were both from Spain, as were Quintilian and Columella.

Apuleius, the author of the Roman novel *The Golden Ass*, quoted earlier, was a famous son of North Africa and had statues erected to him in Carthage celebrating his achievements as an orator and a writer of sophisticated and showy Latin. Members of the provincial nobility in the West had a culture and a language in common with the educated classes at the centre of things in Rome. Apuleius' first language was probably Punic (by his time an established North African dialect, although the Punic settlers were Phoenician in origin), but he boasted of his fluency (oral and written) in Greek and Latin.

Greek was a more widespread means of communication in the eastern half of the empire, but local dialects and languages, like Phrygian for example, were also commonly spoken and the script has been found on inscriptions. The Greeks and the Syrians were featured in Chapter 4. You met them as caricatures lashed and lampooned by Juvenal's disgruntled but possibly fictional friend, Umbricius. I also indicated the ambivalent attitude the Roman authors, or those whom we are able to access, had towards the Greeks and those who inhabited the Greek world.

Whatever disparaging remarks Juvenal makes about the role of the Greeks who had made their home in the city of Rome, Athens maintained her prestige as the intellectual centre of Greece, resting on the cultural laurels of the past but also enjoying patronage from a succession of Roman emperors. The emperor Hadrian (second century CE) was well known for his philhellenism and for his interest and involvement in Athens' urban development and cultural events. This is a different picture from the one we have in Sulpicius' consolation letter to Cicero. In the context of his condolences,

Sulpicius philosophizes on the fragile nature of all human endeavours. Great cities in Greece where he was governor had fallen into ruins in his time.

Do you remember how Juvenal subsumed Syrians from Asia Minor under the heading of degenerate Greeks? Before we launch into the larger picture, it might be helpful to look at a Syrian who seems to have lived at least some of his life and died not in his native land, nor in Rome, but in one of the farther reaches of the empire, Britain. His wife's tombstone was discovered in South Shields (the fort of Arbeia) in the north of England (there is a facsimile cast in the British Museum in London). This dedication to the deceased woman, Regina, is a fascinating illustration of the ethnic and cultural mix we can meet at any point in time or in any place within the Roman empire. It also alerts us to the inexact science of reconstructing even part of the story surrounding one inhabitant of a Roman province.

> If you look at the photograph of Regina's tombstone you might be able to make out the Latin script, but what about the very different lettering at the bottom? What status do you imagine the deceased and her commemorator enjoyed?

The Latin inscription tells us that Barates the Palmyran (Palmyra was a rich trading city on the edge of the Arabian desert) laments the loss of his wife, Regina, whom he had bought as a slave, freed and given a noble name, 'queen' no less. She was originally of the Catuvellaunian tribe, from a region just north of the river Thames, and Barates probably purchased her in the slave market at Verulamium (St Albans). The Palmyran script at the bottom translates as 'Regina, the freedwoman of Barates, alas.' Just by looking at the tombstone – it is rich and in the elaborate Palmyran style – we can assume that Barates was not short of money. He appears to have been a rich merchant and he has been tentatively identified with a Barates who was buried at Corbridge, 40 km (25 miles) away, but commemorated on a humbler slab. The Corbridge Barates is described as *vexillarius*, which could mean flag bearer or possibly flag maker. The B of Barathes has been restored in this inscription.

Some scholars will stick their necks out and identify him as the same man, a maker of military ensigns who became a successful trader after being discharged from service. He was 68 years old when he died. Regina of the elaborate tombstone was only 30. The attempt

Regina's tombstone. Bridgeman © Tyne & Wear Archives & Museums / The Bridgeman Art Library

to fill in details of the Syrian Barates is bound to veer towards speculation. What is interesting about the Regina tombstone is the evidence it provides for emigration within the empire, intermarriage, work and wealth and, particularly pertinent for our discussion, the adoption of Roman epigraphical habits.

Barates, the bereaved, figures prominently on his wife's tombstone. If his own grave was indeed the more downmarket affair discovered at Corbridge, then at least his former and happier circumstances are recorded by the expensive monument he erected in the throes of grief. One wonders, though, if it is the same man, why he did not reserve himself a place in Regina's gravesite (as Lucius Aurelius did, commemorated alongside his Aurelia Philematium, the butcher and his wife featured in Chapter 5). Whether or not there were one or two Syrian Barates, the record of Regina's death doubles as an acknowledgement of her husband and his dutiful affection. Regina's tombstone demonstrates his generosity and devotion. So ends the story of the Syrian who ended up in Britain, rescued a British girl from slavery and called her his queen.

Places imitating Rome

Cassius Dio (*Roman History* 56.46 – NB he writes in Greek) has a telling anecdote about the shrine of the deified Augustus being duplicated, with some communities building them willingly and others only doing it under orders. In Chapter 2 you were introduced to the significance of buildings in Rome and the prominent place official altars or triumphal arches enjoyed in the capital city. In Chapter 3 you took a close-up look at a monument. Similar messages of civic pride, renewal and prosperity appear in the provincial cities throughout the entire empire, and are, on the surface, testament to the pervasive nature of Roman civilization. You heard how the people of Bithynia and Pontus were more eager than efficient in this respect. Having an amphitheatre for organized shows reinforced a feeling of community of empire. The baths were more than amenities but social centres, leisure palaces where business deals could be made and influential contacts formed.

At one time it was accepted and commonplace to talk about processes of Romanization in the empire's provinces. So much could be identified that was Roman in conception and character, especially in the cities where urbanization of a particular pattern seems to have been an obligation expected of and accepted by local aristocracies. As they beautified their towns, they also showed loyalty to the empire and its emperors by erecting triumphal arches, amphitheatres and temples. Some scholars believe (Dio is one ancient witness) that the emperor Augustus may have pioneered a more systematic policy in this respect. He prompted urban designs on Roman lines in new and restored towns, according to some sources, even down to such details as the arrangement of the statuary in the main squares.

Nowadays scholars are both able and motivated to dig deeper in the search for indigenous cultures and to look for lifestyles that have a veneer of Romanness but which have, in fact, stamped Roman customs with a local and individual character. The end result of this symbiosis, or living together, of different cultures can produce a picture which is neither strictly Roman nor wholly 'native'.

We cannot always say whether the process was subversive or accommodating, conscious or spontaneous. The adoption and adaption of Roman styles is sometimes described as acculturation, and one of the best examples of how this might work in practice is the incorporation of Roman deities into the local religion. The Celts combined their goddess Sul with the Roman Minerva and the physical remains of her worship can be seen at Roman Bath in Britain.

Grand Tour: Julius Caesar, Julius Agricola and the Roman world

This brief sketch of two military careers is not a 'romantic' interlude about great men making history. Having said that, these two generals demonstrate some key strategies in subjugation and they illustrate Roman methods of manipulation throughout the empire. They were both masters of the art, which is not to say that the 'art' always worked. There are certain key provinces that they are most famously associated with in history. In tracing their movements we can say something about most of the empire's territory. As ever other, by now, familiar Romans will be brought in to fill in some gaps.

Julius Caesar typifies the successful Roman general and is easily one of the most famous commanders to emerge from the pages of ancient history. Caesar wrote up his campaigns in Gaul. He did this in accomplished prose and referring to himself in the third person. This work demonstrated his writing as well as his fighting ability. Other biographers and historians related Caesar's expeditions to Spain, Egypt and Britain but they tended to be celebratory as well. Truth is usually a casualty of war memoirs, although Roman writers were not generally shy about how they expanded their empire and rooted out resistance. They would not equivocate about pain and punishment where they judged it to be a justifiable response. As the Romans were likely to exaggerate enemy casualties, it was not always a good idea to take Roman estimates at face value, whatever the context.

There were ideal and less than ideal conditions for establishing the Roman way. Michael Grant, in his biography of Julius Caesar (*Julius Caesar*, 1969, p. 34ff.), describes how Caesar was appointed as a *quaestor*, a kind of junior member of the senate, and sent abroad to assist the provincial governor of Further (Southern) Spain. Rome had acquired the territory of Spain and Portugal from Carthage when its empire fell to Rome in a succession of wars in the third century BCE.

The further north one went, towards the mountain range of the Pyrenees, the more troublesome the indigenous tribes became. These were native Iberians who were a fiercely independent people and whose language was not even of an Indo-European origin (the modern-day Basque country). Augustus' general, Agrippa, had to force such tribes out into the open and permanently down into the plains so that their activities could be policed more easily. The Romans' treatment of recalcitrant peoples was never gentle. They were quite capable of ethnic cleansing if there were no stable ruling structures they could adapt to their interests. They would only make so much effort to win over local populations and they preferred the local leaders of the community to do it for them.

Southern Spain was a relatively trouble-free zone with a mixed population of Celts, Iberians and well-established Italian settlers. Caesar was not stretched as an administrator in this area and so he could spend his time in this more 'Romanized' area of the peninsula doing some useful networking among those with influence, potential supporters of his political career back in the capital. Juvenal (Chapter 4), although writing some 150 years after Caesar, directly pointed to how lucrative provincial government could be. However, fleecing the provinces was less expected as a perk. By the time of the emperors there was less pressure on governors and their staffs to make enormous profits out of their time abroad. In the days of the Republic the ambitious politician needed to come back with enough money to recoup his initial outlay and with a tidy amount put by for election campaigning. Possibly, and perversely, some of the profits would be needed for him to defend himself against charges of corruption and extortion. Political and legal activities would require large bribes.

Caesar was to return to Spain later in his career, but on the second occasion as governor. His brief was to sort out bandits around the mountains of Lusitania (Portugal). This was Caesar's first real experience of leading troops into battle. Spain the second time around was an even more positive boost to his career. He cleared his debts and sent Rome large, allegedly voluntary, contributions extracted from Spanish cities. He managed simultaneously to ensure the gratitude of large numbers of inhabitants by modifying repayments of debts.

You have probably realized by now that in spite of focusing on life away from Rome, all roads seem to lead us back to it. I cannot resist concluding this section with a reference to Catullus, the poet whose wedding hymn appeared in Chapter 5. He was contemporary with Caesar. As well as love poetry, Catullus produced some choice and obscene epigrams, three or four liners, on Caesar and other public players in the power game.

Catullus was put out at returning from one province with nothing to show off to friends, not even a litter and a few litter bearers to his name. Expectations of making something out of service abroad were shared by those on the staff of the governor. Catullus' disappointing time was in Bithynia on the Black Sea, Pliny 'territory' 200 years later. In the following extract from Poem 10, Catullus lets us have a laugh at his expense. In trying to impress his friend Varus' girl, he makes up a story about a litter and litter bearers which he acquired abroad. They ask:

'Bithynia, how is it getting on these days and what did you make out of your stay?'

I replied frankly, and explained the situation, that not even the locals, let alone governors or staff, got much out of it; not so much as a drop of hair oil. In my case the governor was such a tight arse that the needs of his retinue totally passed him by.

'But come on,' they say, 'you must have procured their home product, a litter with litter carriers?' Over to me again, I bluffed it out to impress the girl with wealth I did not have! 'Oh, sure, no provincial posting could be that barren, although this was a pretty awful one, you understand. I have eight sturdy litter bearers to my name.' (Actually I didn't have a single man there or in Rome who could be trusted to hoist up a broken bed-leg on his shoulder!)

Then the girl, acting like a tart on the make, started wheedling. 'Catullus, my own, lend them to me for a bit. I want to be carried to the temple of Serapis [an Egyptian cult, associated with cures].'Hang on,' I replied, 'I wasn't thinking straight, when I just said that about my owning a litter myself. My comrade, Cinna, I mean Gaius Cinna [Catullus is flustered and stammering by now], well, he bought it, but it's the same difference, and as far as I am concerned, I have as full a use of them as if I had purchased the thing myself. But as for you, are you always this tactless and irritating, seizing on a casual statement?'

Caesar had himself been to Bithynia twice in his earlier career. At that time it was a client kingdom and Caesar was supposed to be requisitioning some ships for use in the war against Mithridates of Pontus. The king of Bithynia took a fancy to Caesar and this fuelled gossip and jokes for years after. Whatever the personal relationship, Caesar honoured the political connection throughout his life, speaking up for the Bithynian royal family and its interests. During his stay out east he helped in military operations around Anatolia (Cilicia) aimed against, you may not be surprised, persistent pirate activity.

The famous expedition

Caesar finally acquired the province of Gaul, after some notorious political manoeuvring and the formation of the first triumvirate; the other two men sharing out the spoils of power were Crassus and Pompey. When Caesar wrote in his *Gallic Wars* that Gaul was divided into three parts, he was referring not to modern-day France but to the northern area of the province ('Gallia est omnis divisa in partes tres' (Caesar, *De Bello Gallico*, opening to Book 1)). The south of France was well established as Gallia Transalpina – 'Gaul on the far side of the Alps'.

Caesar's campaigning in the north was not simply a military success story. The Gauls were by this time forming larger political units with systems of elected aristocratic magistracies, a situation which eased Caesar's way politically. He won the support of Gaulish chieftains, rewarded and promoted them and ensured their loyalty to Rome's interests. Their attachment to Caesar and to Rome usually secured the acceptance of the empire by those they ruled. If their peoples were sufficiently disaffected by high-handed reorganization of their land and society by the Romans, then these local leaders could quite easily turn on their Roman 'patrons'.

Quintus Varus, presented by ancient historians as an over-zealous and 'Romanizing' governor, provoked just such an outbreak in 9 CE. Under Varus' command, three of Augustus' legions were massacred in Germany in the area of the Teutoberg Forest. The commander of the rebellious tribes was Arminius, a German nobleman who had completed an equestrian career in the Roman army. This spectacular success was difficult for Arminius to follow and he died about ten years later, a popular hero. The Romans, after this massive defeat, never really penetrated beyond the Rhine.

Gaul was far less problematic. Augustus was able to draw on the connections Caesar had forged with local nobilities and to integrate the Gallic aristocracy into Roman systems of education and administration. There is a splendid story of social climbing in the province when Augustus had reorganized it into manageable regions. A Gaul, Licinius had been enslaved by the Romans but freed by Julius Caesar. Augustus made him procurator (financial agent) of the province.

Licinius had learned fast. He made use of his new-found Roman status and dignity to deal with his personal enemies. He was ingenious in making the most out of his position for the amassing of riches. He was responsible for collecting the tribute due to Rome and, as in some areas this was handed over on a monthly basis, Licinius managed to take advantage of the Gauls' ignorance of the Roman dating system. He persuaded them that there were 14 months in the year because December was the tenth month (this is the literal meaning of December, with *decem* meaning ten in Latin. It kept this name from the old calendar when the Roman year had started in March). Therefore, Licinius argued, there must be another two months before the new year started in January.

Eventually a complaint from the provincials reached the emperor Augustus, who was not amused. Licinius showed Augustus the treasure he had accumulated from this opportunist tactic and defended his actions on the grounds that it reduced the Gauls' options for funding a revolt. Licinius claimed that he was simply holding it in trust for his Roman rulers. The name 'Licinius' became a byword for those who fleeced the provincials and retired on great riches. Juvenal uses him for this purpose in his first Satire (line 109) and his fourteenth (line 306). The Licinius episode is reported in Cassius Dio (54.21), where Dio parades him as a combination of barbarian greed and Roman ingenuity.

Playing the administrative system was not the only reason for adopting Roman society and structures. For the local aristocracies, knowing the language of the conqueror became a status symbol in itself and a means of advancement. The sons of leading families attended schools which provided a Roman education and Gaul gained and maintained a reputation for its colleges of oratory for the next 500 years.

An anecdote in Suetonius relates how the Emperor Gaius Caligula staged an oratory competition at Lugdunum (Lyons) during the games there. The loser presented the winners with prizes and also made the congratulatory speeches – all very civilized until we hear that the emperor forced the clear failures to erase their entries with sponges or their own tongues. Refusal to comply met with the threat of being thrashed and thrown into the Rhone. (*Life of Gaius* 20). Caligula was just as likely to play these sorts of sick jokes on citizens of Rome so, perhaps, we should not read too much into this nasty piece of humiliation of the provincials or see it as reminding them of their place. However, there were occasions when this sort of superiority and snobbery did occur and the experience of Caligula's successor, Claudius, is a case in point.

The emperor Claudius was born at Lyons and had a special affection for the area. He even enrolled prominent Gaulish citizens who met the property and wealth requirements into the senate at Rome. In spite of the zeal with which well-off Gauls had for years commissioned Roman triumphal arches, amphitheatres and temples throughout their provinces and the enthusiasm with which they had recreated the Roman cultural milieu, there was still significant hostility to Claudius' policy from the Roman and Italian senators.

Britannia – starting from scratch?

Caesar did not achieve the same effects with his comparatively short campaign in Britain. What was the motivation for his raids? The excuse was rooting out the remnants of opposition the Romans had confronted in Gaul and who, it was rumoured, had taken refuge across the water. There may have been a hope of lavish loot. There was speculation at the time about an abundance of gold, silver and pearls. Perhaps the phrase which best sums up the impulse to cross the sea to Britain is David Braund's 'The excitement of invasion' (in *Ruling Roman Britain*, 1996). Braund recaptures the mood by emphasizing how exotic, how adventurous it was to sail over an ocean believed to be at the edge of the inhabited world to an island Plutarch described as 'incredible in size' (*Caesar* 23.2). Cassius Dio confirms the extravagant claims about the task in hand (39.50).

Plutarch was writing his biographies about 150 years after the event. Cassius Dio, whom you met above, was a Bithynian by birth and was composing his histories in the early years of the third century CE. Both are writing in Greek and they would have had access to some of the biographers already mentioned but who are lost to us. To back up our impressions of Britain we have the familiar voice of Cicero whose brother Quintus served in the campaigns. Cicero expressed disappointment that Britain had proved no more than a source of slaves, and slaves with a limited range of skills at that. The Britons had no gold, no silver and no culture. They were lawless barbarians and about the only thing worth bringing home to Rome (or so Cicero playfully suggests) was the chariot; that at least the British barbarian had perfected (*Letters to Trebatius* 7.7).

The psychological barrier to Britain had been breached. Cicero could now make jokes about the mysterious and outlandish territory and its rough inhabitants. About a hundred years later the emperor Claudius launched an organized invasion of the island. Some scholars believe that the brief expedition to Britain orchestrated by Gaius Caligula, a few years earlier in 40 CE, had provided a useful dress rehearsal and that Caligula's successor and uncle, Claudius, benefited from all previous preparations, including those of his strange and psychotic nephew. Julius Caesar may not have brought Britain into the Roman provincial set-up but he had opened up trade possibilities and made some profitable political connections with willing local kings. It was the arrival in Rome of exiled 'friends' from Britain that prompted Claudius to invade.

David Braund traces the significance and characteristics of the campaigns and conquests and the way in which Roman writers fashioned an identity for the island and its people. The main point for our purposes is that Claudius' venture began to integrate Britain into the empire. Archaeological finds testify to the process, and so does the literature. There were trading centres, state mines and a pacified population as far as the rivers Severn, Trent and Humber. These pockets of adaptation to the Roman presence were large enough to bring Britain to the brink of being a fully fledged province. Then things went wrong. There was some serious misgovernment of Britain and the result was unrest and rebellion, the famous one being Boudicca (known to generations of readers as Boadicea) and the Iceni tribe. Nero seriously considered abandoning the territory altogether.

Agricola, the father-in-law of the historian Tacitus, began his governorship of Britain in 77 CE, under the emperor Vespasian. Agricola had been to Britain before. He had served under Suetonius Paulus at the time of Boudicca's rebellion. He had also been a *quaestor* in Asia but Tacitus is at pains to tell the reader that this did not corrupt his father-in-law, who continued to impress with his self-control and sense of proportion. Asia remained a notorious province for encouraging corruption, so this posting was a good test of moral fortitude. Agricola's first governorship sent him to Aquitania in Spain and Tacitus portrays these three years as a model of good government. Agricola was as much a statesman as a soldier.

The purpose of this little digression on Agricola's career is not to illustrate how Tacitus prepares the reader for Agricola's success on the military and political fronts in Britain. This is dealt with in detail by Braund. Tacitus' technique as an historian does make a fascinating study and he is a Roman writer who comes highly recommended for critical reading. My aim in piecing together bits of

Caesar's and Agricola's career is a more straightforward one – that you become increasingly aware of the continuity of the image of empire over time. You can move ahead several hundred years and find contemporary commentators going over old ground about corruption, mismanagement, the state of education and the proper or improper formation of the ruling-class character. For the Roman historian, the preservation of Pax Romana relied principally on powerful players and their ability or inability to administer the empire.

Back in Britain

The Romans had still not penetrated as far as Caledonia (Scotland) and the rest of the province had not been satisfactorily resettled. Vespasian's own modest claim to fame was being involved in the capture of the Isle of Wight (before he dealt with the Jewish revolt of 70 CE), but the idea of the remote north of Britain was what sparked the imagination of Roman writers. The poet Silius Italicus wrote an epic about the struggle against Hannibal but he took a leaf out of Virgil's book and included a bit of prophecy, a look ahead to Vespasian's triumphs abroad.

This is Jupiter comforting Venus and guaranteeing that the empire of her descendants will weather the storm of the Carthaginian invasions:

Eventually, a warrior family, brought up on the Sabine berry [you might recall Umbricius' claim], shall expand the reputation of the deified Julian emperors. The head of that family will give Rome the conquest of unknown Thule [maybe the Shetlands or Iceland, somewhere beyond the Orkneys] and then will be the first to take the troops into the groves of Caledonia.

Silius Italicus, *Punica* 3.594–8

Perhaps you can see that Britain could still be milked for the romantic image of conquest, but the story of Agricola's defeat of tribes in remoter parts of the island is not a pretty one to modern ears. Persistently rebellious and unco-operative tribes were either obliterated in battle or in the aftermath of defeat. This strategy would not have surprised or disturbed Agricola's admiring son-in-law. Tacitus was not just a dutiful relative; he had his own ideological reasons for recording and embellishing Agricola's military and administrative achievements in Britain. In some ways Tacitus echoes Virgil, too. Agricola is savage against the obstinate but forgiving to those who submit.

Tacitus tells us that his father-in-law had a deliberate policy of 'civilizing' the natives. In a passage scholars love to note, quote and read between the lines, the historian describes how British loyalty was ensured:

> The following winter was spent on some very fruitful strategies. The purpose was to change the habits of men who were neither settled nor cultured but on the contrary receptive to making war, so that they became, instead, accustomed to peace and leisure by means of pleasurable things. So Agricola encouraged individuals and actively supported communities in the construction of temples, town centres and houses. This he did by praising the energetic and reprimanding the slackers. The result was a rivalry to gain prestige, which replaced the factor of coercion.
>
> Tacitus, *Agricola* 21

This was the reality. Agricola had the sons of leading men educated in the liberal arts and promoted the natural talents of the British over the skill specialisms of the Gauls. This in turn produced a situation where those who had but recently rejected Roman speech now had a real taste for eloquence:

> Next came the status conferred by our manner of dress, with wearing the toga at a premium. Gradually, there was a defection to those diversions that underpin luxurious living, porticoes, baths and the sophistication of the banquet. Among the naive this was called being part of the civilized world but actually it was an aspect of enslavement.
>
> Tacitus, *Agricola* 21

We have come full circle with this analysis of Romanization. The cachet of the language and the lifestyles of their conquerors were not lost upon those local leaders who could afford them. Romanization gave them a whole range of outward signs which confirmed their superior status in their own communities and cemented the link with the rulers from Rome. In the end, Britain was pacified and 'provincialized' in the same way as Gaul had been by Julius Caesar and then by his heir, Augustus, by serving the self-interest of a few who could be relied upon to guarantee the acceptance of Rome by the many.

This might sound cynical and a trifle one-sided. Branigan in his chapter 'Images or Mirages of Empire' (*Images of Empire*, ed. Alexander Loveday, 1991, p. 92) concludes, principally from archaeological evidence, 'that many natives of Rome's North Western provinces, from all points on the social ladder, perceived the Romans and their empire as broadly beneficial to them.' Branigan ends his discussion by reminding the reader of the sketch 'What have the Romans ever done for us?' in Monty Python's film *Life of Brian*. The list is impressive – sanitation, medicine, health, irrigation, baths and freshwater systems, roads and public order. Hold some of these features in your mind when we return to the Gaul of the bishop Sidonius Apollinaris, in the fifth century CE, for our farewell look at Roman civilization.

Insight

David Mattingley's 2006 book, *An Imperial Possession*, is a thought-provoking reassessment of Roman Britain which emphasizes the negative consequences of colonization in such fundamental areas as the land, trade and social amenities. He also expands the idea of resistant adaptation (local customs and deities being insinuated into Roman practices and rituals) and argues that the native population actively rejected aspects of the conquerors' culture and social organization. But how uniform was each community's response? In 2000 I wrote in an essay on 'The Language of Dissent' (p. 288) that local leaders in Britain and elsewhere were inclined to accept Roman rule if they retained their positions and privileges: 'Better still, these positions were enhanced by the wider range of status symbols Roman political culture was able to provide.'

Places change

Near the beginning of this chapter you were given a glimpse of late antiquity, the end of the fourth century CE, and the time of the poet Claudian and the Western regent Stilicho. The reason for returning to late antiquity is to find out more about the 'remains' of Roman civilization at a time of geographical fragmentation, when Roman culture and institutions survived and sometimes revived across barbarian landscapes.

By the fifth century CE the Roman world was under constant threat from invasion or encroachment. Vandals and Goths had to be bought off or fought off. The Vandals seem to have started out from the territory of modern Poland, the Goths from the Ukraine and the Crimea. The Goths' division into Ostrogoths and Visigoths is a rough and ready way of distinguishing between eastern and western-based tribes. Goths and Vandals alike seem to have had a mix of Germanic and Slavonic origins.

Stilicho, the Romanized Vandal who reached the dizzy heights of the western regency and the position of overall commander of the Roman army, is referred to as German by the historian Bury in his *History of the Later Roman Empire*. Perhaps the modern designations are confusing. With regard to their ethnic identities we are working with imponderables. As far as the Romans were concerned, what really separated these tribes out and characterized them were their distinct ways of coexisting or conflicting with the Roman empire whose boundaries they had crossed.

By the fifth century CE the Vandals had made their presence felt in Gaul. (They crossed the river Rhine at Mainz in 406.) From the Pyrenees they forged on into Spain and eventually to North Africa. They were invited into Africa by the ruling count, Boniface, who had already aroused the suspicions of the imperial court at Ravenna by building a personal power base in the province. Augustine (St Augustine), bishop of Hippo, records the despair of the clergy in the face of terrible Vandal atrocities. In Epistle 228 he instructs his fellow bishops to let their people flee but to stay in post themselves as long as their presence is required.

After various battles, a compromise was devised whereby the Vandals held on to territory in Numidia and all of Mauretania. They paid an annual tribute to Rome for the privilege, but not for long. The Vandal leader Gaiseric made a complete conquest of Roman Africa. The Roman emperor in the West, Valentinian, had to put up with a rapid moving of the goal posts and be grateful that the Vandals were not preparing to annex Sicily, Sardinia or Italy itself. Italy continued to receive surplus corn from Africa, but, as Bury points out (*History of the Later Roman Empire*, vol. 1. p. 257), the corn was now an export, not a tribute.

Things were no better for the Balkan peninsula in this century of sea changes for the empire. In the 440s the Huns made a big push on Roman territory. The Huns were essentially nomadic peoples from Mongolia who migrated from the Ukraine to the Rhine in the fifth century. Their 'irruptions' had been a big factor in displacing Visigoths and Ostrogoths from their home territories. They were a military match for the Goths and dangerous both as enemies and allies of the Romans. They were paid a tribute by the imperial government, an annual sum of 700 pounds of gold, but Attila, undoubtedly then, as now, the most famous ruler of the Huns, found reasons for breaking the peace and appearing with force of arms at the Danube. By 448 Attila could dictate his own terms and the price of peace was high. The emperor in the East, Theodosius II, paid up until his death. At this time, Attila was effective ruler in modern Hungary, Romania and southern Russia.

Attila not only received tribute from the emperors in both the East and West; he was also a supplier of essential troops to their armies and defences in Gaul, where Hunnish contingents were a crucial factor against German settlers. For centuries of empire, Gaul had seemed the most Roman of provinces, an unassailable part of the imperial power structure. Now it relied on the barbarian invaders of the East for its very survival. Ironically, the Huns themselves had to adapt to the ways of both their German vassals and their Roman 'clients'. Attila employed private secretaries who were fluent in Latin – they were often Roman subjects. Attila justified his own position as an overlord by quoting Roman law. We are lucky enough to have a detailed account about Attila and his court from Priscus, a learned Thracian, who accompanied the Roman ambassador Maximinius on a mission to Attila in 449.

Maximinius and Priscus travelled for some time with the barbarians and still had not received an audience with Attila by the time they had crossed the Danube. An important thing to remember – as so much of this book has concentrated upon the first 200 years of the empire – is that the imperial capital was now Constantinople and that the two ambassadors set out from the East. After one brief interview with the king, Attila, the Scythians (as the Huns were called) kept the ambassadors at arm's length during much of the journey.

The waiting around and the travelling must have been frustrating. At one point Maximinius and Priscus, and servants, lost their cooking utensils in a storm by their lake encampment. There were also western Romans in the queue to see Attila. It was a mission full of incident and anecdote. During one wait, Priscus encountered a Greek-born man who had started a new life among the Scythians. Priscus reports the Greek's criticisms of Roman rule, complaints which covered the fragility of Roman protection in war and the rapacity of Roman tax collection in peacetime.

Andrea Giardina's introduction to the excellent 1993 book, *The Romans,* discusses this episode as evidence of a polarization of views on Rome's civilizing mission. (See Vegetius' quote in Chapter 2, which is cited by Giardina.) Was there any advantage in being Roman in an era when key institutions were so corrupt? This is an interesting question, when Roman historians themselves could at times lament the loss of an ethical core in their society. Tacitus seems to have established a trend when he identified simpler and nobler values in barbarian communities and imagined their family and kinship structures as similar to those of the early Romans.

Priscus' defensive reply focused on the value of Roman constitutional law, something that differentiated the civilized from the barbarian and something the Greek had voluntarily relinquished. The efficacy of the law was a longstanding motif among the defenders of Rome and her empire. For example, the lawlessness of the Britons was the object of a scathing comment made by Cicero in one of his letters to Quintus about 500 years before.

The influence of Roman law on the modern world is almost incalculable. Legal digests and case studies were being produced as late as the fifth and sixth centuries CE under the emperors Theodosius II and Justinian respectively. (Priscus' companion, the official ambassador, Maximinius, was a leading light in the compilation of the Theodosian code.) These works have preserved for us practices and precedents going back to the beginning of Rome. The Justinian code was applied to the Roman East on its publication in 533 CE, and reached the West when the emperor's general Belisarius recaptured Italy from the Ostrogoths and Africa from the Vandals.

Although this resurgence of Roman power was relatively short-lived, Roman law, as R.H. Barrow points out in his 1949 book *The Romans* (p. 213), 'exerted no little influence on the "barbarian" codes. For, when successive barbarian races overran the West and Italy was subject to a foreign government, the barbarians incorporated into their own legal codes great masses of Roman law.' We might not want to go as far as Barrow and describe the Roman digests and compilations as a thousand years of practical wisdom, but the legacy is impressive all the same. Justinian's Digest opens with the words of the prestigious jurist Ulpian:

> Anyone intending to study law (*ius*) ought to know the origin of the word *ius*. It derives from justice: As Celsus neatly defined it, the law is the art of the good and the fair. It is for this reason that a man might call us priests; for we worship justice and we proclaim a knowledge of the good and the fair, separating the one from the other, and distinguishing what is and what is not legitimate. We desire to make men good not solely because they are afraid of penalties but because there is the encouragement of rewards. We claim, if I am not deceived, a true not a false philosophy.

Lawyers of any era might receive this image with a wry smile. Priscus' Greek acquaintance suggests that the reality of Roman law was inequality of access; the rich man was not punished for wrongdoing and the poor man had to pay the judge and the judge's clerks to obtain any justice at all. Whatever fallible humans and fallible systems produce as an end product, the enduring influence of Roman law seems to rest in its comprehensiveness. All social and political interaction, local, national and international, could be adjudicated upon with a previous ordinance or judgement to draw upon or a new interpretation to conjure with. Firmness of principle and flexibility of tactic were certainly among the strengths of its approach, tempered, too, with some acceptance of society's evolution from below. Custom and practice were, within reason, allowed for in legal developments. Studying Roman law is a bit like studying a branch of political science and simultaneously digesting philosophical and ethical concepts basic to Roman thinking and doing.

Elsewhere in Priscus' account of his travels with Attila, we find that, in spite of his defence of the Roman way and his very Roman distinction between barbarian behaviour and civilized life, he is patently unhappy about the weakness of Roman rulers who have been reduced to bribing the Huns and their leader. Priscus should make an honest witness to the merits of the barbarian leader. He may have felt that the humiliation of the situation was in some way compensated for by the dignity of the king who was holding the Roman empire to ransom. Priscus admired the strength and the bearing of Attila, although he was not to know that Attila probably had quite a lineage. The Hunnish king may have been able to trace his royal ancestry back 1,000 years and there had probably been family associations with prestigious Chinese dynasties.

When we were all appropriately seated, a cup bearer went up to Attila and offered him a wooden cup of wine. He accepted this and toasted the first in precedence. The one who had been thus honoured by the salutation rose to his feet and did not presume to sit down until the king had tasted or drained the wine and had returned the cup to the wine bearer. All those present then honoured him in this fashion; we drank from our cups and saluted the king. [When all the decorum of toasting had been completed, tables for three or four were placed below Attila's table.] Attila's servant came in first with a dish full of meat, followed by attendants who laid bread and meats on our tables. For us and for guest barbarians there were luxury meals on silver platters but Attila ate only meat from a wooden trencher.

He was restrained in other ways, too. His cup was wooden whereas we were served with golden and silver goblets. His dress was modest and distinguished only by its cleanliness. The sword at his side, the fastenings of his Scythian boots and his horse's bridle were all unadorned with gold, or gems or the sorts of costly accoutrements used by his fellow barbarians. [Further courtesies of toasting are observed before the next course.] When evening had approached, pine torches were lit and two barbarians came forward to Attila and sang songs of their own composition; these were celebrations of the king's victories and brave deeds of war. The guests turned their eyes to the singers, some taking pleasure at the poetry while others became aroused by the memories of battle. Still others who were now weak with age and their fighting spirits of necessity subdued, gave way to weeping.

(Priscus' full account of the embassy can be read in translation in Bury, pp. 279–88)

Discussion

The epic/Homeric feel to this scene is quite striking. The courtesy code is pronounced and was probably reassuring to both Priscus and Maximinius. They did not know what to expect of a barbarian banquet. This is a hospitable court. Priscus also admires the simplicity and unpretentiousness of Attila although his pre-eminence and prestige are obvious; perhaps there are shades here of the old ideals of Rome, the plain and restrained style of a past long since corrupted. Attila's banquet must have been quite a contrast with the ostentatious courts of the Roman emperors by this time.

Nor were Priscus and Maximinius aware that the hidden purpose of this embassy of which they were part was the assassination of Attila, which would have made them otherwise even more uneasy guests. Others in the party had been primed to plan this and the two companions were in a potentially highly dangerous situation during their attendance on Attila. Whatever the strategy, paying off the barbarian kings or attempting to murder them, the military might of Rome was certainly not what it had been and this was truly a very different world for the educated and Romanized official from the days when foreign kings had themselves been clients of Rome.

Song of a falling world?

My last heading is borrowed from a book on the later Roman empire written by Jack Lindsay in1948 (published by Dakers, London). In it Lindsay combines comment and interpretation with large chunks of translated text. Of our last author, Gaius Sollius Modestus Sidonius Apollinaris, bishop of Clermont in France in the fifth century CE, Lindsay writes (p. 127):

> *in his work we see the sad fate that had come over the official defender of the fixed imperial culture. Yet he clearly has an almost frantic enthusiasm for the worn devices of rhetoric, and the stereotyped literary activity in which he and his friends delighted was felt by them as a noble expression of the tradition in all its fullness.*

This is harsh stuff and not every student of Sidonius would agree. Ancient writers, like modern ones, go in and out of fashion. There has been something of a revival of later empire literature in recent decades and Sidonius is enjoying a bit of a comeback in this respect. I don't intend to try and defend him against Lindsay's charges of bad writing, but you should be aware that many scholars could make a good case for Sidonius and his literary art. There had been a significant shift in art and literature to very ornate and showy styles and Sidonius could hardly help being a man of his time.

Our interest lies in what sort of Roman civilization this man inhabited. He collected up his large number of letters with the example of the

Younger Pliny in mind. Throughout his literary output, which included a great deal of poetry, he makes reference to and he emulates many of the writers you have read during the course of this book. The point is that he had a Classical education and saw himself as a bearer of Roman cultural traditions. Sidonius was a firm believer in Roman values. He had a circle of cultured friends whose villa estates he visited when he could. These were the literati of the region, the standard bearers of Roman culture and the Latin language:

> I am convinced, most skilful of men, that I would be perpetrating an outrage against learning, if I postpone the praises that should honour you, because you have put off the evil day, the extinction of literary culture. You are to be acclaimed as the reviver, the patron, the champion of what was virtually buried. Throughout Gaul with you as the guardian the Latin language has reached a haven amid storms of war.
>
> Sidonius' letter to Iohannes, *Epistles* 8.2

It is typical of Sidonius' letters that they tantalize us with snippets of information about the current situation embedded in sometimes forced metaphors and tortured expressions. (The style is far removed from Cicero's or Pliny's, his declared role models.) In his lifetime the Auvergne was to pass from the orbit of the Roman empire. Sidonius and his circle of friends became subjects of the Visigoths. As John Percival points out in his 1997 article, 'Desperately seeking Sidonius: the realities of life in fifth-century Gaul', the letters of Sidonius are those of a man who actually lived through the process known as the 'Fall of the Western Empire' and saw it happening almost literally on his doorstep.

Amid all this upheaval, Sidonius' harping on about the Latin language and literary traditions might seem eccentric. He had to defend his human flock during the horrors of the Visigoth invasion. He mediated between the Gallo-Romans and the new rulers. He suffered imprisonment. Clearly, crisis or no crisis, his life as a bishop, celebrating mass, preaching, teaching and dealing with disputes, was a far cry from the leisure of those senatorial predecessors of the earlier empire. However, he was like many educated Christians who were deeply committed to preserving the Classical traditions and who were the only hope for Roman civilization to survive, or at least large facets of it, into a restructured Europe.

You have only to hear from Christian as well as pagan authors the words of shock and horror, almost an apocalyptic feeling some 50 years before when Rome was sacked by the barbarians. It did not matter in these traumatic times that in practice the capital of the empire and the seat of the emperors was now Constantinople in the Greek East, that when the emperors came west they held court at Milan or Ravenna and that Rome remained something of a faction centre for unreformed pagan senators. It was still the centre and symbol of Roman civilization and the original seat of Pax Romana.

It is not so surprising that Sidonius, born of a senatorial family in Lyons about 430 CE and living out much of his life in this long-established Roman province with its reputation for Latin oratory and its years of imitating Rome, should set great store by preserving the language and culture we have been looking at throughout this book. Even under the rule of the Visigoths Sidonius and his friends seem to have retained estates and on the surface they managed to preserve a civilized lifestyle, with baths, good food and what Jack Lindsay describes as 'a sumptuous literary life' (p. 133).

A closer look at the letters reveals that the baths are not always functioning, the roads are dangerous and the villas are in need of repair. In his letters, Sidonius warns a visitor of advanced years about the hazards of travel in winter:

It is a long journey and the days are short. There is plenty of snow but a dearth of provisions along the way, long stretches of wide open spaces but very constrained hostels. The potholes in the roads are dripping with the damp of the rains or they are dried out by the frosts and jagged. Moreover, the highways bristle with rocks and the rivers are slippery ice flows, the hills make for rugged climbing and the valleys are eroded by constant rockfalls.

[...itinerum videlicet longitudinem brevitatemque dierum, nivium copiam penuriam pabulorum, latitudines solitudinum angustias mansionum, viarum voragines aut umore imbrium putres aut frigorum siccitate tribulosas, ad hoc aggeres saxis asperos aut fluvios gelu lubricos aut colles ascensu salebrosos aut valles lapsuum adsiduitate derasas.]

Sidonius, *Epistles* 3.2.3

Thinking back to Horace's journey through Italy in Chapter 2, the years do seem to have taken their toll on the civilization of Rome. On the other hand, the careful arrangement in the Latin of Sidonius is all neat and satisfying. Percival suggests that the elaborate greetings Sidonius' friend is told to expect, the triumph over nature, the elements (and the bad upkeep of the roads) which his safe arrival will signify, all this points to 'a literary concoction, a piece of imaginative writing'.

Sidonius did live in hard times and the material conditions of Roman civilization were rapidly changing around him. He makes a fitting endnote all the same. Educated citizens of the Western empire were still composing elegant pieces of Latin around a familiar topos or theme, drawing on their literary predecessors and suppressing the realities which did not, at that moment, concern them. This has been your last lesson on how to read, enjoy and learn from an authentic Roman voice.

POINTS TO REMEMBER...

1 The origins of Rome's standing army are of particular historical interest. As Rome colonized through Italy and beyond into present-day Europe and Asia, the Senate needed farmers to be soldiers and frequent campaigning took its toll on agriculture. Whether this was really a principal factor in the growth of large estate farming is a subject of vigorous debate among Roman historians. Once the army became professional, veteran soldiers put pressure on their commanders to obtain land settlements for them in return for years of service.

2 The presence of the army in the provinces could be accepted and resented in equal measure. There is a rich variety of evidence about the effects of Rome's expansion across the Mediterranean which undoubtedly changed the face of trade, local economies, institutional structures and the cultural horizons of the colonized. The Romans did, however, show religious toleration with regard to indigenous deities and cultic practices.

3 Provincial governors and their military and administrative staff expected to profit from their periods abroad. Once autocratic rule had been established, emperors kept a tighter rein on their colonial civil service and by Trajan's time an astute ruler expected to be consulted and updated on day-to-day issues, not just crises in security. From Vespasian onward, emperors were frequently drawn from those in active military command.

4 Roman Britain makes an interesting case study since, once the Romans had left, the social structures and ways of life they had imported seem to have relatively rapidly disappeared. David Mattingly has rather turned around the joke about 'What did the Romans ever do for us?' (in Monty Python's *Life of Brian*, set in Judaea, the rebels are forced to come up with sanitation, education, roads, etc.) because he deconstructs the picture of their civilizing improvements.

5 Historians cannot gloss over the ruthlessness with which Roman commanders dealt with those peoples unwilling to submit to imperial rule. Sometimes it was a deliberate policy to obliterate tribes on vulnerable borders who were too nomadic or unstructured to be massaged (with the co-operation of local chieftains) into a Roman-style settlement.

6 Longstanding provinces from Gaul to Spain and North Africa had more than a veneer of Roman civilization about them. They formed part of a political entity. Claudius thought it fit to introduce Gallic leaders into the Senate during the 60s BCE. By the beginning of the first century CE, Spain and North Africa were places producing skilled commanders who subsequently became emperors.

7 There was a strong cultural dimension and diversity to Rome's expansion. In the time of Antoninus Pius (second century CE), the African-born orator and author Apuleius benefited from being part of a Romanized local nobility in Madauros. He studied Greek and Latin as well as speaking the local Punic and promoted the philosophical and literary learning that flourished in the West and the Greek East.

8 The Roman world was very differently configured by the fifth century CE. Movements of peoples at the edge of the empire had radically altered its demographics and its landscape, but there were many cultural constants, not least the continuation of literary traditions and the intellectual pursuits of the educated.

9 The art and poetry of late antiquity was ornate and ostentatious. Literature of the Christian era used pagan imagery to reinforce notions of heroism and to underline Rome's destiny to rule the known world. It did not matter that the city of Rome was becoming more of a symbolic than a geographical and administrative heart of Roman civilization.

10 There are many places the world over where the material signs of Roman civilization can be viewed, visited and admired. Alongside roads, aqueducts, palaces, villas, granaries, amphitheatres, forums (fora) and the remains of whole cities, we can also engross ourselves in the literary pictures of Rome and its provinces and peoples. With luck, this will make us more reflective about the way our own societies (and empires) might be scrutinized and judged from the outside.

Appendix 1: Timeline of Roman history

The traditional date given for the founding of Rome was 753 BCE. In dating, the abbreviation a.u.c. stood for *ab urbe condita* (from the city being founded). Greek civilization boasted the poets Homer and Hesiod in this same century. Rome was ruled by kings until 509 BCE. We are dealing with all sorts of uncertainties but Roman legend named them as Romulus, Numa, Tullius, Ancius Martius, Tarquinius Priscus, Servius Tullius and finally Tarquinius Superbus. It seems to be the Etruscan dynasty that was finally ousted and replaced by a republican government, the rule of consuls and the Senate. A temple to Jupiter was established on the Capitoline Hill.

The island of Lesbos, in the meantime, produced the poets Alcaeus and Sappho (*c.*610–575 BCE). Greeks had settled around the Asia Minor coastline. In mainland Greece, Attic black-figure pottery was appearing. By 546 BCE the Greeks were involved in a major conflict with Persia.

Rome settled into some form of constitutional government, with the ruling body gradually, and often unwillingly, providing the rest of the citizen body with magistracies, a measure of protection and access to a legal system. *The Twelve Tables*, their first codified laws, were published in 450 BCE. During this period, the fifth century BCE, Athens reached cultural heights in sculpture, vase painting (red figure) and literature. (See the companion book, *Teach Yourself Greek Civilization*.) Some names you might know: the poet Pindar, the playwrights Aeschylus, Sophocles, Euripides (tragedy) and Aristophanes (comedy), the historians Herodotus and Thucydides, and the philosopher Socrates.

In the fourth century, the Celts were in Italy and Rome was sacked by the Gauls in 390 BCE. By 264 BCE, after wars with the Samnites, Rome was in control of Italy south of the river Po. The Greek world was also changing. From 336 to 323 BCE Alexander the Great was in power. There was a new cultural centre in Egypt, the city of Alexandria, where poets who were to prove very influential in Roman literature were associated with the library there: Callimachus, Theocritus, Apollonius. The fourth century was the age of Plato, Aristotle and the orator Demosthenes. After Alexander, three distinct empires emerged, the Seleucid, the Egyptian and the Macedonian.

Ruling Rome	The Roman orbit	Cultural connections
	310 Rome expanding territory into Etruria (north of the river Po)	Roman coinage around this time
	280–275 fighting off Pyrrhus of Epirus in the Greek South of Italy	
	256–255 The Roman general Regulus is sent to Africa (not a success)	First tragedy in Latin (by Livius Andronicus)
	264–241 First (Punic) war with Carthage – Romans win	
	227 Sicily, Sardinia and Corsica are now Roman provinces	Cato the Elder writes on agriculture
217 Fabius Maximus, the 'delayer' is at the helm in Rome		
	219–202 Second Punic War – Romans win again	**212** Plautus writing and producing Latin comedies
	215–205 War against Macedon. The general Scipio is in Spain in 210 (where Carthage had established an empire)	**202** Fabius Pictor writes prose history of Rome
		196 Rosetta Stone with hieroglyphic, demotic and Greek scripts telling of the coronation of Ptolemy V (Egypt)
	198 Rome gets involved in Greece	**189** Ennius writing tragedies in Latin
	197 Spain becomes a Roman province	
		166 Terence, a North African, write Latin comedies
	149–146 Third Punic War (Carthage defeated on their own ground). Africa and Macedonia become Roman provinces	Greek marble now being used in Roman temples
	135–132 Slave war in Sicily	

Ruling Rome	The Roman orbit	Cultural connections
133–121 Tiberius Gracchus and Gaius Gracchus utilize people's magistrates to initiate agrarian reform. Senate has them killed	**133** Asia becomes Roman province	Lucilius writing satire
	120 Creation of province of Gallia Narbonensis	
107 Marius becomes consul **107–100** Marius restructures Roman army	**106** Marius fights Jugurtha in North Africa	
	91–88 Fighting disaffected Italians (the Social Wars). Italians defeated but are conceded citizenship	**95** Meleager (of Gadara) produce Greek epigrams
88 Sulla, Marius' rival, marches on Rome	**88–66** Mithridates (of Pontus) attempting to liberate Greeks from Rome is defeated by Pompey. Sulla captures Greece in 86	
83–82 Sulla back in Italy. Civil war between him and Marius. Sulla resigns dictatorship in 80	**73–71** Spartacus heads slave revolt in Italy; defeated by Crassus **74–62** Bithynia and Pontus made provinces	**70–52** Cicero publishing political speeches
70 Trial of Verres, corrupt governor of Sicily. Cicero on the attack **63** Consulship of Cicero and the conspiracy against the government by Sergius Catilina	**66–63** Mithridates finally defeated by Pompey who reorganizes East. Judaea ceases to be an independent kingdom	**63** Cicero's orations against Catiline **59–54** Catullus publishing his love poems

Ruling Rome	The Roman orbit	Cultural connections
	58–50 Gallic Wars **55–54** Caesar in Britain. Crassus and army defeated by Parthians in 55	**58–52** Caesar writes up his Gallic campaigns **55** Lucretius' philosophical poem *De Rerum Natura* published posthumously. Pompey's theatre in Rome, the first to be built in stone
49 Caesar crosses river Rubicon, taking his army into Rome **46** Caesar is dictator at Rome **44** Caesar is assassinated on the Ides of March. Chief conspirators: Brutus and Cassius **43** Octavian, Antony and Lepidus form a triumvirate (Cicero killed)	Celtic Gaul becomes a Roman province **42** The Battle of Philippi: Brutus and Cassius defeated by triumvirate and troops	**44** Cicero starts on philosophical works **44** Strabo, Greek geographer, start many years of activity **40** Sallust writes history of Jugurthan Wars **39** Virgil's writing career starts with the *Eclogues*
40 Antony and Octavian make pact at Brundisium **36–35** Campaigns against Sextus Pompeius, son of Pompey the Great		**37–30** Horace, *Satires* Book One and *Epodes* **36** Varro's *On Agriculture*
31 Antony and Cleopatra defeated at battle of Actium **30** Egypt occupied	**29** Spanish campaigns	**29** Virgil's *Georgics*, Propertius' *Elegies* Book One **28** Building begins on triumphal arch and imperial mausoleum
27 Octavian 'restores' Republic and becomes Augustus	**27–19** Agrippa secures Spain	**27–24** Tibullus' poems; Propertius continuing *Elegies*; Horace publishes *Odes*; Ovid starting his poetic career with the *Amores*; Vitruvius writing *On Architecture*

Ruling Rome	The Roman orbit	Cultural connections
23 Conspiracy against Augustus **19** Constitutional reinforcements of Augustus' powers **18** Augustus' social reforms and marriage legislation **12** Death of Agrippa. Augustus becomes Pontifex Maximus, chief priest of the state religion	**25** Galatia becomes a province **20** Settlement with Parthia	**20** Temple to Mars the Avenger begun **19** Deaths of Tibullus and Virgil **17** Horace writes *Carmen saeculare* for secular games **13–11** Theatre of Marcellus **12** Horace's *Epistles* **9** Ovid's *Art of Love;* last books of Livy's *History of Rome;* dedication of *Ara Pacis* (Altar of Peace)
6 Tiberius retires to Rhodes for eight years **2** Augustus' daughter Julia in sex scandal with political overtones	**8–6** Tiberius campaigns in Germany	**8** Death of Horace and Maecenas **2** Second edition of Ovid's *Art of Love* (*Ars Amatoria*) **2** Forum of Augustus dedicated

CURRENT ERA (Common Era) STARTS HERE

Ruling Rome	The Roman orbit	Cultural connections
2–4 Augustus' grandsons and heirs, Lucius and Gaius, die. Tiberius made emperor's heir	**6** Judaea becomes Roman province	**1–4** Ovid writes *Fasti* (festival calendar in verse) **3** Maison Carrée built at Nîmes
8 Scandal surrounding Younger Julia, Augustus' granddaughter. Ovid exiled the same year **14** On the death of Augustus, Tiberius becomes emperor, which signals the start of the **JULIO-CLAUDIAN DYNASTY**	**9** Disaster in Germany (massacre at Teutoberg Forest). Rhine becomes Roman frontier **6–9** Pannonian revolt **10** Pannonia become a province **17** Cappadocia becomes a province Germanicus in the East to deal with rising of Tacfarinas.	Death of Livy and Ovid

Ruling Rome	The Roman orbit	Cultural connections
19 Death of Germanicus **23** Death of Tiberius' son Drusus **26** Tiberius retires to Capri's leaving his lieutenant's Sejanus, prefect of the praetorian guard, in charge of Rome	**26** Pontius Pilate becomes prefect of Judaea	Manilius writing poems on astronomy Velleius Paterculus writing histories
31 Sejanus is executed on Tiberius' orders **37–41** On the death of Tiberius GAIUS CALIGULA becomes emperor	Caligula on the Rhine	**c. 30** Preaching and death of Christ Death of elder Seneca, writer on oratory
41 Assassination of Caligula; CLAUDIUS, his uncle, is made emperor (41–54) **43** Port of Ostia is established	**42** Mauretania organized as two provinces **43** Britain invaded under Aulus Plautius **45** Province of Thrace	
47–48 Moves to admit Gallic aristocracy to Roman Senate **54** Claudius dies in suspicious circumstances; NERO (54–68) becomes emperor. His tutor, Seneca, and Burrus rule on behalf of the young emperor for five years	**58–59** Campaigns in Armenia and Parthia	Satire on Claudius circulated and attributed to Seneca (Pumpkinification) / (*Apocolocyntosis*). Lucan, epic poet, Calpurnius Siculus (*Ecolgues*), Persius (satirist) and Petronius (*Satyricon*) make up the literary talent
59 Murder of Agrippina by her son, the emperor	**61** Revolt of Iceni (led by Boudicca) in Britain	

Ruling Rome	The Roman orbit	Cultural connections
62 Burrus dies; Seneca's star wanes	**66–73** Jewish Revolt	**67** Josephus, Jewish historian, defects to Romans
64 Nine-day fire in Rome, followed by persecution of Christians		
65 Conspiracy of Piso; Seneca and his nephew Lucan forced to suicide		
66 Petronius forced to suicide		
68 Nero forced to suicide; a year of four emperors follows (candidates of the army): OTHO, VITELLIUS and GALBA, followed by Vespasian		
VESPASIAN (69–79) – **THE FLAVIAN EMPERORS**	**70** Destruction of temple at Jerusalem	**74** Frontinus, technical writer, becomes consul
74 Expulsion of philosophers and astrologers from Rome	**72–78** East reorganized	**79** Pliny the Elder (*Natural Histories*) dies in eruption of Vesuvius
	77–84 The general Agricola in Britain	
79 Vespasian dies; his son TITUS succeeds (79–81)	**79** Volcanic eruption of Vesuvius destroys Pompeii and Herculaneum	
80 Dedication of the Colosseum and inaugural games. Fire at Rome and destruction of Capitoline temple		Poets Statius, Silius Italicus, Martial and Quintilian (prose writer on rhetoric) all active; Plutarch, Greek biographer, begins long literary career
81 Death of Titus; accession of his brother DOMITIAN (81–96)		

Ruling Rome	The Roman orbit	Cultural connections
	83 Campaigns in Germany **85** Germany becomes two provinces (a frontier defence line developed) **85–92** Campaigns against Dacians. **86** Moesia divided in two	**88–97** Clement I, Pope **95** Gospels and Revelation of St John
94/95 Expulsion of philosophers including writer/moralist Epictetus **96** Domitian assassinated; NERVA succeeds (96–8) **ANTONINE DYNASTY BEGINS** (97 Tacitus consul) Poor relief project		**98** Tacitus' *Agricola* and *Germania* Greek orator Dio Chrysostom active
98–117 TRAJAN (from Spain) is emperor **112–13** Trajan's forum and Trajan's column dedicated	**100** Foundation of Timgad **101–106** Trajan conquers Dacia (Romania) **114–117** Parthian wars; Armenia and Mesopotamia annexed	**100** Pliny writes *Panegyric* to Trajan **100–111** Pliny consul and governor of Bithynia (112-letter about Christians); Tacitus writing *Histories, Annals*
117 Trajan dies; HADRIAN succeeds (117–38) **118** beginning of rebuilding of Pantheon	**115–117** Jewish Revolt **121–125** Hadrian's tour of the provinces **122** Hadrian's Wall in Britain **123** Peace with Parthia **128–134** Hadrian journeys to provinces again **132–135** Bar Kochba's revolt and final dispersal of the Jews	**120** Suetonius' *Twelve Caesars* Juvenal writing (*Satires*) Greek writers Lucian (satire), Appian (historian), Ptolemy (astronomer)

Ruling Rome	The Roman orbit	Cultural connections
138 Death of Hadrian; accession of ANTONINUS PIUS (138–161) **143** Herodes Atticus (Greek orator) and Fronto (Latin orator) are consuls		**140s** Pausanias (Greek) writes description of Greece; Apuleius (North African orator, philosopher, novelist) writing; Galen (medicine) active. **144** Eulogy to Rome by Greek Aelius Aristides
161 Death of Antoninus; MARCUS AURELIUS emperor (161–180)	**162–166** Parthian wars; Roman commander Lucius Verus (co-ruling with Marcus Aurelius) **165–167** Plague through Roman empire	**165** Justin, Christian apologist, martyred
169 Death of Lucius Verus	**167–180** German wars	**174–180** Marcus Aurelius writing *Meditations*
177 Commodus, son of Marcus, becomes co-emperor **180** Marcus dies; COMMODUS emperor (180–192)	Christian martyrs at Lyons	**178** Celsus' *True Account* **180–196** In these years Aurelian column completed
192 Assassination of Commodus **193** Another year of four emperors, PERTINAX, DIDIUS JULIANUS, CLODIUS ALBINUS but with SEPTIMUS SEVERUS (193–211) finally triumphant **SEVERAN DYNASTY STARTS HERE** (Pescennius Niger proclaimed emperor by Eastern legions, but defeated at Antioch in 194)	**197** Clodius defeated at Lyons **197–200** Campaigns in East and journey of Septimius to Egypt **208–11** Campaigns in Britain. Rebuilding of Septimius' home town, Lepcis Magna (North Africa)	**197** Christian apologist, North African Tertullian writes *Apologetica* **200** Christian school at Alexandria (including Clement and Origen, early Christian fathers); Neo-Platonic philosophical school established Literary activity of Herodian (history), Philostratus (literary biographer)

Ruling Rome	The Roman orbit	Cultural connections
211 Septimius dies at York; CARACALLA emperor (212–17), briefly co-rules with Geta, who is assassinated **211–216** Baths of Caracalla built **217** Assassination of Caracalla (brief interlude with Macrinus ruling); ELEGABALUS emperor (218–22)	**212** Caracalla grants citizenship to all inhabitants of the Roman empire **213–14** Campaigns on Danube **215–17** Campaigns in East	**200–254** Christian philospher Origen active
222 Assassination of Elegabalus; accession of SEVERUS ALEXANDER (222–35). Severus assassinated **235–80** 50 years of chaotic affairs with 20 different emperors	**224** Sassanid dynasty in Persia (400 years of desultory war with Rome to follow) **234–5** Campaigns in Germany Wars with Alemanni, Dacians, Sarmatians, Carpi and Goths; wars with Franks, Alemanni (both peoples in Gaul by 253 and Alemanni in North Italy by 258)	**229–30** Cassius Dio's *Roman History* (written in Greek) Ulpian – Roman jurist and praetorian prefect murdered by his troops (223) **257–8** Persecution of Christians **260** Decree of toleration of Christianity
276–84 Emperors PROBUS, CARUS, NUMERIUS, CARINUS, DIOCLETIAN (284–306)	Diocletian divides empire into four administrative sections. Tetrarchy, rule of four emperors, established.	**274** Cult of Sun gaining primacy **297** Law against Manichean strand of Christianity **303–4** persecution of Christians **305** Lactantius writes on *The Tetrarchs* and *Human and Divine Institutions*
306–37 CONSTANTINE is emperor	**312** Rival Maxentius defeated at Battle of Milvian Bridge, Italy	**313** Edict of Milan ends persecution of Christians; Christianity becomes state religion; Christian basilica in Rome

Ruling Rome	The Roman orbit	Cultural connections
337 Death of Constantine – his sons come to power, CONSTANS and CONSTANTUS II (CONSTANTINE II dies 340)	**337** Attack by Persians	**341** First ban on pagan sacrifices **325** Council of Nicaea (dealing with diverse trends and heresies in Christian religion) **324–30** Constantinople founded as Christian city and alternative capital of the empire **340** Death of author Eusebius of Caesarea
357 CONSTANTIUS II journeys to Rome		
360 Emperor JULIAN		**361** Paganism officially reinstated
361 Death of Constantius II	**363** Peace with Persians. Wars against Scots and Saxons	**358** Julian writes *On Royalty*
363 Julian is assassinated; JOVIAN is emperor for one year **364 VALENTINIAN DYNASTY –** VALENTINIAN I (364–75) and THEODOSIUS (378–95) **383–94** Usurpations, Maximus and Eugenius (latter defeated at battle of river Frigidus)	**366–9** Attacks by Goths and Alemanni **378** Defeat at Adrianople **380** Treaty with Goths **390** Treaty of Constantinople with Persians **396** Gildo's revolt in Africa. Empire divided on death of Theodosius between two young sons, HONORIUS in West and ARCADIUS in East. Regents respectively STILICHO and RUFINUS, later supplanted by eunuch EUTROPIUS	**387** Baptism of St Augustine **390** Libanius writes *On Behalf of Temples* **391** Ban on pagan worship **394** Deaths of St Gregory of Nyssa and St Martin Claudian (Alexandrian writing poetry in Latin) starts successful literary career **396** St Augustine bishop of Hippo, North Africa; Christian poet Prudentius writes on the sufferings of the Martyrs and *The Battle of the Soul*; also produces rebuttal of Symmachus' paganism
408 Stilicho is executed; THEODOSIUS II becomes emperor in East (408–450) **410** Alaric and Visigoths capture Rome	**398** Invasion by Huns **401** Victories over Visigoths and Ostrogoths in Italy **406** (Very end of) Suebi; Vandals and Alani cross Rhine **408–50** THEODOSIUS II emperor in East	**397–8** St Augustine's *Confessions* **397** Death of Ambrose **c. 400** *The Augustan History – Historia Augusta* **407** Death of St John Chrysostom

Ruling Rome	The Roman orbit	Cultural connections
411–21 CONSTANTIUS III in command of West		**411–51** Various councils to deal with persistent heretical trends in Christian religion
425–55 VALENTINIAN III and Aetius as master of the military		**413–26** St Augustine writing *City of God*
		429–38 Theodosian Code
		430 Death of St Augustine
		435 Ban on pagan sacrifices reinforced
457–72 RICIMER (son of Gothic and Suevian royalty) becomes master of the militia in the West; emperors after Valentinian (455–75): MAXIMUS, AVITUS, MARJORIAN, SEVERUS, ANTHEMIUS, OLYBRIUS, GLYCERIUS JULIUS NEPOS	**450–71** Aspar (of Alani) in command of the East. Emperors after Theodosius: MARCIAN, LEO I, LEO II, ZENO, BASILISCUS (very briefly), ANASTASIUS 1, JUSTIN I	**472** Sidonius Apollinaris becomes bishop of Clermont-Ferrand
	476–93 Barbarian ODOACER is king of Italy, having deposed emperor figurehead of West, Romulus	
476 Emperor ROMULUS AUGUSTUS is deposed	**490** Ostrogothic presence in Italy. Theoderic and, later, brother Euric German rule has extended into Gaul and Spain. Patrician THEODERIC ruling in Italy from 490 to 526	
	527–65 JUSTINIAN	Greek Procopius writes celebration of Justinian and victories against Persians, Vandals and Goths
		534 Code of Justinian

Endnote – for a while Justinian's wars, at great cost in lives and treasure, reclaimed the Roman world around the Mediterranean. Merchant shipping was again possible in African, Italian and Spanish ports. The Lombards and the Arabs proved the downfall of the empire in the West.

Appendix 2: Food for thought

You have encountered more than one meal during the course of this book and learned something of the reliance on wheat in the Roman diet. Learning about eating habits in any civilization becomes an open-ended process because it leads to questions about agriculture, trade, industry and social divisions. Fascinating but perhaps even more complex and controversial are the investigations into the psychology of eating in ancient society or approaches which treat eating as a cultural activity.

Margaret Visser's book *The Rituals of Dinner: The Origin, Evolution and Meaning of Table Manners* (HarperCollins, Canada, 1991) was described by *Publishers' Weekly* as 'a smorgasbord of cross-cultural insights, delectably served,' so the reviewers quickly fell into an appropriate language of food to describe the book. Margaret Visser has several bites at the Roman world and their social rituals of eating in her wide and stimulating survey.

Even closer to Rome is Emily Gowers' book *The Loaded Table: representations of food in Roman literature* (Oxford, 1993), which reveals a whole range of imagery and hidden agendas in the ancient writers when they turn to the subject of food and feeding:

> **As an ordered form created out of selected, transformed ingredients and offered to others, the meal has a great deal in common with literary composition. The Greeks and the Romans could describe the whole process of creating, presenting and consuming a literary text in alimentary terms. (p. 41)**

One of the most famous and over-the-top dinner parties ever thrown in fictional Latin literature is the banquet of the self-made millionaire Trimalchio, which features in a satirical novel, the *Satyricon* (first century CE). One exotic and elaborate course appears after another, punctuated by conversations and by Trimalchio, the host, holding forth on a variety of subjects. Clearly, the bizarrely configured food plays its part in the satire. The *Satyricon*, which has not survived complete, is attributed to Petronius, a sophisticated favourite at Nero's court. It was freely interpreted on film by Federico Fellini. Petronius is available in various paperback editions.

The significantly more modest intention of this section is to revisit two dinners from the text and to add a few trimmings, recipes which might have refined the foodstuffs at Pliny's meal, the one mentioned in the preface as a broken date; to start, some suggestions about what might have embellished Horace's grilled thrushes, had they not gone up in smoke (Horace's journey in Chapter 2). If this whets your appetite, the Roman gourmet Apicius, whose cookbook I have used, is available (translated) in paperback. Apicius' book is the basis for a number of slim volumes of selected Roman recipes and menus which can be found in museum shops the world over.

HORACE'S THRUSHES

Apicius, recipe 5, to accompany 'high birds' of any type: pepper, lovage, thyme, dried mint, filbert nut, Jericho date, honey, vinegar, wine, *liquamen* [a sauce made out of salted fish entrails – best varieties red mullet, tunny fish, sprats or anchovy; leave innards in the sun and shake frequently; leave in a vessel for two months or longer, preferably in a fine-meshed basket, which allows the liquid through. This fish sauce was known as *garum*], mustard and *defrutum* [a cooking wine, pre-boiled and reduced to about a half to a third of its volume; no sloshing wine straight into the saucepan in Roman cooking]. Apicius hints that you get a more flavoursome bird if you wrap it in pastry prior to baking in the oven. The pastry was to be made of oil and flour; this was also a popular 'parcel' for bacon joints smeared first with honey – sugar was not known to the Romans.

PLINY AND THE DINNER DATE

Pliny had on offer lettuce, snails, eggs and *alica*:

we had a lettuce each all laid out, three snails apiece, and two eggs, barley[?], and wine with honey ... there were olives, beetroots, gherkins, and onions, and a thousand other treats.

[paratae erant lactucae singulae, cochleae ternae, ova bina, halica (alica) cum mulso et nive ... olivae betacei cucurbitae bulbi, alia mille non minus lauta.]

Pliny, *Letters* 1.15

Apicius, Recipe 18

Lettuce (and endive): To avoid indigestion, dress lettuces with vinegar and a little *liquamen*. This dressing also helps prevent flatulence. Add 2 oz of cumin (pounded and moistened with the vinegar), 1oz of ginger, 1 oz of fresh rue, 6 oz of dates, 1 oz of pepper, 9 oz of honey.

Snails (Recipe 18): Fed on milk – get your snails and clean out with a sponge. Take out the membrane so that they slide out of their shells. Put in a pot with milk and salt for a day. Keep adding milk over the next days and clean out the excrement hourly. Once the snails are too fat to get back in their shells fry them in oil. You can also add pure salt, asafoetida, *liquamen* and pepper. Alternatively, soak snails alive in milk mixed with wheat flour; when fat enough, cook.

Eggs (Recipe 19): Can be served with *liquamen*, oil and wine (and with pepper and asafoetida); a good sauce for soft-boiled eggs is pounded pepper, lovage, soaked pine-kernels (in water overnight). Add honey, vinegar and blend in with *liquamen*.

Pliny's unnamed treats! Home-made sweets? (Recipe 13): Stone the dates and stuff with nuts, pine kernels or pounded pepper. Sprinkle on salt and fry in cooked honey. Serve. [dulcia domestica: palmulas vel dactylos excepto semine, nuce vel nucleis vel pipere trito interficies. sale foris contingis, frigis in mello cocto, et inferes.] Take best wheat flour and cook in hot water until it turns into a good hard paste. Spread on a plate and leave to cool. Cut it up as sweets and fry in very good-quality oil. Then pour over honey, sprinkle with pepper and serve.

Measure milk in pan, mix with honey, and add five eggs per pint. Blend eggs and milk to smooth mix and strain into an earthenware pot and cook over a slow heat. When set, sprinkle with pepper and serve.

Mix four eggs, a half-pint of milk and 1 oz of oil. Sizzle a little oil in a shallow pan, and add mixture. When cooked on one side, turn out on a round plate and pour over honey. Sprinkle with pepper. [In case you are wondering about the frequency of pepper in the Apician sauce – he seems as wedded to it as the cook in *Alice's Adventures in Wonderland* – this relates to the absence of sugar in the Roman diet; pepper accentuates sweetness.]

Pliny's 'barley cakes': I have left this item to last because it is not a straightforward one. You may recall the brief digression on grain in Chapter 4 (under the headings of 'bread and circuses'). According to Thomas Braun ('Barley Cakes and Emmer Bread' in J. Wilkins, D. Harvey, M. Dobson (eds), *Food in Antiquity* (University of Exeter Press, 1995), the early Greeks were very appreciative of barley cakes (p. 29). Lesbos' fine barley meal was praised in verse.

For the Roman soldier, though, barley rations instead of wheat signified a collective punishment and, according to Vegetius, who wrote on military matters, recruits who failed in their tasks were given barley (*De Re Militari* 1.13). Barley beer was more palatable and seems to have been drunk in areas of Roman Spain and of Gaul, on the Rhine frontier and in Britain. *Polenta* (which was mentioned in Chapter 4) was, according to Braun, barley groats and their presence at the table generally signified a very poor diet. (Polenta in modern-day Italy is made from maize.)

Getting back to Pliny's 'barley', the Latin for barley is *hordeum* and yet the word Pliny uses in his letter is *alica*. Latin dictionaries translate this as spelt or emmer groats. However, more than one commentator on Pliny's letters confidently asserts that Pliny is referring to a barley drink and they cross-reference to a Martial poem to reinforce the point. The commentators note the contrast between the barley and the rich man's tipple of wine and honey and they wonder why Pliny mentions them in the same breath.

So, what was Pliny doing boasting about barley cakes or barley water? Is Pliny careless with his terms or are we being careless with our translations? It might be that earlier hulled forms of wheat, like emmer, were regarded as so similar to barley grain that the word *alica* did for both. Or does it make more sense to assume Pliny is actually referring to tasty emmer groats which his absent friend has missed?

Braun tells us that *alica*, emmer groats, were of fine quality in Campania where the emmer wheat thrived on the volcanic soil. In Campania a slang term for prostitutes was *alicariae* because they congregated around the spelt mills. (Prostitutes were usually called *meretrices*; the English word 'meretricious' derives from it.) I certainly did not imagine that elaborating upon Pliny's dinner would send me off in so many different directions, but Latin word searches are rarely straightforward and invariably intriguing. In some ways, refining the recipes has led us into another exercise on reading sources in their cultural context and on the pitfalls of always taking translations on trust.

Appendix 3: The Roman pantheon

Apollo   The god of culture and creativity. A god of light for the Greeks, he became indistinguishable from the sun god who had once been a distinct deity (Helios) belonging to the earlier generation of gods, the Titans. According to Greek mythology, these gods had been superseded by the Olympians. (Saturn was a Titan, as was Oceanus.) Apollo was also a god of healing and of disease and death. The swan, the hawk, the raven and the crow were all associated with him. In art he was frequently depicted in his capacity as an archer or holding the lyre.

Bacchus   Also known as Liber and a version of the Greek Dionysus. He was originally much more than a god of wine and the vine. Bacchus released inhibitions generally and symbolized abundant fertility. Many of the legends about the god in both his Greek and Roman guise indicate his immense power and his mercilessness against those who resisted his influence.

Ceres   The goddess of the crops, she corresponded to the Greek goddess Demeter and absorbed her famous legend, that of the loss of her daughter Proserpina (Greek Persephone) to the god of the Underworld. In Italy and Rome, her cult was a plebeian one. She was the goddess of the lower classes in Rome and was offered the first fruits of the crop in the countryside.

Diana   Like Minerva, a virgin goddess and a keen huntress. She was the twin sister of Apollo and known to the Greeks as Artemis. She, in turn, was the moon goddess, so represented the other light source (the one reflected from the sun). This naturally associated her with night and magic; and she was regarded as a goddess of triple identity, incorporating Selene (the goddess of moon) and Hecate (a deity associated with witchcraft). In spite of representing and upholding chastity, she was, like Juno, called upon in childbirth.

Dis   God of the Underworld (Hades), he was honoured in Rome with a subterranean altar on the Campus Martius. He shared his worship with the consort he had kidnapped for himself, Proserpina, daughter of Ceres. Black animals were his sacrificial victims.

Juno   The queen of heaven, sister and wife of Jupiter, she represented marriage and childbirth. The peacock was associated with her (from the myth of many-eyed Argus, her servant, who was transformed into a peacock with his eyes eternalized on the plumage). To the Greeks she was known as Hera.

Janus   The god of doorways, of endings and beginnings. He was the first to be named in official prayers. His underlying power was considerable as he sanctioned all divisions of time from break of day to the seasons and the new year (hence the English word January). He also represented the sources of things from the springs to the seas. He had no Greek equivalent and his origins were not clear even to the Romans.

Jupiter The greatest of the gods, and the ruler of gods and men, his origins can be connected to the elements. He was a sky deity and controller of the weather. He presided over oath taking, laws of hospitality, and all aspects of sovereignty. The eagle was sacred to Jupiter. He was the counterpart of the Greek Zeus.

Mars Most famous as the god of war, he was in origin a god of agriculture, protector of crops, and may have started out as a storm god. He was particularly important to the Romans as the father of the twins Romulus and Remus, founders of Rome and famous for being suckled by a wolf. He was the counterpart of the Greek Ares.

Mercury The god of trade and commerce, of theft, of communications, of travel and of eloquence. He also escorted the dead souls to the Underworld. In his capacity of protector of the corn trade, he was an important figure for the Romans and his worship increased along with the activities of the merchants in the empire. His Greek counterpart was Hermes.

Minerva A warrior virgin, born from the head of Jupiter, she fostered the arts of war, but also domestic crafts, such as weaving. She was the goddess of wisdom and the owl represented her and accompanied her in artistic images. Her Greek name was Athene.

Neptune As god of the sea, like Jupiter, he was a powerful elemental force. One of his Greek titles was earth shaker. He was also the god of horsemanship (like his Greek counterpart, Poseidon).

Venus The goddess of love and particularly sexual passion. She was a Latin spring deity. Roses were among her special blooms but also myrtle. Her association with the sea arose from her conflation with the Greek Aphrodite, who in legend was born from the ocean foam. As mother of the Trojan Aeneas, she was an important founder of the Roman race. As well as doves and a variety of birds who drew her chariot, sparrows were particularly associated with Venus. In the ancient world, sparrows were renowned for their lasciviousness.

Vesta Goddess of the hearth and of the eternal fire of Rome, tended by the six Vestal Virgins. She was automatically revered at any place of sacrifice where a sacrificial fire was involved. During her own festival in July millers and bakers took a holiday. Her Greek counterpart was Hestia.

Vulcan The blacksmith god who overlooked the fire and the forge. His lameness is worth mentioning as such a deformity was unique among the Olympians. He was the god of technology. As a smelter of metal, he was also called Mulciber. The Greeks knew him as Hephaistos.

Taking it further

Bibliography

Barrow, R.H. *The Romans*. Pelican, Harmondsworth, Middlesex, 1949

Beard, M., Crawford, M. *Rome in the Late Republic*. Duckworth, London, 2004

Beard, M., Henderson, J. *Classics: A Very Short Introduction*. Oxford University Press, 1995

Berry, J. *The Complete Pompeii*. Thames and Hudson, 2007

Bradley, K. *Discovering the Roman Family*. Oxford University Press, 1991

——. *Slavery and Society in Ancient Rome*. Cambridge University Press, 1994

Branigan, K. 'Images – or Mirages – of Empire: an archaeological approach to the problem', in L. Alexander (ed.). *Images of Empire*. Sheffield Academic Press, 1991

Braund, D. *Ruling Roman Britain: Kings, Queens and Emperors from Julius Caesar to Agricola*. Routledge, 1996

Braund, S.H. (ed.). *Satire and Society in Ancient Rome*. University of Exeter Press, 1989

——. *Latin Literature*. Routledge, London and New York, 2002

Brown, P.M. *Horace: Satires I*. Aris and Phillips, Warminster, 1993

Bowman, A.K. *Life and Letters on the Roman Frontier*. British Museum Press, London, 1994

Bury, J.B. *History of the Later Roman Empire* (vol. l). Dover Publications, New York, 1958

Butterworth, A., and Laurence, R. *Pompeii: The Living City*. Phoenix, 2006

Carcopino, J. *Daily Life in Ancient Rome*, trans. by E.O. Lorimer. Penguin Books, 1937; republ. 1962

Cyrino, M.S. *Big Screen Rome*. Blackwell, Oxford, 2005

——. *Rome Season One: History Makes Television*. Blackwell, Oxford, 2008

Dixon, S. *The Roman Family*. Johns Hopkins University Press, Baltimore and London, 1992

Edwards, C. *Writing Rome: Textual Approaches to the City*. Cambridge University Press, 1996

Favro, D. *The Urban Image of Augustan Rome*. Cambridge University Press, 1995

Ferguson, J. *Juvenal: The Satires*. Macmillan Education, 1979

Flory, M.B. 'Family in Familia: Kinships and Community in Slavery'. *American Journal of Ancient History*, 3 (1978): 78–95

Flower, H. *Ancestor Masks and Ancestor Power in Roman Culture*. Clarendon Press, Oxford, 1996

Freudenberg, K. (ed.). *The Cambridge Companion to Roman Satire*. Cambridge University Press, 2005.

Gardner, J.F. *Women in Roman Law and Society*. Croom Helm, London, 1986

Garnsey, P., and Saller, R. *The Roman Empire: Economy, Society and Culture*. Duckworth, London, 1987

Giardina, A. (ed.). *The Romans*. University of Chicago Press, 1993

Gowers, E. *The Loaded Table: Representations of Food in Roman Literature*. Oxford, 1993

Gransden, K.W. *Virgil Aeneid VIII*. Cambridge University Press, 1976

Grant, M. *Julius Caesar*. Weidenfeld & Nicolson, London, 1969

——. *The Routledge Atlas of Classical History* (5th edition). London, 1994

Graves, R. *I, Claudius*. Penguin Books, Harmondsworth, repr. 1986 (first publ. 1934)

Hope, V.M. *Death in Ancient Rome: A Sourcebook*. Sourcebooks for the Ancient World. Routledge, 2007

Hopkins, K., and Beard, M. *The Colosseum*. Profile Books, London, 2005

Hollis, A.S. *Ars Amatoria, Book I*. Clarendon Press, Oxford, 1977

Huskinson, J.A.R. (ed.). *Experiencing Rome: Culture, Identity and Power in the Roman Empire*. Routledge with The Open University, 2000

Johnson, B. *The Dream of Rome*, Harper Perennial, 2007

Jones, D. *Bankers of Puteoli: Finance, Trade and Industry in the Roman World*. Tempus, 2006

Lindsay, J. *Song of a Falling World: Culture during the Break-up of the Roman Empire, AD 350–600*. Dakers, London, 1948

Lomas, K. 'Roman imperialism and the city in Italy,' in R. Laurence and J. Berry (eds), *Cultural Identity in the Roman Empire*. Routledge, London, New York, 1998

McKay, A. *Virgil's Italy*. New York Graphic Society, 1970

Mattingly, D. *An Imperial Possession: Britain in the Roman Empire, 54 BC–AD 409*. Allen Lane History, 2006

Parenti, M. *The Assassination of Julius Caesar: A People's History of Ancient Rome*. The New Press, New York, 2003

Percival, J. 'Desperately Seeking Sidonius', in *Latomus* 56 (1997): 279–92

Rawson, B., and Weaver, P. (eds). *The Roman Family in Italy: Status, Sentiment, Space*. Clarendon Press, Oxford, 1997

Rickman, G. *The Corn Supply of Ancient Rome*. Clarendon Press, Oxford, 1980

Robinson, O.F. *Ancient Rome: City Planning and Administration*. Routledge, London and New York, 1992

Rosenstone, R.A. *History on Film, Film on History*. Pearson Education, Harlow, 2006

Saller, R. 'Framing the debate over growth in the ancient economy', in W. Scheidel and S. von Reden (eds), *The Ancient Economy*. Edinburgh University Press, 2002

Toner, J.P. *Leisure and Ancient Rome*. Polity Press, Cambridge, 1995

Treggiari, S. 'Jobs in the Household of Liva', in *Papers of the British School at Rome* 43 (1975), pp. 48–77

Veyne, P. *Bread and Circuses*, trans. B. Pearce. Allen Lane, 1990

Visser, M. *The Rituals of Dinner: The Origin, Evolution and Meaning of Table Manners*. HarperCollins, Canada, 1991

Warde Fowler, W. *Aeneas at the Site of Rome*. Oxford University Press, 1917

Wiedemann, T. *Emperors and Gladiators*. Routledge, London, New York, 1992

Wilkins, J., Harvey, D., and Dobson, M. (eds). *Food in Antiquity*. University of Exeter Press, 1995

Wilkinson. L.P. *The Roman Experience*. Paul Elek, London, 1975

Winkler, M.M. (ed.). *Gladiator: Film and History*. Blackwell, Oxford, 2004

Wistrand, E. *The So-called Laudatio Turiae: Introduction, Text, Translation, Commentary*. Acta Universitatis Gothoburgensis and Oxford University Press, 1976

Wyke, M. *Projecting the Past: Ancient Rome, Cinema and History*. Routledge, New York and London, 1997

Where to find the ancient authors

There are paperback editions of most of the authors featured in this book, for instance Virgil, Horace and Ovid from Chapter 2, Tibullus from Chapter 3 and Juvenal from Chapter 4. Cicero's letters (a selection) and all of Pliny's correspondence (Chapter 4) appear in paperback. Livy's history – not all of it has survived – is also in paperback. Apuleius' *Golden Ass* (Chapter 6) has been recently reissued by Penguin in a new translation by E.J. Kenney. Also obtainable are Caesar's *Gallic Wars*, Suetonius' *Twelve Caesars* and Tacitus' *Annals*, *Histories*, *Germania* and *Agricola*.

Strongly recommended are the Oxford University Press paperbacks of Virgil's *Aeneid* (C. Day Lewis translation) and Ovid's *Love Poems* and *Metamorphoses* (translated by A.D. Melville). David Raeburn's translation of *Metamorphoses* for Penguin Classics includes an excellent introduction. Some Classical authors can also be found in Wordsworth publications: Petronius and Apuleius, for example (with informative introductions). Statius, Sidonius and Claudian are less accessible but there are editions in well-stocked Classics sections in the major bookshops (and there is always the possibility of picking up Classical authors second-hand).

Carry on studying!

There are plenty of opportunities to read more about Roman civilization. There are general histories of Rome and its empire, and many excellent, thorough and well-referenced books on the market. I recommend a browse around the libraries and the bookshops.

Some of the older books of the 'everyday life in Rome variety' are often both fascinating and painstaking. The age of some books still in circulation does not in any way detract from their scholarship and their insights. Edward Gibbon's multi-volume *The History of the Decline and Fall of the Roman Empire* (1776–88) is in many ways as educational about the author's cultural and political context as it is thought-provoking in its judgements and conclusions about the Romans.

There are plenty of modern works on problematic aspects of Roman civilization, from the corn supply to the Roman psyche. The study of the influence of Roman ideas on modern thought is also a growth industry; artistic and literary genres are traced through from Roman culture to the present day, so the extent of our *imitatio* (imitation) of past models becomes clear.

Resonances of Rome, historical, mythological and literary, can be detected in unexpected places, for instance in the genre of science fiction (in novels, graphic novels and on screen). Classical figures and narratives might be refashioned and refreshed by the modern media partly because they have acquired so many cultural layers through the centuries.

A close interpretation of ancient texts in context reveals the intellectual sophistication of the Classical authors. The tools of modern literary criticism are applied to the poetry and prose of Roman writers and there is a constant buzz in research and teaching about the history and the culture of this past civilization.

The Open University Classical Studies department offers degree-level modules in the cultural history of the ancient world and in 2010 introduced a study of *Myth in the Greek and Roman Worlds* (at Honours level). There is a whole block devoted to Ovid's *Metamorphoses* and the reception of myth from the medieval period to the present day. OU students can also learn Latin and Greek as absolute beginners. Campus universities and colleges have also developed courses for part-time study and the Internet offers all kinds of opportunities for learning about the Romans, although some sites are more reliable than others. There are a few suggestions in the section below to get you started. The Open University has an Open Learn area on the Internet where material from current and past courses can be accessed.

Index

Acknowledgements

Dr Dominic Montserrat (1964–2004) cast a keen and Classical eye over this book in 1998 and saved me from many errors and misplaced witticisms. He was a dear friend and colleague. Dr Lynette Watson (Open University Associate Lecturer) provided material and insightful interpretations for the relationship between town and country. Dr Tony Keen (Open University Associate Lecturer) gave invaluable help in correcting and updating the text. My family – John, daughters Tanith and Jessica, my sister Karen Barratt and husband Mike – did lots of reading and encouraging when I first embarked upon the book 15 years ago.

Photographic credits